Mythmaking in the New Russia

Mythmaking in the New Russia
Politics and Memory during the Yeltsin Era

Kathleen E. Smith

CORNELL UNIVERSITY PRESS

Ithaca and London

First published 2002 by Cornell University Press

Printed in the United States of America

Library of Congress Cataloging-in-Publication Data

Smith, Kathleen E.
  Mythmaking in the new Russia : politics and memory during the Yeltsin era / Kathleen E. Smith.
    p. cm.
  Includes bibliographical references.
  ISBN 0-8014-3963-9 (cloth: alk. paper)
  1. Russia (Federation)—Politics and government—1991- . 2. Political culture—Russia (Federation) 3. Post-communism—Russia (Federation) I. Title.
  DK510.763.S6 2002
  947.086—dc21 2001006052

Cornell University Press strives to use environmentally responsible suppliers and materials to the fullest extent possible in the publishing of its books. Such materials include vegetable-based, low-VOC inks and acid-free papers that are recycled, totally chlorine-free, or partly composed of nonwood fibers. Books that bear the logo of the FSC (Forest Stewardship Council) use paper taken from forests that have been inspected and certified as meeting the highest standards for environmental and social responsibility. For further information, visit our website at www.cornellpress.cornell.edu.

Cloth printing   10 9 8 7 6 5 4 3 2 1

The struggle for power is the struggle to tame the past, to seize it, to make it both intelligible and useful by objectifying it, by simplifying it. The invention of a future thus presupposes the invention of a past.

—DAVID KERTZER

Contents

Illustrations

Acknowledgments

S tudying Russia is more than a vocation, it is a constant adventure, replete with excitement, frustration, fascination, and sometimes elation. I have been absorbed in watching Russians try to come to terms with their past for over a decade now. This book distills some of my observations of Russian culture and politics after 1991. It could not have been written, however, without the help and support of numerous individuals and institutions.

I thank first those professionals in Russia who made this work possible. My friend Boris Belenkin, librarian of the Interregional Memorial Society, not only let me rummage through his collection of election materials but always greeted me with refreshing good humor and plenty of tea. Thanks also to Elena Strukova of the Historical Library, Moscow, who let me work with an uncataloged collection of election posters and leaflets, and to the attendants at the periodical room of the Social Sciences Library (INION), who day after day let me order more than my fair share of newspapers. The courteous and efficient workers at the Central Moscow Archive for Documents on Special Media (TsMADSN) graciously helped me find many of the wonderful photographs that illustrate this book. Of the many archives I visited in Moscow, theirs was the most pleasant place to work.

Other friends in Moscow made me want to keep coming back. I'm grateful for the company over many years of Irina Granik, Irina Iurna, Sasha Kliachin, Lilia Shevtsova, and Valia Zhdanova. Thanks also to Maura Reynolds, Ol'ga Kazmina, and Margaret Paxson for their friendship and encouragement during the final stretch of my work in Moscow.

Kathryn Hendley and William Pomeranz read and commented on the entire manuscript, and Catherine Wanner and David Mendeloff shared their thoughts on key chapters as well. Michael Urban and Veljko Vujacic gave their opinions on early drafts of chapters presented

at the AAASS conference. My work on monumental propaganda benefited from participation in the Social Science Research Council workshop "Architecture and the Expression of Group Identity: The Russian
Empire/Soviet Union, 1500–present." Franklin Sciacca shared his
considerable knowledge of the Cathedral of Christ the Saviour with me.
Discussions with Blair Ruble and Shari Cohen also helped me conceptualize this project. At the Kennan Institute, Heather Frank provided
valuable research assistance. I'm grateful to all of them for their insights.

A portion of Chapter 6 appeared earlier as "An Old Cathedral for a
New Russia: The Symbolic Politics of the Reconstituted Church of
Christ the Saviour," in *Religion, State & Society* 25, no. 2 (June 1997):
163–175. *Religion, State & Society* is the journal of the Keston Institute, a leading center of research and information on religion in communist and postcommunist countries. More details on the activities
and publications of the Keston Institute can be found on its website,
http://www.keston.org.

Partial support for the research and writing for this book was pro-
vided first by a grant from the National Council for Eurasian and East
European Research (NCEEER) under authority of a Title VIII grant from
the U.S. Department of State. The International Forum for Democratic
Studies in Washington, D.C., kindly hosted me during my NCEEER grant.
A Mellon Foreign Area Grant from the Library of Congress and a Title
VIII–supported research fellowship from the Kennan Institute of the
Woodrow Wilson International Center for Scholars funded my work at
later stages. The staffs of the Office of Scholarly Programs and the European Reading Room at the Library of Congress and at the Kennan Institute provided me with great working conditions and pleasant company. Hamilton College also generously supported early fieldwork and
tolerated later leaves of absence. In this regard, thanks are due especially to Professor Alan Cafruny and Dean Bobby Fong. In no way, however, should this work be construed as representing the opinions of any
of the persons or institutions I have named.

Special thanks are due to my sister, Pamela Nakahata Smith, and her
family for hosting first me and then all three of us as we made the transition home from Moscow. Pam and my parents, Michael and Eleanor
Smith, also provided the baby-sitting and hand-holding necessary to finally get this book launched. The friendship of Kathryn Hendley, Hilke
Kayser, and Jane Dawson also helped me keep going through many
moves.

My husband, William Pomeranz, brought a critical eye, a tolerant temperament, and his own extensive knowledge of Russia to the writing of this book. Over many years he has given unflagging support to this project and all of our joint ventures. The arrival of our daughter, Kira, helped me set a firm deadline for finishing this book. She also contributed many long naps to its final stages. Thanks to Will and Kira for making it all worthwhile.

KATHLEEN E. SMITH

Alexandria, Virginia

Mythmaking in the New Russia

[1]

Memory and Postcommunist Politics

O n the evening of August 22, 1991, a crane entered the square in front of KGB headquarters in Moscow, hoisted the statue of Feliks Dzerzhinskii from its pedestal, and lowered it onto a flatbed truck. Cheers and catcalls from the boisterous crowd that had been trying to knock down the monument to the Soviet Union's first head of the secret police accompanied the statue's ignominious exit. Many of those in the jubilant gathering had spent the previous nights on the barricades around the Russian White House, which had been the center of resistance to an attempt by conservative Communists to remove Mikhail Gorbachev from the presidency of the USSR by force and to thwart the political decentralization and economic liberalization that he had introduced five years earlier. Led by the president of the Russian Republic, Boris Yeltsin, thousands of citizens had confronted the tanks brought into the capital by the coup plotters. After three tense days, the hard-line Communist junta had crumbled, and the victorious people of Moscow thronged into the streets to mark their triumph, in part by defacing the symbols of Communist Party rule.

The toppling of Dzerzhinskii seemed to represent a giant step away from Russia's totalitarian past and toward democracy. At that moment, the populace appeared to have decisively repudiated the legacy of repressive rule. Russian citizens had shown their willingness to defend their new freedom to speak out, to travel, to vote. It looked as if Gorbachev's tentative reforms had given way to a real liberal revolution. Who would have imagined then that less than a decade later, in December 1998, a popularly elected Russian legislature would vote in favor of restoring that statue to its old location in front of the security service's headquarters in downtown Moscow? In the intervening years, monumental art had become just one arena in which politicians battled over what should be remembered from the national past.

Intense interest in Soviet history had characterized the years of po-

Crowds besiege the monument to Feliks Dzerzhinskii in front of KGB headquarters, Moscow, August 22, 1991. (Photo by V. Marin'o. Courtesy of TsMADSN.)

litical reform that culminated in the defeat of the August 1991 coup. When Gorbachev introduced the idea of glasnost, or "openness," in the mid-1980s, he reasoned that increased freedom of expression would attract intellectuals to his plan for economic reform. He predicted that small doses of investigative journalism and constructive criticism would lead to more responsive governance, and hence strengthen the authority of the Communist Party and its system of government. Many journalists took the opportunity to crusade for social justice, and numerous intellectuals contributed to discussions of how to reinvigorate the planned economy, but one of the topics of greatest interest to both the media and the intelligentsia turned out to be recent national history. Revelations about Stalinist purges and the brutality of collectivization soon filled the pages of the daily press. It seemed by 1989 as if every aspect of the past was being scrutinized. Even Lenin was no longer sacrosanct. By the time of the conservative Communist backlash in August 1991, antistalinist and antileninist interpretations dominated discourse about the past in the USSR.[1]

Admittedly, attacks on the idols and legitimacy myths of the Soviet system had never passed unanswered. For example, when liberal politicians in the Leningrad city council voted to add a referendum on the city's name to local ballots for the upcoming election for president of the Russian Republic in the spring of 1991, the Communist press and Party organizations lobbied hard to preserve the name that paid homage to the leader of the Russian Revolution. Appealing to popular memories of different layers of national history, the defenders of Leningrad pointed not only to the city's status as the "cradle of the Revolution" but also to Leningrad's association with one of the bitterest battles of World War II. They identified the proposed return to St. Petersburg with the age of autocracy and sharp class distinctions. In this instance, anticommunists won, with slightly over half of the two-thirds of eligible voters who participated endorsing St. Petersburg. Nevertheless, their opponents' clever manipulation of historic symbolism had put democratic reformers on the defensive.[2]

The collapse of the Communist system of rule did not put an end to explorations of Soviet and Russian history. In the aftermath of August 1991 those loyal to the old regime could be observed seeking to salvage their dreams by rejecting some aspects of the past and embracing others. While keeping such slogans as "For our Soviet motherland," for instance, leaders of the revamped Communist Party of the Russian Federation declared that theirs was not "the party of Trotsky and Beria, Vlasov and Iakovlev, Gorbachev and Yeltsin." They rejected the legacy not only of those long identified in Soviet historiography as traitors and miscreants—such as General Andrei Vlasov, who organized Russian prisoners of war in Germany to fight against the USSR during World War II—but also of perestroika-era reformers such as the former Politburo member and liberal ideologue Aleksandr Iakovlev.[3]

By contrast, "democrats" or "liberals"—terms that can be only loosely applied to the assortment of Russian anticommunists who supported a mixture of market economics and political pluralism—hesitated to indulge in patriotic mythmaking, a practice that they associated with heavy-handed Communist Party propaganda rather than with the Western capitalist democratic societies that they took as their models.[4] In moments of crisis, however, they too turned to the national past, first reviving antisoviet themes popular during perestroika and later searching for positive grounding for a new state patriotism. After the Russian Communist Party made a strong showing in the December 1993 parliamentary elections, for example, Yeltsin suddenly announced that he had rehabilitated the persons executed on Lenin's orders for their participation in the 1921 Kronstadt uprising against the Bolsheviks. By late 1996, however, he was calling for reconciliation and asking the public to help identify a unifying "idea for Russia."

Does it matter whether the representatives of the Communist Party managed to sidestep accountability for their messy past, or whether democrats found or forged positive, patriotic images of their own? In view of the myriad pressing economic, security, and institutional problems facing Russia, why would politicians devote so much attention to versions of the past? Politics always has a symbolic dimension. Politicians in general have a particular interest in shaping versions of past events because shared memories of nationally significant events provide grist for the formation of collective identities. Politicians who can convert past glories into symbolic capital in the present can not only woo supporters but also give an aura of legitimacy to their claim to be worthy wielders of power. Moreover, new rulers face the problem not just of "forming a government" but of "fostering emotional attachment" to a new system of government and, in the case of Russia, to a new state.[5] Neither the achievement of sovereignty nor a sharp break with a political system guarantees the quick adoption of new identities or the rapid reconstruction of new historical narratives that explain how the present came to be.

Russian political actors had particular cause to delve into the past. Periods of turbulent change always seem to foster waves of looking backward, whether with nostalgia or with distaste. Revolutionaries may fear the counterrevolutionary nature of too much memory, but even they need an image of the old regime to serve as a foil for their own government. In the case of the collapse of communist regimes and planned economies, values and understandings of national and other identities, as well as institutions and policies, required rethinking. The anthropologist Katherine Verdery argues that postsocialist change "is a problem of reorganization on a cosmic scale, and it involves the redefinition of virtually everything, including morality, social relations, and basic meanings. It means a reordering of people's entire meaningful worlds."[6] If one agrees even to some degree with her assessment, then one can understand why political activity in the wake of communism centered not just on the creation of market institutions and the holding of electoral contests but also on sorting out questions of what lessons should be taken from the past.

In Russia, compared to its former East European satellites and to the other Soviet republics, the problem of salvaging something from national history was bound to be acute. As the imperial center, Russia could not effortlessly shift blame for its problems onto another nation. It could not easily attribute the ills of Soviet-style socialism to some alien force, though some extreme nationalists would try to make Jews the scapegoats for Russia's woes. Nor after nearly seventy-five years of Communist rule could Russians easily pick up where they had left off.[7] Nevertheless, despite the unpleasantness or remoteness of much of the national past, perceptions of history continue to inform judgments in present-day Russia.

This book rests on the assumption that framing collective memory matters not just on the individual level, where it shapes group identity and provides moral imperatives, but also on the societal level, where it informs a variety of political choices. As Michael Schudson contends, "A nation 'remembers' institutionally as well as individually, its organs of government altered, its political language rewoven, its repertoire for speaking or doing politics redesigned by past events."[8] Dramatic and traumatic events in a nation's history are processed by the media, politicians, and cultural figures in ways that affect the popular legitimacy of regimes and policies. Comparisons with past regimes, in particular, shape notions of good government. Moreover, in the ideological vacuum that sometimes follows political and cultural upheaval, symbolic politics may provide the easiest means for voters to distinguish between competing parties.

In this book I attempt to understand how and to what effect memories of the national past were being negotiated and propagated in Russia during the Yeltsin era. I trace battles over representations and interpretations of the past in the nation's political life and explore how political elites in particular tried to construct or appropriate versions of the past or historical symbols. By analyzing the forging and remaking of collective memory in a variety of arenas over the first eight years of Russian independence, I seek to illuminate the bases of legitimacy of competing political forces. Obviously, an assessment of their mythmaking efforts is only one way to measure the strength of various political groups. But, as sporadic efforts from above and below to set a commemorative calendar, to popularize historical stories and symbols, and to find viable heroes give way to more coherent narratives of national history, clues to attitudes that will shape Russian politicking and policy making in future decades become evident. As the anthropologist Mary Catherine Bateson points out,

Wherever a story comes from, whether it is a familiar myth or a private memory, the retelling exemplifies the making of a con-

nection from one pattern to another: a potential translation in
which narrative becomes parable and the once upon a time
comes to stand for some renascent truth. . . . Our species thinks
in metaphors and learns through stories.[9]

If one thinks of national identities not solely as some sort of mystical
cultural bonds formed in the distant past but as something continuously under construction, then one can study them to "learn more
about those who deploy them and whose interests they serve."[10]

Political scientists studying the transformations under way in Eastern Europe and the former Soviet Union have tended to focus their efforts on institutional change and to operate on the assumption that political actors are motivated by rational self-interest. Rational choice
theories leave little room for cultural considerations.[11] While not deny-
ing the importance of studying economic and political institutions, I
have adopted an approach to politics that views symbolic activity as
the root of authority, which in turn makes possible the exercise of
power in modern states without direct application of force. By ap-
proaching the consolidation of a new political regime through the
analysis of mythmaking and commemoration, social remembering and
forgetting, I have taken my lead from anthropologists, sociologists, and
cultural historians.[12] But, as a political scientist, I have tried not to lose
sight of either the political intent that often lies behind the mobilization of collective memories or the impact of interpretations of the past
on battles for influence.

Having made a case for the analysis of collective memory as a means
of illuminating current Russian politics, I feel it necessary before pro-
ceeding to consider how social scientists have conceptualized collective memory, and where the pitfalls lie in studying it. The investigation
of memory has become increasingly popular among cultural historians,
but one might wonder what is meant by "collective memory" and how
it differs from "ideology" or "history." Maurice Halbwachs began his
fundamental work on collective memory by contrasting individual, au-
tobiographical memories with the memories held in common by
groups. People remember collectively, he argued, in that they recall national events that touched their lives even when they did not personally witness them.[13] Such memories, though partial and often inaccurate, bind people together by forming the basis of a perceived shared
past. For his fellow cultural historians, according to Alon Confino, collective memory "has come to denote the representation of the past and

the making of it into a shared cultural knowledge by successive generations in 'vehicles of memory' such as books, films, museums, commemorations, and others." Therefore, collective memory can be seen as
popularized representations of the past located in a variety of sites, or
lieux de mémoire.[14]

Though political actors often take great interest in how the past is
interpreted, collective memory—unlike ideology—is not a set of connected principles. Shared images of the past may inform political decision making, but they are not the same as explanatory theories or complex political worldviews. Even when marshaled into commemorative
rituals, memories do not always form coherent building blocks in larger
national narratives. Moreover, collective memory is invariably rooted
in—though by no means an accurate representation of—history,
whereas ideology is generally grounded in abstract ideas. Finally, ideology is in principle open to all consumers, whereas collective memories
belong to sometimes exclusive groups.[15]

Collective memory, though it is a matter of recalling and retelling
the past, should not be equated with history, either. Collective memory
is more fluid than history. Unlike an account of events that exists at a
remove from social life, collective memory "continuously negotiates
between available historical records and current social and political
agendas."[16] It is not formed in accordance with the rules of a professional discipline. Its "undisciplined" nature means collective memory
has more in common with the modern notion of heritage. As David
Lowenthal explains, "History explores and explains pasts grown ever
more opaque over time; heritage clarifies pasts so as to infuse them
with present purposes."[17] But, whereas heritage seeking is often a
highly personal activity and one in which individual memories are sub-
stituted for the history of a group, collective remembering has to do
with framing the past in ways that attempt to capture the common experience that defines group identity. Collective memory, in short, provides a means to conceptualize the omnipresent phenomena of mythmaking and "invention of tradition."[18]

Although offering a useful lens for the analysis of the formation of
versions of group identities, the concept of collective memory is not
easily applied. Popular elements of a society's imagined past may be relatively simply identified and tracked over time in literature and the
media. The challenge, as the historian Alon Confino notes, is to go further, to look for action inspired by memory. "To make a difference in
society," he argues, "it is not enough for a certain past to be selected. It

must steer emotions, motivate people to act, be received; in short, it must become a sociocultural mode of action."[19] Hence, one cannot escape from the difficult methodological task of trying to identify and evaluate the reception of collective memory. Moreover, Confino contends that studies of how elites represent the past should not pretend to be about collective memory, since they do not address the way in which memories are offered up by or altered in civil society.[20]

The problem of assessing the reception of representations of the past is endemic in the field of memory studies. But Confino's concern with the internalization of historical mentalities and his case study in which the local bourgeoisie and civic associations were active in the invention of tradition need not define the range and nature of useful inquiries into memory and national identity. A study of the mobilization of collective memories by an elite can provide insight into an important aspect of the process of forming a national identity—the proffering of potentially acceptable beliefs about what it means to be a member of a certain nation. Without ignoring the negotiation that produces collective memory—for interpretations are contested among elites as well as from below—one can still usefully approach representations of the past as part of politicians' activities, especially in postcommunist states with their legacy of weak civil societies.

In this book I focus on the production or adoption and propagation of collective memories by the central Russian political and cultural elite. Of course the selection of important precedents is not the sole privilege of actors in national politics. Local myths and countermemories may frequently be set in opposition to overarching narratives propagated by national authorities.[21] A thorough study of local memories and their relation to national narratives in Russia would be fascinating, but I do not aspire to tell a story of center-regional relations here. I further leave to the pollsters to try to capture all the vagaries of public sentiment toward holidays, symbols, and other expressions of political mythmaking, and to the ethnographers to attempt to map how individuals internalize representations of the past. When possible, however, I have been attentive to indicators of popular acceptance or rejection of myths and symbols, such as voluntary civic participation in public rituals, letters to newspapers regarding historical controversies, and jokes aimed at new icons.

Ultimately, however, this book investigates the efforts of competing elites on the level of national politics to mobilize collective memory to increase their stature among at least some sectors of the public. Admittedly, such an approach runs the risk of treating conflicting memories as simply the result of preexisting political differences.[22] Although one can see in Russia collective memory and political divisions being renegotiated simultaneously, these processes are so interwoven that causal relationships seem very ambiguous: when is collective memory driving political decision making and when is political pragmatism driving selective representation of the past? It may not be possible to sort out this causal tangle, but one can bear in mind that memory is not entirely malleable. Hence, while political actors may promote self-serving interpretations of history, they are neither unconstrained by history nor free of their own bonds of memory.

A last concern raised by Confino is analysts' tendency to focus on narrow questions, such as how a certain event is remembered or how the past is represented in a single medium, rather than look at "broader questions about the role of the past in society."[23] I would not be so quick to dismiss "narrow" studies; Nina Tumarkin's fascinating survey of how World War II is remembered in Russia and Victoria Bonnell's probing study of Soviet political posters demonstrate that "fragmented" approaches can offer great insights into particular state-society relations.[24] Readers will have to judge for themselves to what extent the present analysis of collective memory in Russia contributes to larger issues of memory and society; but it does attempt to avoid the problem of fragmentation by looking at memories of a variety of events and personages in several arenas. Drawing on a survey of the media, an analysis of political texts, and numerous months of fieldwork in Moscow over a decade, I have selected cases that were highly visible, hotly contested, and explicit in their use of historical referents. These cases come from such varied forums as election campaigns, legislative battles, and court cases.

This investigation of memory and politics in the new Russia begins with an account of how loyal Communists, in the wake of the unsuccessful coup attempt in August 1991, fought in the Constitutional Court for the right to preserve their old name. In the course of the court proceedings, one can see Communists struggling in the aftermath of their political humiliation to redefine their own group identity and to rehabilitate themselves in the eyes of the public by rewriting their own history. Chapter 3 looks at how, by contrast, for the ruling democrats August 1991 marked a positive turning point. It considers their somewhat laissez faire attitude[25] toward commemorating their regime's founding moment, and the erosion of the triumphal myth of August after the events of October 1993 and the Russian parliament's subsequent amnesty of the coup plotters.

Beginning in 1994, contestation over the past and particularly over notions of patriotism increased in Russia. Chapters 4 and 5 trace the evolution of the mobilization of collective memories of the recent past in two distinct cases: debates over what to do with trophy art from World War II, and celebrations of commemorative holidays. Both of these situations reveal renewed efforts by the Communist Party to capture the patriotic mantle, and defensive shifts by liberals—that is, people who shared a commitment to political pluralism and individual rights and to some degree of market reform—away from previous harsh criticism of the Soviet era.

Subsequent chapters consider nascent efforts by various so-called democrats to assert their own notions of appropriate versions of the national past. Chapter 6 examines the means by which the mayor of Moscow, Iurii Luzhkov, injected his conception of Russian heritage into the capital's landscape. Chapter 7 turns to the head-to-head confrontation between liberal reformers and nationalist-oriented Communists in the 1996 presidential race. The campaign is analyzed from the perspective of the use of historical referents and symbols. Finally, Chapter 8 considers Yeltsin's final efforts to promote a usable past by searching for a positive basis for a democratic patriotism and by seeking the reconciliation of historic opponents.

Rewriting Communist Party History in the Constitutional Court

Trials of the old regime after political upheavals are not un-common. New democracies in Greece and Argentina, for instance, tried and convicted former authoritarian leaders. Truth commissions have also gained popularity as a means of publicizing previous human rights abuses. But Russian leaders, although they sanctioned the arrests of the organizers of the August 1991 coup attempt and banned the Communist Party, did not attempt to try the old regime either through the judicial system or before the court of public opinion. In Russia, the vanquished took the victors to court by challenging President Boris Yeltsin's decrees that suspended and later outlawed the Communist Party of the Soviet Union (CPSU) and its Russian branch (CP RSFSR) and nationalized their property. Only when the Constitutional Court agreed to hear this case did the victors respond with a more comprehensive attack on the former ruling party.

Although they were free to form new parties of a communist orientation, many former CPSU leaders chose instead to defend their old organization. Angry with Yeltsin's charge that the CPSU had led the country to a "historical dead end,"[1] Communist loyalists praised their party, but without lauding every aspect of seventy years of Soviet history. Some would-be heirs to the leadership of the CPSU also opted to fight for their heritage through a new democratically created institution—the Russian Constitutional Court.[2] The Party's defenders realized full well, however, that a legal victory would not mean much unless they could simultaneously raise the Party's authority among the citizenry. They had to craft not just persuasive legal arguments for the court but also an effective moral appeal for a broader audience. Hence, though they constantly reminded their opponents that the courtroom was not the place for historical judgments, they themselves sought during the course of the trial to recast Party history.

Obviously, a court hearing does not have the same shape as an unfettered public debate. The representatives of all sides had to shape their arguments to respond to the specifics of the presidential decrees and to conform with the legal framework, most notably the 1978 Brezhnev constitution, which had been only somewhat amended between August 1991 and the start of the high court's hearing in July 1992. Moreover, the justices tried to avoid "politicization," often chastising representatives and witnesses for "polemics" and "digressions."

Nevertheless, the trial setting—especially the cross-examination of witnesses and experts—forced the parties into a dialogue that frequently hinged on evaluations of the past. Although the hearing failed to hold the public's attention over the six months of its duration, presentations in the Constitutional Court and polemics in the press regarding the trial reveal both sides' first cuts at framing new usable versions of the Soviet past. Before we can understand the contents of this dialogue, however, we must briefly consider the situation that sparked it.

The August Coup

On the morning of August 19, 1991, broadcasts by a new organization calling itself the State Committee for the State of Emergency (GKChP) flooded the Soviet airwaves. Composed of seven top officials—including the vice president of the USSR, Gennadii Ianaev; the head of the KGB, Vladimir Kriuchkov; Prime Minister Valentin Pavlov; and Defense Minister Dmitrii Iazov—and the head of the Peasants' Union, the GKChP informed the public that it had taken power because President Mikhail Gorbachev was incapacitated by health problems. The early decrees broadcast that day, however, demonstrated that the GKChP aimed to reverse Gorbachev's increasingly liberal political and economic reforms. For instance, the GKChP suspended new political parties, arguing that "taking advantage of the liberties that have been granted . . . extremist forces have emerged, embarking on a course toward liquidating the Soviet Union, ruining the state, and seizing power at any cost." The committee members promised to preserve the USSR by preventing the signing of the new decentralizing union treaty scheduled for August 20, to lower prices on food and vital consumer services, and to improve housing, medicine, and education. In short, they presented themselves as saviors of a nation in which the security of Brezhnev-era socialism had given way to political and economic chaos.[3]

Although the GKChP had isolated Gorbachev and his family at their vacation home in the Crimea, it had not taken the precaution of arresting other potential opponents. On the morning of August 19, the Russian Republic's government, with Yeltsin at its head, took the lead in opposing the GKChP's seizure of power.[4] Perhaps to the surprise of the coup plotters, Yeltsin sprang to the defense of his long-time rival Gorbachev. Within hours of the GKChP's first announcement, Yeltsin and his close associates had drafted a public statement charging the GKChP with illegally removing the elected president of the USSR. Yeltsin, Ivan Silaev, the chair of the Russian Council of Ministers, and Ruslan Khasbulatov, the acting chair of the Russian Supreme Soviet, signed the appeal labeling the seizure of power a "putsch" and declaring all of the GKChP's actions to be unconstitutional.

Over the next two days, a standoff developed between the army units that had moved into Moscow at the direction of the GKChP and crowds of civilians mobilized by Yeltsin, with the assistance of journalists and democratic activists. Individually and collectively, civilians appealed to soldiers not to obey any orders to fire on the crowd. On the second day of the coup, over 100,000 citizens attended rallies in Leningrad and Moscow. Fearing that an attack might come under cover of darkness, hundreds of protesters spent the night at makeshift barricades around the Russian parliament building, known as the White House, where Yeltsin and his team had set up a command center. On the night of August 20–21, three young men were killed when they tried to prevent some tanks from moving closer to the White House. But, whether by design or not, the coup plotters never initiated a military attack on the Russian government.

The coup leaders' weakness stemmed in part from the terrible impression they created with their first press conference. TV cameras zoomed in on Acting President Ianaev's shaking hands, and the plotters spluttered ineffectually when a young Russian journalist dared to call the events a "coup." The GKChP also failed to prevent the state television's news program from broadcasting footage of crowds at the White House and a summary of Yeltsin's appeal delivered from atop a tank.[5] Strong negative reactions from abroad and a lack of enthusiasm from many republican and local leaders further shook the committee members' confidence. Seeing their authority slip away, a delegation of demoralized putschists rushed to the Crimea on the afternoon of the 21st to try to curry favor with Gorbachev. The USSR president, however, sided with the Russian government, which arrested the chief plotters, with the exception of Interior Minister Boris Pugo, who committed suicide.

Two days after the defeat of the coup, Yeltsin summoned Gorbachev to the White House to appear before the Russian legislature. After congratulating those gathered on the victory over reactionary forces and naming those who had been arrested for their role in the coup attempt, Yeltsin gave the floor to Gorbachev. The USSR president paid homage to the Russian parliament and president, putting himself and Yeltsin together in the "vanguard of democratic forces" that were the main targets of the putschists. He spoke of feeling betrayed by those he trusted. Yet Gorbachev took credit for having transformed society so that it could successfully resist the coup attempt. Dissatisfied with Gorbachev's failure to acknowledge that he shared some of the blame for the behavior of his handpicked subordinates, however, Yeltsin humiliated Gorbachev by forcing him to read out evidence of their disloyalty. Then he signed a decree suspending the activity of the Russian Communist Party, and suggested to a startled Gorbachev that he do likewise for the Communist Party of the Soviet Union.[6]

The Decrees

Arguably, the rapid collapse of Soviet power after the unexpected coup attempt caught democratic politicians unprepared. Instead of seizing credit for the dramatic developments, Yeltsin, in a radio address to the nation on August 29, described the historic political developments of the preceding weeks as if they were entirely self-generated. Moreover, rather than emphasizing his own role or the efforts of democratic groups in bringing down the Communist system, Yeltsin spoke of how "the main levers of power are falling from the hands of those forces that have ruled the nation for decades." He referred to the collapse of the center and of the security forces without setting out any interpretation of cause and effect. He even urged Russians to resume their "normal working rhythm," and suggested "a halt to the euphoria of victory."[7]

Nevertheless, in the days that followed the defeat of the putsch, Boris Yeltsin used presidential decrees to increase the Russian government's power and to continue his earlier efforts toward decommunization of Russian society. With the central figures behind the putsch al-

ready under arrest, Yeltsin removed from office those regional execu-
tives who had openly supported the coup plotters, and named his own
temporary representatives to oversee the actions of local governments
across the Russian Federation.[8] To reinforce his authority over the
state, Yeltsin suspended the activity of the recently formed Russian
branch of the CPSU, the Communist Party of the Russian Republic,
and took its property under guard. The president accused the CP RSFSR
of having supported the GKChP in trying to oust Gorbachev from office, and of having hindered the fulfillment of his decree of July 20,
1991, ordering the cessation of political parties' activities within Russian state institutions.[9]

Although Yeltsin apparently did not feel in August 1991 that he had
jurisdiction over the fate of the all-Union Communist Party, he
nonetheless took control of its archives, as well as those of the USSR
KGB, to prevent their unlawful destruction. Finally, on August 25,
Yeltsin decreed that all CPSU/CP RSFSR assets on Russian territory
would become the property of the Russian state.[10] The seizure of CPSU
and KGB archives might have been seen as a portent of investigations,
arrests, and firings to come. But Yeltsin ordered democrats not to abuse
their victory. He vowed that there would be no dictatorship of the democrats, no single party dominating the government. In particular,
Yeltsin renounced the legacy of witch-hunts. Referring to his own experience in being "worked over" by the collective for his temerity in criticizing the pace of Gorbachev's reforms, he swore that he would not
allow any persecution of ordinary Communists.[11] Having become the
unexpected beneficiary of a nearly bloodless revolution, the president
found it easy to be gracious to what he saw as a clearly defeated foe.

Gorbachev's attitude toward the Communist Party, its prospects,
and its culpability for the coup attempt differed markedly from
Yeltsin's. As noted above, Gorbachev was slow to assimilate the change
in popular opinion that occurred during his three-day imprisonment.
On his return, he expressed his confidence that the Communist Party
could be reformed. Only on August 24 did Gorbachev resign as general
secretary of the CPSU and suggest to the Central Committee that its
members "adopt the difficult but honorable decision to disband itself."
But Gorbachev wanted to let the Party masses have a say in the CPSU's
future, so he left it to republican and local Party organizations to "determine their own fate."[12]

When the CPSU did not act quickly to dissolve itself, however,
Yeltsin issued a harsher decree. Timing the announcement for the eve

of the anniversary of the Bolshevik Revolution, on November 6, 1991, Yeltsin ordered that both the CPSU and the CP RSFSR cease their activity and that Party property be handed over to the government. In this decree, Yeltsin began by averring that the CPSU was never really a political party per se, but rather a special mechanism for realizing political power by combining with or subordinating state structures. "The leadership structures of the CPSU," he charged, "implemented their own dictatorship and created the material basis for their own unlimited power at the state's expense." Yeltsin accused the Party of violating the 1978 constitution of the Russian Federation by having incited religious, social, and national discord. He dubbed the Party's activities "antipopular" as well as "anticonstitutional" and blamed the CPSU leadership for the current collapse. Efforts to "reanimate the gigantic mechanism" of the CPSU would not be tolerated. But, Yeltsin cautioned, neither would he permit "attempts to tar millions of ordinary Communist Party members, who had nothing to do with the arbitrariness and violence carried out in their names."[13]

The Reaction

Carefully drawing attention away from the highly placed coup plotters, the Communist Party's defenders argued that the new government's "repressive decrees" violated the human rights of those 19 million citizens who belonged to the CPSU. The freedom to join some other association did not compensate for the loss of the preferred organization. Adopting the democrats' own language and principles, Communists accused Yeltsin of breaking the USSR law on social organizations by not working through the courts to dissolve the CPSU. They further claimed that the ban was a move by Yeltsin to disband the "only real opposition force" and hence "a dangerous precedent for the punishment of any dissent." Communists even cast the CPSU in the role of a victim of Stalinism, describing it as having been subject to acts of "arbitrariness and illegality" and as awaiting "rehabilitation."[14]

As a practical response to the ban, in late December 1991 a group of deputies to the Russian Supreme Soviet appealed to the Constitutional Court to consider the legality of the president's decrees halting the Communist Party's activity and nationalizing its property. Given the suspension of Party activity, the Party's representatives were self-selected and thus seen by some as ineligible to speak for the organization as a whole. Mikhail Gorbachev, the last CPSU general secretary, not only declined to defend the Party but later even refused to obey the Constitutional Court's summons to appear as a witness. Similarly, few of the millions of members frequently referred to by the Party's advocates publicly rallied behind their party or hastened to join one of the several successor parties that had formed by the time of the trial.[15]

In autumn 1991, many liberal political observers expected that the trial would in effect deliver a postmortem on an organization that had already died. The CPSU had been suffering from internal schisms and steadily losing members before the coup. Hence one journalist surmised that the ban was meant not to humiliate the defeated or to demonize a political opponent but to prevent provincial Party structures from continuing to obstruct reform. She doubted that Communists would have to defend themselves against witch-hunts. After all, the president himself relied on many former Communists to staff his administration.[16] In fact, as the radical democratic mayor of St. Petersburg, Anatolii Sobchak, explained, "In the new Russia no one even thought that the CPSU should be tried and declared a criminal organization. The new Russian leadership was too closely connected to the Party—one could say it emerged from the heart of the Communist Party."[17] Since so many people, and not just a few high-ranking politicians, had voluntarily broken with the Communist Party and changed their ideals, a Nuremberg-style trial of the CPSU seemed superfluous to many democrats. Most liberal politicians assumed a sufficient break with the past had already occurred naturally.[18]

But when the court decided in the spring of 1992 to hear the appeal of Yeltsin's ban of the Communist Party, several ad hoc groups of liberals rushed to prepare a countersuit. Oleg Rumiantsev, a deputy who headed the Russian Supreme Soviet's commission to draft a new Russian constitution, filed a petition signed by more than seventy fellow legislators asking the court to evaluate the constitutionality of the CPSU and CP RSFSR. He argued, essentially, that the Constitutional Court should consider whether these political parties' ideologies and behavior were in accord with the basic laws governing social organizations. In May 1992, the Court decided—over the protests of the original petitioners—to combine the two appeals.[19]

With good reason, both democratic and Communist newspapers labeled the Constitutional Court's subsequent joint hearing the "trial of the CPSU." The representatives of the banned CPSU and CP RSFSR[20] who took on the task of defending their organizations against Rumiantsev's accusations certainly had cause to regard themselves as being on trial. Meanwhile, despite the fact that they had initiated the hearing with their attack on Yeltsin's ukases, those Communist deputies who petitioned the court to review the ban also saw themselves as on the defensive against a powerful executive branch. Hence, although they sometimes contradicted each other, these two teams can be looked at as essentially engaged in the same task—fighting for the honor and right to life of the CPSU.[21]

The president appointed two members of his administration with law degrees—Sergei Shakhrai and Mikhail Fedotov—and his close adviser Gennadii Burbulis to defend his decrees. Andrei Makarov, a well-known defense lawyer, represented the group of deputies who signed the Rumiantsev petition.[22] The two democratic teams at the joint hearing were also not entirely united. The president's defense hinged on the contention that the CPSU was not a real political party, but rather a part of the state apparatus and therefore subject to the president's disposition. The Rumiantsev appeal, by contrast, relied on wording in the constitution regarding social organizations. Shakhrai, Fedotov, and Makarov, who conducted the courtroom portion of the cases, sought to smooth over this inconsistency by circumlocution: they referred to the Party as "the organization calling itself the Communist Party." They worked together in sorting through archival documents and presented a united anticommunist front.[23]

Communists Make Their Case

The Communist Party's adherents began their case on the offensive, arguing in their opening statements that the CPSU was in fact a popular institution. They cited its size—some 19 million members allegedly before its suspension, making it by far the largest social organization in the former Soviet Union. Moreover, they pointed to the Party's successful leadership of the nation in World War II. If the Party were "antipopular," Deputy Iurii Slobodkin averred, the Soviet people would not have rallied around it during the war. Wartime behavior showed that Soviet citizens were loyal, not "oppressed." The rapid rebuilding of the Soviet economy after the war and the nation's technical achievements, especially in the realm of space flight, were also held up as signs of the enthusiastic support that underlay CPSU rule.[24] With these examples, the CPSU's advocates unerringly pointed to the least controversial, most untarnished national achievements during the seven decades of Soviet rule.

The defenders of the CPSU also touted the positive changes within the Party and its role in reforming Soviet politics. The Party, they noted, initiated reform both at the Twentieth Party Congress in 1956, where Khrushchev denounced Stalin's "cult of personality," and again in the 1980s. By abolishing the Brezhnev constitution's article 6, which had enshrined the leading role of the CPSU, the Party itself had cleared the way during perestroika for a multiparty system. It might even be considered the "midwife" of such independent liberal groups as Democratic Russia.[25] Arguably, the CPSU had not completed the transition to a parliamentary party, but what counted was trajectory. As the former head of the Central Committee of the CP RSFSR, Valentin Kuptsov, contended: "The president banned a party that had undergone cardinal reforms, that was already acting only by political means, and that had carried out enormous work in the democratization of [Soviet] society."[26] In view of the CPSU representatives' evident disdain for Gorbachev and hatred of the "architect of perestroika," Aleksandr Iakovlev, their defense of the Party based on its commitment to democratization rang somewhat hollow.[27] Nevertheless, numerous CPSU witnesses pointed to the Party's steps toward internal and external democratization as virtues.

In fact, Party representatives argued that the abolition of article 6 in March 1990 so significantly transformed the CPSU that only its actions after that date should be subject to judicial scrutiny. In a debate regarding the admissibility of documents pertaining to the Soviet massacre of captured Polish officers at Katyn on the eve of World War II, the law professor Feliks Rudinskii highlighted the differences between the Stalin and Gorbachev eras by comparing the Politburo of 1940 with the Politburo of 1991. He asked rhetorically,

I wonder, can a Politburo in which one of the leaders can arrest the wife of another, which in general arose on the basis of the repression of the Seventeenth Party Congress, and when the NKVD was raised above the Party, be looked upon as embodying the will of the Party? What bearing can all this have today for our generation of Communists?[28]

When it suited them, he and his colleagues equated analysis of other historical periods with politicization, charging that the lawyers for the other side dwelled on the actions of past generations of Communists because they were unable to prove the unconstitutionality of the living generation's policies.[29]

Despite drawing a line in Party history at March 1990, CPSU representatives could not, and did not try to, avoid discussion of the past altogether. Besides referring to past achievements, they acknowledged the existence of some of the most tragic events of the Soviet period. They expressed their horror at the many abuses of human rights under Stalin, but simultaneously praised themselves for having admitted their mistakes after Stalin's death.[30] Moreover, the Party's defenders attempted to minimize the scope of the purges and to present the Party as the main victim of the purges. Several Communists recounted their own families' sufferings in the Stalin era, and one of them, Deputy Dmitrii Stepanov, stated: "More people died at the hands of the fascists than [died] here during the years of the Stalin cult of personality. And it's not entirely correct to measure everything by the numbers of those who suffered. For instance, in our century the number of those killed in car accidents far outweighs the number killed in all wars."[31] The Communist newspaper *Pravda* praised Stepanov's zeal and drew attention to his status as the son of a victim of repression, but did not cite his dubious statistics.[32]

Other CPSU representatives avoided the subject of how many people had suffered in the purges and focused instead on the victims' identity. The side's consensus was aptly captured by Valentin Falin, a former Central Committee official:

> Against whom was Stalin's first and main blow, when he carried
> out a counterrevolutionary coup in the nation? Among what so-
> cial groups, parties, if one can speak of parties, were there the
> greatest number of victims? Among the Communists. This was
> the case in the 1930s and in the 1940s.[33]

Only by repressing many Communists could Stalin realize his dictatorship. It followed that the Party was not the source of evil intentions, but rather a victim of circumstances.[34]

To create a mix of sympathy and respect for their heritage, the Communist Party's defenders balanced their claims of victimization with accounts of deliberate sacrifices made for the nation. They pointed to the Party's leadership and human losses in the Civil War, the Revolution, and World War II. In weighing the Party's services and faults, the former prime minister Nikolai Ryzhkov proclaimed:

> The history of the Party is complex, just as the history of our nation is complex. Despite its tragic pages, the people themselves, at the cost of their comfort, made our great nation a superpower. And in this, in the first place, millions of Communists participated. Can one now reproach them for this? For this reason, I do not consider my party criminal.[35]

Similarly, in response to the charge of having usurped state functions, Party officials defended their "interference" as well-intentioned, generally successful efforts to make better public policy and to increase economic efficiency. In other words, the Party might have technically overstepped its mandate, but only in its quest to improve the nation's standard of living. Even former Communists who willingly acknowledged that in their time they had acted unconstitutionally admitted that they had done so with the intention of serving the people's interests.[36]

To account to the court for misdeeds of the past and to exculpate themselves in the public eye for responsibility for the collapse of Soviet power, some Communists began to advance the notion that the CPSU had always been divided. There had been two parties—one composed of self-serving careerists and the other consisting of sincere, dedicated believers. The honest members, claimed Rudinskii, always fought against uncommunist activities such as the Terror of 1937 and the bureaucratic corruption of the 1970s.[37] Some CPSU representatives characterized the split as between good reformers and bad Stalinists. Others elumped Gorbachev with those who had betrayed the Party and the nation. Thus Kuptsov railed:

> [Our side] defends here not Stalin and not Gorbachev, not those scoundrels who operated using the name of the Party as cover. It defends the Communist Party of the Soviet Union as a political organization that represents the interests of the working people, and that CPSU which by November 1991 had cleansed itself of chameleons who were seeking profit in the embraces of the new authorities.[38]

Whatever their views on Gorbachev, the Party's courtroom advocates concurred that rather than applying an unjust notion of collective guilt to the Party as a whole, certain leaders could be charged with violating both the constitution and Party norms.[39]

On a similar note, Party representatives denied Yeltsin's claims about the Communist Party's collective culpability for the August 1991 coup attempt. Not by accident, the Communist team began the trial with witnesses from its regional organizations who could sincerely swear to a lack of information regarding the coup and boast of their inactivity during the three days of emergency rule. Other witnesses testified that the coup plotters kept even the Central Committee in the dark, and that Ianaev had told its members to mind their own business.[40] Whatever happened in August 1991, the Communist side argued, could not be construed as the result of decisions properly adopted by the Party's leading organs. Moreover, CPSU representatives reminded the justices that the case against the GKChP members had not yet begun, and that no charges had been filed against additional participants by local prosecutors. In the absence of any official conclusions as to the nature of the August events, many issues, including Gorbachev's own role in the coup, remained open to speculation. Hence, individuals could even theorize that the coup was somehow masterminded by forces that wanted to liquidate the CPSU.[41]

To earn further sympathy, Communist Party representatives had several tactics designed to make all present or former CPSU members—a category that included the opposition lawyers and nearly all of the justices—reflect on their presumably clean consciences. They asked all Party members who appeared before the court as witnesses whether they personally had committed any unconstitutional acts. Those who testified against the Party were also questioned as to why they had ever joined an "unlawful organization." The Communist Party's defenders also flung the charge of hypocrisy at witnesses whose testimony contradicted earlier writings that followed the Party line. Frequently witnesses responded by defending their own honesty, calling themselves "law-abiding" but also sometimes admitting that in the past they had never judged their actions by the criterion of constitutionality. Many liberal witnesses told of how they had come to reevaluate their actions, whereas loyal Party members generally defended their behavior and attributed all of the Party's failings to corrupt individuals unrepresentative of the Party as a whole.[42]

Lastly, Communist Party loyalists tried to highlight the failings of the current government by drawing historical parallels. Though they had initiated the trial, they accused their opponents of using the hearing to distract the public from the "collapse of the once powerful fatherland and economy, from the destruction of science, culture, and the army, and from hunger and spiritual genocide launched against our own people."[43] They repeatedly pointed to the interethnic situation as far worse now than under Communist rule. In terms that must have resonated with his fellow pensioners, the former Politburo member Vladimir Dolgikh complained about food prices and the high rate of crime.[44] Party representatives also swore that they were concerned with reclaiming Party property primarily because the current government had not turned it over to needy social groups or used Party buildings to house local courts, as promised. If they were to regain their holdings, they vowed, they would donate Party sanatoriums, hospitals, dachas, and the like to organizations for the disadvantaged, keeping only publishing houses and other property necessary for the revitalization of a political party.[45]

CPSU representatives, in sum, presented their party as self-sacrificing, public-spirited, and reform-minded, and hence as unjustly victimized by the new government of Russia. They called up images of World War II and the postwar reconstruction to enhance their characterization of themselves as noble and unselfish. By recalling improvements in the standard of living under communism, they wooed those Russians who felt themselves injured by the current economic reform. Interestingly, Party representatives rarely mentioned Lenin or the Revolution. They focused instead on events still preserved in the memory of living generations. They tried to link collective memories of positive events in Soviet history with the personal lives of those involved in the case. They asked people to judge the Party by its achievements, to recall the Party as it had depicted itself at the time. Though they felt compelled to discuss the purges as the most unpleasant episodes in Party history, they twisted their interpretation of the times to make themselves the chief victims of repression. The mantle of victim clearly had strong appeal, not only because it fitted the dismay and chagrin of Party members upon finding their organization banned, but because it fitted a popular mood as well. With the dissolution of the USSR and the loss of superpower status, many Russians felt like the vanquished rather than the victors.[46]

The Democrats Respond

The democrats, too, built their case around several broad themes. First, spearheaded by the side that petitioned the court to examine the constitutionality of the CPSU, the democrats did their best to reveal not only the most egregious human rights violations committed during Soviet rule, but also Party bureaucrats' routine violations of constitutional norms in their administrative work. They produced witnesses from the human rights movement, the censors' office, and law enforcement to tell of the Party's unconstitutional behavior, especially its interference in the legal system. They introduced testimony regarding the history of the secret police from 1917 to 1991, and they buried the court in archival documents regarding Stalinist repressions, the invasion of Afghanistan, and the use of state funds to support left-wing movements overseas. They simultaneously made many of their archival discoveries available to liberal journalists. A typical result was *Moskovskie novosti*'s publication "The Party Is the Court, Press, Army, and Secret Police of Our Epoch" (a parody of the once popular slogan "The Party is the mind, honor, and conscience of our epoch"), which reprinted documents pertaining to the arrest and trial of dissidents, the CPSU's financial support of the Italian Communist Party, and its assignment of political officers—often drawn from the KGB—to military units.[47]

Second, the democrats strove to prove that, though the Party's methods had changed over the past few years, its activities and ideology had remained essentially intact. The lawyer Andrei Makarov drew parallels between the Revolution of 1917 and the putsch of August 1991, both of which he characterized as violent attempts to seize power. No period of Soviet history was sacred. When asked whether he considered even the CPSU's activity during World War II to have been unconstitutional, Makarov retorted:

> If you have in mind the extrajudicial punishments, replacement of state organs of leadership by the organization calling itself the CPSU, if you have in mind the repressions, violations of the rights of whole nations included in this period, then yes, I consider that without a doubt this activity was unconstitutional.[48]

From the time of the Revolution up to the present moment, the anticommunists contended, the Bolsheviks had based their rule on force, but concocted high-minded documents that simply did not correspond to their real actions. To counter the Communists' use of passages in the Party's public statements as evidence of the Party's real nature, the anticommunists often found themselves engaged in extracting evidence of the most banal details. On being asked to comment on whether the Party ever used state property, one frustrated witness said, "I think we're trying to break down open doors, we want to prove what, in my opinion, is known by 99 percent of the population who have lived in these conditions."[49] This sort of legalistic maneuvering neither brought respect to the democratic side nor encouraged public interest in the trial.

Third, the democrats raised the theme of repentance. They accused the Communist representatives of being incapable of truly atoning for the terrible mistakes of the past, and challenged the claim that the Party had voluntarily embraced destalinization, democratization, and economic reform.[50] In explaining the motivations for his countersuit, Rumiantsev stated forthrightly that he believed the Party had not been sincere about embracing constitutional principles after the abolition of article 6, or it would have disassociated itself from past illegalities, returned its ill-gotten wealth to the people, and stopped carrying out government functions. In addition, Shakrai and Makarov cited the refusal by the overwhelming majority of delegates to the final Party congress in 1990 to endorse a resolution that all previous programmatic documents had lost force.[51] The advocates of banning the CPSU also noted their opponents' propensity for casting all blame on a few Party leaders. Ironically, witnesses for the democratic side frequently spoke of their own repentance, of their willingness to take some of the responsibility for the tragedies of Soviet history. Even when asked whether Yeltsin too, as a member of the CPSU leadership, bore some responsibility, Makarov replied that there were no "islands of legality"—everyone should shoulder some of the blame.[52]

Lastly, both in the courtroom and in the press, the representatives of the presidential administration and the liberal deputies impugned the motives of the Party's defenders. Sergei Shakhrai defended Yeltsin's ban by explaining that the CPSU, "having let power slip away, lost its purpose. Having lost the atmosphere of universal terror, having choked on the air of freedom, this organization died." Hence Russia's legally elected president had simply "certified" the Party's disintegration and "eased its legal exit from the stage." He reasoned that Party loyalists were trying to "resuscitate a corpse" because they held out some hope that eventually the Party would return to power.[53] The anticommunists also insisted that the Party's current representatives were motivated by greed for power and for property. After all, individual Communist Party members lost none of their rights to profess their beliefs or to participate in political life. Despite talk of witch-hunts, one could see former leaders freely traveling abroad, writing their memoirs, and living as they pleased. For the anniversary of the October Revolution, which fell during the course of the trial, the Communist Party representatives even participated in a public demonstration permitted by Moscow authorities.[54]

In sum, the democratic side stressed episodes of violence that the Party's representatives preferred to omit from their narrative of Soviet history. The Revolution, the August coup, use of the armed forces to interfere in the politics of other sovereign states, the purges, the persecution of dissidents, the slaughter of prisoners of war at Katyn—all were held up as evidence of the Party's true nature. The "organization calling itself the CPSU," argued Shakhrai and Andrei Makarov, should be remembered as ruthless and power-hungry from beginning to end. Moreover, the democrats sought to counter memories of national achievement under Soviet rule with fresh examples of waste and impropriety, such as funneling millions of dollars to Communist parties abroad. The trial, however, produced little in the way of new revelations about Soviet rule, and hence drew scant attention from a public that had been inundated over the past five years with sensational stories about Communist crimes. The drawn-out, legalistic nature of the proceedings, of course, also contributed to popular indifference.

The Decision and Its Ramifications

The Constitutional Court justices faced numerous problems in evaluating the status of the CPSU and CP RSFSR. Most notably, the court faced gaps in the existing legislation regarding social organizations and a constitution that had originally been drawn up by the CPSU to enshrine its leading role and to preserve its rule. There was something Orwellian about charging the authors of the constitution with constant violations of its norms.[55] Moreover, several justices later admitted to journalists that they were acutely aware of the political implications of either completely invalidating Yeltsin's decrees or wholeheartedly endorsing the charge that the Party was unconstitutional. Consequently, they carefully crafted a compromise verdict.[56]

At the core of their November 1992 ruling, the justices made a distinction, introduced by Yeltsin and refined by legal experts, between the Party's leadership structures and its base organizations. The majority of justices agreed with the president that the CPSU at its higher levels did not resemble a social organization, and that, even after the removal of article 6, the Party's leading organs had continued to carry out state functions in violation of the constitution. Furthermore, they approved of Yeltsin's decision to suspend the Party, given the support for the GKChP evinced by many of its leaders. Yet, like the president, the court did not want to punish ordinary members of the Party for actions taken by the leadership without their input or knowledge. Therefore, they supported a ban on the Party's organizational structures from the level of *raikom* (regional committee within a city Party organization) upward, but annulled the dissolution of primary CPSU organizations formed on territorial principles.

Despite its often harsh criticisms of the CPSU's practices, the court declined to rule on Rumiantsev's petition challenging the constitutionality of the CPSU and CP RSFSR's behavior. The justices noted that by the time Yeltsin issued his ukase of November 1991, the republican organizations that made up the CPSU had "ceased to exist . . . as a result of disbanding, suspension, prohibition, and other transformations." Since the CPSU—including its Russian branch, which Yeltsin had legally suspended for usurping state functions—no longer existed, the matter of its constitutionality was moot.[57]

What did the ruling mean for the Party's future? The court allowed that base territorial organizations could generate new leadership structures and register in accordance with existing Russian law on an equal footing with other political parties.[58] But, with the exception of pensioners, most CPSU members belonged to primary organizations at their workplaces, not at their places of residence; therefore, by specifying the legality of territorial Party cells, the justices tacitly reinforced Yeltsin's earlier decree excluding political activity from the workplace. Party members could also petition civil courts for the return of some Party property. In another compromise ruling, the judges distinguished three types of property falling under CPSU control at the time of Yeltsin's ukases—state property, legitimate CPSU holdings, and property belonging to other unspecified owners—and concluded that Yeltsin could decide the future only of that portion of the CPSU holdings that constituted state property.[59]

Immediately after the verdict, the Communist press published an appeal for the revival of Communist Party activity. Its authors, who included such notables from the trial as Gennadii Ziuganov, Valentin

Kuptsov, Viktor Zorkal'tsev, and Ivan Rybkin, called upon primary Party organizations to reactivate themselves and announced a new plenum for February 1993. The publicity for that gathering labeled it a "revival-unification congress," thereby revealing its organizers' intention to claim the mantle of the old Communist Party. Indeed, plenum delegates voted to declare themselves the legal heir to the Communist Party of the Soviet Union, though in accord with territorial reality they dubbed their organization the Communist Party of the Russian Federation (KPRF). Justice Ernst Ametistov and others later argued that the actions of this congress already violated the spirit of the Constitutional Court's decision, but no legal steps were taken to challenge the KPRF's pretensions.[60]

Democratic Communism?

The old adage holds that history is written by the victors. The very genesis of the trial of the Communist Party, however, demonstrated the unusual nature of the ruling Russian democrats' attitudes toward the past. It is not uncommon for the leaders of new political systems to condemn the past in some ritualistic fashion, but the trial of the CPSU did not fit this pattern.[61] Some members of Russia's vanquished political establishment called upon a relatively new judicial institution to evaluate their past actions. Moreover, the court had to use the old regime's almost intact constitution to judge its heirs. Hence, rather than mark the beginning of a new system of rule, the trial emphasized continuity between the Gorbachev period and the postcommunist era. The case was not about revolutionaries drawing a thick line between the past and the present but about yesterday's functionaries brushing the dirt from their suits as they crawled out of the dustbin of history to which they had been gently relegated. Yeltsin came to the trial of the CPSU not to seek retribution against the old regime but to face very real charges that he had abused his authority. The trial brought home to democrats the difficulty of making a revolution by democratic means. Not only did they have to answer in court for actions during the "revolution," but they were bound by the old regime's laws, which they had not had time to replace.

Meanwhile, the very nature of the battle in front of an independent judicial institution showed how the Communists had mastered the language and the means to fight the democrats on their own turf. The liberal press poked fun at their rhetorical style, saying that the "smell of mothballs" emanated from their speeches, which resembled so many old propaganda accounts of progress and declarations of moral and ideological superiority.[62] But the representatives of the CPSU successfully used the language of the human rights movement to protest against the notion of collective guilt and against any limits on their right to free association. Moreover, by pursuing a remedy for their problem through the legal system, the representatives of the CPSU demonstrated their own willingness to work through the new democratic system.

Though the advocates for the Communist Party occasionally contradicted each other, they presented a unified front in their depiction of the Party as always having been committed to pursuing the overall good of the nation. Tension over how much and for what to apologize was assuaged by pride in past economic, scientific, and military achievements. Old myths about struggle, self-sacrifice, and victory were resurrected. The Party's leadership role and consequent heavy losses in World War II, in particular, were held up as shining examples of suffering for the benefit of others. The trial gave stalwart Communist officials a chance to polish their reputations and that of their party as well. Their appearance allowed them to demonstrate that not all had foresworn the communist cause or come to scorn the achievements of the past.

The Party's new status as a victim of repressive government policies also made for good publicity. At a time when many Russians felt themselves to be the casualties of current policies, the claim of victimization evoked great empathy. In defending themselves, the old men in bad suits could also claim to be sticking up for a whole generation whose contributions of labor and even life for their country were now being demeaned or disregarded. Moreover, by challenging the democrats' nonchalant dismissal of national history as a source of positive inspiration, the Communist loyalists had set the stage for a battle over the meaning of patriotism for the new Russia.

Remembering August 1991:
Founding Moment or Farce?

During the August 1991 coup attempt, journalists captured and reproduced the spectacle of Russian President Boris Yeltsin standing atop a tank, appealing to a crowd of anxious men and women to resist the unconstitutional actions of the GKChP. The image of Yeltsin heroically presiding over a peaceful civic movement would seem to have provided fodder to Russian democrats eager to distinguish the new regime from the old. But only two years later the image of Yeltsin defending the nation from his base in the Russian parliament building was tarnished and perhaps superseded in the public mind by new reportage of Russian tanks firing on the White House on Yeltsin's orders. Today the area that Yeltsin dubbed "Freedom Square" in August 1991 is partially occupied by a "Memorial Territory" for the victims of October 1993. Members of the Communist and nationalist opposition have decorated a weedy lot bordering the White House with wooden crosses, ribbons, flowers, and bulletin boards covered with photos of victims and political commentary. The contest over this territory is only part of the intense conflict over constructing and reconstructing the recent past for political ends.

Although consensus on how to evaluate the past is unlikely during times of political upheaval, even at times of great discord opposing forces can often agree on the identity of distinct historical turning points as such. In Russia, August 1991 marked such a moment. In the aftermath of the failed coup the democrats seemed to have won a great victory in the six-year struggle over the course of political reform. August 1991's standing as the defining moment in recent Soviet/Russian history, however, was challenged in October 1993 by the equally dramatic shelling of the Russian parliament building. For some observers, the assault on the Supreme Soviet signified the failure of democracy at the hands of Yeltsin, while for others it seemed like a final step in an arduous process of democratization that had really begun only in August 1991. The national legislature's decision in 1994 to amnesty the coup plotters and those opposition politicians accused of starting the bloody clash in October 1993 before any trial took place opened the door wider to a myriad of interpretations of these events.

August 1991 had the potential to serve as a founding moment in the mythology of the new Russian state. Governments have substantial resources with which to direct public attention to specific historic moments, but they do not always use them. Nor can they guarantee that the public will be receptive to the efforts they do make. All sorts of contingencies may arise to supersede efforts to canonize a certain version of history, and a pluralist political environment permits opposition groups and critical observers to commemorate their own memories of key events.

Marking a Victory

In the wake of the arrest of the coup plotters, Yeltsin and the Russian government acted decisively to set a tone of popular victory. They immediately marked their achievement by making August 22, 1991, a national celebration—Freedom Day. They also christened the territory in front of the White House Free Russia Square, honored the citizens who participated in the resistance to the coup with a new medal, and adopted the old tricolor of Peter the Great, carried by many of the defenders of the White House, as Russia's flag. The Russian government also organized funerals for the three young men who were killed in a confrontation with army troops near the White House during the coup attempt.

At a massive rally preceding the funeral, Gorbachev expressed his sense of obligation to the young people. But Yeltsin stole the show with his use of the highest patriotic rhetoric—"We do not bid farewell to their names because henceforth their names have become sacred for Russia"—and his remarkable plea to the victims' families to "forgive me, your president, for not being able to defend, to protect your sons."[1] In a continued display of humility, Russian politicians marched with the crowd to the cemetery for the last rites. The patriarch of the Russian Orthodox Church led the service for the two ethnically Russian victims, while a rabbi presided over the burial of the third. The funerals were broadcast live on national television with reportage switching back and forth between the Orthodox and Jewish burial rites and stressing the diverse class backgrounds of the three martyrs. Coverage was, in the eyes of two Western observers, scripted to depict Russia as a nation newly "committed to common citizenship in civil society."[2]

The popular response to the end of the coup consisted of far more than attendance at state-sponsored rallies. The first popular celebration began spontaneously on the afternoon of August 21, before officials even felt secure enough to announce victory over the GKChP, when rock musicians put on an impromptu concert at the White House barricades. On the evening of the next day, a jubilant crowd roamed through Moscow, threatening to break into CPSU offices and to topple the statue of the founder of the Soviet secret police, Feliks Dzerzhinskii. The public mood was militant and revolutionary.

Some of the civic defenders of the White House also sought to play an active role in commemorating and institutionalizing the achievements of August 1991. While still on the barricades, activists proposed the formation of a permanent volunteer defense force. In the words of an appeal to defenders of the parliament composed on the night of the 21st: "But God save us from giving in to euphoria. The monster is still alive and will destroy many of us one by one if we presume to disperse with a feeling of having done our duty." The author of the manifesto therefore called on people to unite in a "living ring" that could instantly gather wherever the "monster" appeared.[3] Less than a month later, the Living Ring union held its founding conference in Moscow and proclaimed as its main goal "to be an active participant in the democratic transformation and the formation of rule of law in Russia, and to be a popular guarantee against totalitarian regimes." The union's members chose not be a political party with a distinct ideology, but instead adopted the tasks of preserving memories of August and disseminating facts about what had happened.[4]

Remembering August as Liberation

The Russian government's preferred mythical version of the events of August 1991 can be easily identified in Boris Yeltsin's public addresses on the first anniversary of the coup attempt. On August 21, 1992, Yeltsin welcomed the media in the Kremlin, where he had moved from the Russian White House after the end of the USSR, and congratulated

them "on the day of victory . . . of the forces of democracy and the supporters of change, of the whole Russian people, over reaction." He
thanked journalists for their role in showing the world "the new Russia, previously unknown, the Russia that could overcome its old in-
stinct of resigned submissiveness." In an earlier television address to
the nation, the president had praised the unselfish patriotic impulses
that had sent citizens to the barricades. The defenders of the White
House also knew, he claimed, that most Russians in other cities and
towns were with them. And he compared the rejoicing in the wake of
the defeat of the plotters to the celebrations that marked the Soviet victory over Germany in 1945. Once again, civic unity had been the formula for defeating a monstrous enemy. Yeltsin also used the anniversary to try to reinforce a connection between support for Russian
sovereignty and support for his sweeping economic reform program by
announcing the start of voucher privatization. He told citizens that
their active participation in economic change in 1992 was just as vital
to the fate of the nation as their actions in fighting the coup in 1991.[5]

Yeltsin's interpretation of August 1991, however, almost immediately faced several challenges. At the press conference, a journalist del-
icately raised the idea that the GKChP's clumsy efforts to seize control
of the state could not be seen as a serious attempt at revanche. When he
asked the president's opinion of conservatives' references to the putsch
as an "operetta," Yeltsin testily replied that the death threats made
against his person and the presence of tanks in the streets of Moscow
were not the stuff of farce. Yet the suggestion that the putsch had not
constituted a serious threat to reform highlighted a key problem with
the preferred version of August: the centerpiece of the drama of August
was a nonevent—the expected but never realized storming of the Russian White House. Thus a commentator in 1992 could refer to the living ring around the White House as a big festive happening and compare its canonization to the Bolsheviks' dramatization of the storming
of the Winter Palace—an event that was also disappointing from a
mythical point of view until it had been rewritten by dramatists and
screenwriters.[6] If the coup plotters were bumbling idiots with no
chance of success, then their defeat could hardly serve as proof of the
strength of the democratic movement.

The democratic myth of August was further weakened by its re-
liance on the claim that the Russian people had overwhelmingly
demonstrated in 1991 that they had been transformed into ardent and
irrepressible supporters of democracy. In reality, mass resistance to the

coup in the Russian republic was limited largely to Moscow and Leningrad. In the provinces, journalists and activists publicized Yeltsin's appeals, but local officials and citizens tended to wait till the outcome was fairly clear before publicly adopting a democratic stance.[7] Journalists also had not uniformly supported the Russian government during the coup. Alone among liberal observers, Vitalii Tret'iakov, the outspoken and often controversial editor of *Nezavisimaia gazeta*, reminded the public in 1992 that only a minority of Muscovites had turned out and that outside of the city the general response was inertia. But Tret'iakov nevertheless defended the interpretation of August as an occasion of common civic resistance by noting that those who did take to the barricades represented a cross section of the population.[8]

Also problematic for Yeltsin's preferred version of August was the tenuous nature of any link between anger with the unconstitutional seizure of power and support for far-reaching economic change. Opposition to a return to Brezhnevite socialism with its stultifying, puritanical censorship or to the reimposition of a one-party dictatorship did not necessarily translate into enthusiasm for market reform. One could disagree with radical economic reform and still not be aligned with the GKChP, argued the speaker of the Russian Supreme Soviet, Ruslan Khasbulatov. In 1992 he and Vice President Aleksandr Rutskoi, both of whom had defended the White House alongside Yeltsin, had already begun to voice disagreement with the president's economic strategies, though they were careful to distinguish their views from those of the GKChP.[9] Yet in general, liberal criticism of Yeltsin in 1992 was quite mild, consisting mostly of complaints about the scarcity of democratic activists in high state offices and the retention of the old CPSU elite in important institutions such as the KGB.[10]

Pravda, still a mouthpiece of the Communist Party, challenged Yeltsin's interpretation of August 1991, putting the anniversary headline "A year ago tomorrow everything looked totally different . . ." not over a picture of tanks in the streets but over a chart showing increases in the prices of consumer goods since 1991. *Pravda* also featured interviews with citizens complaining about the emergence of a superrich elite. And on August 22 it published a poll in which 32 percent of respondents claimed that their view of August had changed for the worse (as opposed to 2 percent for the better) and 41 percent favored releasing the imprisoned members of the GKChP. Material disappointments, *Pravda*'s editors suggested, had already led people to reevaluate what August meant.[11]

Overall, neither the executive nor the legislative branch of the Russian government tried to use the first anniversary of the defeat of the coup for educational or entertainment purposes. The anniversary of August was not an official holiday in 1992. Thus, while Yeltsin called upon citizens to reaffirm the ideals of August by participating in voucher privatization, his administration did not create a forum for a collective display of solidarity. Yeltsin himself expressed disagreement with the idea of any lighthearted celebrations, given the tragedy of the three deaths.[12] Nevertheless, civic activists, entrepreneurs, and the city governments of Moscow and St. Petersburg did organize both festivities and solemn ceremonies.

The Moscow organizing committee, despite losing a big sponsor at the last minute, promoted the "Vivat, Rossiia!" festival, which included a restaging of the "Rock on the Barricades" concert. Despite poor weather, Living Ring members met on the 19th, without official speakers, at the site of their former barricades. And at a general democratic meeting, which attracted some 8,000 to 12,000 people, Khasbulatov spoke, followed by Yeltsin's right-hand men, Egor Gaidar and Gennadii Burbulis. State representatives also participated in the unveiling

Memorial to the three youths killed during the August coup on the first anniversary of their deaths, Moscow, August 25, 1992. (Photo by V. Marin'o. Courtesy of TsMADSN.)

of a special memorial to the three victims of the coup at the Vagan'kov cemetery. Museum displays added to the official canonization of August as the triumph of democracy over communism in Russia. The political opposition, by contrast, marked the anniversary very quietly. One ultranationalist organization held a conference at which conspiracy theories of the putsch were discussed. Several others gathered at the grave of Marshal Akhromeev, the last USSR minister of defense, who had taken his life in the wake of the coup's collapse.[13]

Remembering August as a Failure

A year later, August 1991 no longer stood as a sacred founding moment. In 1993, while increasingly outspoken Communists and nationalists questioned whether the coup had been an act of heroism or of treachery, those who had stood together on the barricades in August disagreed as to whether August 1991 marked the culmination of a revolution or only its beginning. Yeltsin had suggested in December 1992 that the victory in August had not been consolidated, and accused the rebellious legislature of trying to achieve "what was not successfully carried out [by the GKChP] in August of last year."[14]

The atmosphere of confrontation persisted throughout the spring of 1993 as Yeltsin and the legislature battled over economic policies and the balance of power between the two branches of government. Valerii Zorkin, chairman of the Constitutional Court, intervened several times to try to work out a lasting compromise. Prolonged negotiations produced a national referendum on the popularity of reform and on whether either the president or the parliament or both should be forced to face early elections.

A majority of the 64 percent of eligible voters who turned out for the April referendum expressed their faith in Yeltsin and his reform policies. But initiatives to force early elections failed to garner the votes of 50 percent of eligible voters necessary to make them binding. Yeltsin interpreted the referendum results as a sign of confidence in him, but he could not break the stalemate. On the second anniversary of August, he and the parliament remained deadlocked.[15]

In August 1993, Yeltsin once again gave a press conference in honor of the anniversary, but this time his address was more political and rather defensive. He still insisted that August marked a turning point, the moment when the fate of reform and Russian sovereignty were decided. And he defended the memory of August against attempts to "cast doubts on the noble impulse of many thousands of Russian people who had come to the defense of democracy and freedom." Yeltsin did not, however, shy away from the unpleasant fact that Rutskoi and Khasbulatov, his key lieutenants in August 1991, now stood in opposition to him. Nor did he hesitate to lay out the lines of dispute between him and the Supreme Soviet. Lamenting that the White House had "turned into a bulwark of revanchist forces today," Yeltsin castigated legislators for their resistance to his economic policies and his proposed new constitution. As for the future of relations between the executive and the legislature, he noted that "the remainder of August will be artillery preparation [*artpodgotovka*], as I call it. Then there will be September, the most crucial month." Though he later reassured citizens that the struggle he contemplated was political, not military, Yeltsin clearly meant to send the opposition a strong warning.[16]

Those opposed to radical market reforms and to President Yeltsin's high-handed behavior toward the legislative branch continued to question the nature of the events of August 1991. Gennadii Ziuganov, leader of the KPRF, and others now publicly argued that the GKChP was not a real coup attempt at all. Questioning the seriousness of men who failed to take the basic step of cutting off their rivals' phone lines, Ziuganov labeled the whole affair some sort of provocation, perhaps abetted by Gorbachev. He also openly admitted that his sympathies lay with the goals laid out by the so-called coup plotters. Indeed, though not a participant in the coup, Ziuganov had joined several future members of the GKChP in signing a manifesto threatening revanche in the summer of 1991. Meanwhile, the head of the Agrarian Party, an ally of the KPRF, claimed that those he had encountered on the White House barricades had not evinced fear of attack—clear evidence, he argued, that not even the democrats had taken the GKChP seriously.[17] Given their nostalgia for empire, Communists and patriots together labeled the August anniversary an occasion for mourning the death of the Soviet Union.[18]

Democrats, in the loose sense of liberals and anticommunists, also expressed their unhappiness with the state of affairs. Few romantic illusions remained from 1991. A survey showed that, although the number of respondents who condemned the GKChP's aims had not changed since 1991, in 1993 only 15 percent thought the August coup would go down as a glorious page in history; 30 percent believed that it would be remembered as a misfortune, and 43 percent predicted it would be viewed as insignificant.[19] August was no longer seen as the end of a fight but rather as just the start of another round of battles for power among politicians. By the second anniversary, moreover, democrats had become concerned about the delays in proceedings against the coup plotters. The inability of the prosecutor's office to bring the case to court seemed to show the weakness of the new system.[20]

Yet, although they blamed Yeltsin for not having consolidated what might have been a decisive victory in August, many leading civic activists had not defected to the side of the legislature. In fact, Lev Ponomarev, a leader of the Democratic Russia Movement, when asked by an interviewer about the danger of a "GKChP-2," replied: "Yes, in a drawn-out, crawling form a new putsch is already under way. Khasbulatov, as leader of the Supreme Soviet, has totally gone over to the side of the GKChP, of the extremist forces . . . demonstratively ignoring the results of the April referendum, in practice they're carrying out a coup."[21]

In August 1993, Yeltsin's supporters and opponents in Moscow organized competing rallies in front of the White House. The democrats wished to recapture their shining moment, the opposition to show that "the genuine supporters of democracy—including those who were here two years ago—as before are on the side of the White House [i.e., supporting Khasbulatov and Rutskoi against Yeltsin]."[22] Democrats rallied without Yeltsin's support. At his press conference on August 19, when a journalist asked about the potential for anniversary rallies to end in violence, Yeltsin said he saw no need for such activity. Nevertheless, at the democratic rally on August 20, Yeltsin's chief of staff, Sergei Filatov, spoke, as did key economic reformers.[23] Ultimately, neither camp drew a large crowd—a few thousand on each side. The festival side of "Vivat, Rossiia," however, with the now traditional rock concert for young people, remained popular in Moscow.[24]

The Second Defense of the White House

On the evening of September 21, 1993, President Yeltsin made his plans for a "fighting September" clear. He announced in a live television broadcast that he had issued a decree dissolving the existing legislature—the Russian Supreme Soviet—and mandating the rapid election of a new Federal Assembly. Yeltsin stated bluntly that he was violating the existing constitution in order to break the deadlock that was preventing the adoption of a new one. The leaders of the Supreme Soviet responded with a midnight session where, guided by the judgment of the Constitutional Court—which had already held its own special session—they declared Yeltsin's decree unconstitutional. Though short of a quorum, they swore in Vice President Aleksandr Rutskoi, whom Yeltsin had fired in a decree of dubious legality earlier in the month, as the new president of Russia.[25]

In the week that followed, approximately 180 deputies, mostly socialists or ultranationalists, refused to leave the White House. Some of their supporters also moved into the White House to help in its defense. From inside the building the deputies frantically lobbied local legislatures and the military for support. As in August 1991, when Yeltsin asked the public to rally not around him personally but around democratically elected institutions of state, Rutskoi appealed to the public "to defend the constitution and the law." Using the language of August, the opposition leaders called Yeltsin's decree a "governmental coup." Their supporters also adopted this perspective; they referred to Yeltsin's "dictatorship" and dubbed themselves "defenders of the constitution."[26]

On September 28, Yeltsin ordered the White House to be surrounded by barbed wire and guards. Hoping to drive the resisters out without using force, the presidential administration cut off first the telephone service and then the electricity to the building. Name-calling escalated as Yeltsin and his allies described the defenders of the White House as mutineers and fanatics who were ignoring the people's wishes for economic reform expressed in the April referendum. The pro-Yeltsin media focused on the ultranationalist youths—some sporting swastikas—who had flocked to support hard-liners in the besieged White House

By using the terms "fascist" and "red-brown" to describe the opposition, liberals played on World War II associations to try to provoke strong emotional responses against the rogue deputies.[27] The defenders of the White House, by contrast, sought to depict themselves as the true heirs of August in the sense of real elected representatives and as the recipients of genuine civic support. By surrounding the White House with barbed wire, one homemade leaflet declared, the "false democrats" had set up a "concentration camp for dissidents."[28] This text combined powerful language connected to the two great populist achievements in modern Russian history—the victory over the Germans in World War II and the victory over the totalitarian system—to stir up civic consciousness.

Peace talks organized by the patriarch of the Russian Orthodox Church failed to soothe tempers. Meanwhile, civic supporters of the parliament increased their activity in Moscow. A street protest on October 2 ended in a bloody clash in which the police and Interior Ministry troops did not hesitate to use extreme force. On the afternoon of October 3, a crowd of several thousand demonstrators broke through a cordon of troops with surprising and, some would argue, suspect ease and approached the White House. The besieged parliamentarians, encouraged by this visible display of support and perhaps confident that it represented a broader trend in society and in the military, came outside to speak to the crowd. From the White House balcony Rutskoi and Khasbulatov urged their followers to storm the nearby building of the Mayor's office and to move on the Kremlin and the television center at Ostankino.

The crowd turned on the Mayor's building, smashing windows and taking up posts inside. Then, commandeering some vehicles and taking weapons from the White House armory, a delegation headed by the Communist hard-liner and former general Albert Makashov sped off to attack the Ostankino tower. At the television center the White House forces encountered fierce armed resistance. After a violent battle in which passers-by also lost their lives, the defenders of the White House were repelled.[29]

Fearing for the safety of his employees, the head of Ostankino ceased all broadcasting at the onset of the attack. The break in television service alarmed viewers across the country. Most had no idea of the turn that the day's events had taken; only a privileged few in Moscow who had access to CNN could watch live coverage of the unfolding events. Channel 2 did manage to restore service that night by using a remote studio that it maintained elsewhere in Moscow. Soon liberal writers, intellectuals, and politicians were making their way there to plead with citizens to support the president in the effort to restore order. The well-known liberal economist and former deputy premier in the Yeltsin government Egor Gaidar issued an appeal to democrats to rally in front of Moscow's city hall, and by one estimate some 40,000 Muscovites gathered in response. But the members of the crowd had little idea of what they could do in the dangerous situation that had developed.[30]

Yeltsin responded to the outbreak of violence by declaring a state of emergency in Moscow and informing citizens that the "armed fascist-Communist mutiny" would be put down as quickly as possible. Early on the morning of October 4, the Russian government brought in tanks to shell the White House. By afternoon, those opposition leaders still inside the White House had surrendered. But, as soldiers cleared the parliament's defenders from the building's basement, the top floors of the White House turned black from the fires ignited by tank shells. In the aftermath of the storm, officials set the number of victims at 145, though opposition accounts and human rights organizations cited much higher figures.[31]

The sudden denouement of the October crisis produced none of the euphoria of August 1991. While many liberals concurred with Yeltsin's assessment that the opposition had been starting a civil war, they lamented Yeltsin's failure to foresee and prevent the violence that erupted from within the opposition camp. Indeed, October 1993 differed from August 1991 in that both sides turned to violence to try to further their aims. The Interior Ministry troops roughed up demonstrators; the defenders of the White House stormed several buildings; snipers allied with the White House allegedly fired on government troops; the army at Yeltsin's command shelled the legislature; and the police beat many oppositionists when they fled the burning building. Other liberals worried that Yeltsin's temporary suspension of the Constitutional Court and his outlawing of a number of opposition organizations and papers, including the KPRF and *Pravda*, would taint the upcoming elections for the new parliament.[32]

Amnesties and Acquittal

The 1994 anniversary of the defeat of the August 1991 coup attempt was affected not only by new memories of the October events but also by the resolution of the legal proceedings against the alleged putschists and mutineers. The fate of the leaders of the August coup and the October opposition must be explored before returning to the arena of annual commemorations.

When the members of the GKChP were placed under arrest after their failure to seize power, other officials who had supported them, including General Valentin Varennikov, Gorbachev's aide Valerii Boldin, and Anatolii Luk'ianov, former chairman of the USSR Supreme Soviet, were detained as well. Their case came to trial only in April 1993. The delay can be ascribed in part to the problem of how to try the defendants for treason after the country they allegedly betrayed had ceased to exist in December 1991.[33] The GKChP members' assorted illnesses and numerous appeals also contributed to the delays in their trial, but they insisted that they wanted the trial to go forward so that the truth about

The Russian White House is blackened by fire after shelling by government troops, October 4, 1993. (Photo by S. Pominov. Courtesy of TsMADSN.)

their efforts would be revealed. They even complained that the designated courtroom could not seat enough spectators.[34]

The defendants' opening statements showed their intent to make the trial a platform for spreading their own theories of blame for the USSR's disintegration. Ianaev, for instance, explained that in 1991 the country was in a state of crisis, the government paralyzed by a war of laws with the republics, the nation riven by ethnic conflict. The GKChP had therefore sought to block the union treaty because it would have meant the end of a strong state. It had never intended to turn back the clock or to attack the democratic movement. Pavlov similarly contended that the GKChP members had acted out of patriotism, not self-interest. And Luk'ianov argued that their goal was to preserve the constitutional structure. Moreover, he and others challenged the widespread belief that Gorbachev had opposed their efforts. What kind of conspiracy could the state of emergency have been, they asked, when they had informed Gorbachev of their intentions ahead of time?[35] Before the trial could proceed past the defendants' opening statements, however, events intervened to cut it short.

In January 1994, when the new parliament settled into its temporary quarters, far from the old White House, political society was still reeling from the bloody conflict of October 1993. Yet, with a new constitution and legislature in place, observers and participants dared to hope that politics might take a more constructive form. Before the Duma deputies could get down to work, they needed to set the procedures that would govern their daily functions. Amidst debates regarding the rules of order, however, the legislators found time to address the painful and divisive topic of past political conflicts.[36] As the Russian prosecutor's office prepared to move forward against the GKChP and the persons accused of inciting and committing violence during the standoff between the Supreme Soviet and the president, Communist and nationalist deputies sought a pretext for the Duma to intervene.

By early February, members of the inappropriately named Liberal Democratic Party of Russia (LDPR), led by the ultranationalist Vladimir Zhirinovsky, had prepared an initiative aimed at freeing the persons charged as a result of the October events and the August putsch. Meanwhile, another group of deputies had begun drafting a proposal to liberate persons convicted during the Soviet era for economic activities that were no longer illegal, such as feeding bread to cattle and possessing hard currency.[37] When Yeltsin proposed marking the adoption of the new constitution with an amnesty for women, the elderly, youths, and former servicemen who had been convicted of relatively minor criminal offenses, the Duma—which had been given the power to declare broad amnesties under the new constitution—hijacked his humanitarian gesture. Leaders of several factions united to insist that the president's criminal amnesty be tied to political and economic amnesties.

At first a political amnesty seemed unlikely to succeed. It would free people who had not yet been convicted, whereas amnesties normally apply only to those already sentenced by the courts. Moreover, it actually did not address some category of crimes labeled "political," but rather concerned the fate of politicians who had been charged with criminal acts.[38] To muster support, however, the amnesty package was altered to include resolutions that would dissolve the newly formed parliamentary investigative commission on the October events and add a "memorandum on accord." The memorandum on accord suggested a basis for consensus, one that it was hoped the president and various political parties would choose to endorse. It consisted of a general statement of nonpartisan agreement on the goals of strengthening democracy, raising economic output, sharing the burdens of reform equally across regions and social groups, and "overcoming the moral degradation of society." It also included a commitment to "conduct political battles strictly within the framework of the law, not turning to or inciting violence, ethnic strife, or persecution of dissent in any form."[39]

Under the slogan "reconciliation," Communist deputies marshaled support for the new package from their Agrarian Party allies, as well as from moderate factions. In the words of one KPRF deputy, the amnesty package would facilitate better relations between the legislature and the executive by "removing the cancerous tumor" of the October events from the forefront of political life. Presumably the release of the "martyrs" of October would lessen the passions of their supporters. Even Sergei Shakhrai, who just two years earlier had defended the Yeltsin administration in the trial of the CPSU, now joined with the KPRF, arguing that no one could emerge victorious from a civil war, and that this amnesty would keep such a conflict from reigniting. The leader of New Regional Politics, in throwing his faction's support behind the amnesty deal, also referred to the costs of civil war, and suggested that Russia follow Spain's example of mutual forgiveness in the name of reconciliation and stability. The regions, he noted, would like to get on with the business of government, rather than indulging in a prolonged round of settling accounts.[40]

Zhirinovsky went even further. In the spirit of reconciliation, he declared, "We have the right to forgive them all—from Kaliningrad to Kamchatka—for ninety years from the first Russo-Japanese war to the most recent Soviet-Afghan war. . . . No one is guilty of anything." Zhirinovsky even developed the idea of institutionalizing this gesture of reconciliation: "This could be a holiday. We haven't had a holiday in Russia for nine years now. Not one holiday. Every holiday—there's bloodshed. Someone doesn't like that day on the calendar. So let's introduce a new day. Many people and states have as their national day— a day of national reconciliation."[41]

Zhirinovsky's appeal for a patriotic consensus came at an opportune moment. The vote on the amnesty took place on February 23, the national holiday formerly known as Soviet Army Day but since renamed Defenders of the Fatherland Day. The Duma had opened that day with a heartfelt speech from a representative of the Women of Russia faction, who congratulated her colleagues who had served in the military, but registered her hopes that "your battles in words never cross over into hand-to-hand fighting . . . and that our line for the microphone is never transformed into a line for the armory." Having called up memories of the October events, she reminded deputies of their duty to work together to save the Russian state and its military.[42]

Although the amnesty deal passed by a vote of 252 to 67, not all deputies were so willing to forgive and forget.[43] In a highly charged speech, Anatolii Shabad, a representative of the liberal Russia's Choice Party, declared: "I am deeply convinced that one of the most important causes of the acts of civil war that occurred in the time periods [covered by the amnesty] is the fact that the Communist regime's crimes, carried out over the course of seventy years, have gone unpunished." He was not categorically opposed to a political amnesty, he said, but it should be offered only after the prisoners' guilt had been proved. By supporting an immediate amnesty, he contended, deputies were promoting a sense of impunity, and hence lending legitimacy to the idea that violence was an acceptable means for pursuing political ends. In effect, Shabad argued for a moral judgment, if not necessarily for punitive measures.[44]

President Yeltsin also showed himself unwilling to forgive and forget. In his State of the Union address to the parliament, delivered on the day after the amnesty package had been approved, Yeltsin diverged from his prereleased text to protest:

Let's be realists and admit that part of the opposition still wants
to take forceful revenge. On both sides there are those who are
blinded by the need to take revenge on their ideological adver-
saries. But hatred and a thirst for revenge can only worsen Russia's grave illnesses. And another thing, I want to say that societal reconciliation is not forgiveness of everything. Mercy is
mercy only when it does not contradict either the law or moral
norms.[45]

This oblique criticism of the amnesty deal, which in the opinion of the
administration had tainted the president's first appearance before the
legislature, was the only bitter note in Yeltsin's speech as he hailed the
new constitution and identified numerous areas in which the parliament and government could work together. Those close to the president spoke out more sharply against the amnesty resolution, which
they saw as an attack on Yeltsin. One irate adviser declared: "There
cannot be a situation in which there are corpses but no culprits." Moreover, the president's representatives accused the Duma of usurping the
courts' role by taking a decision that presumed the accused were guilty
and in need of amnesty.[46]

The amnesty deal, by forestalling trials and parliamentary inquiries,
would seem to have left each camp with its own version of events intact. This delicate balance, however, was upset in May 1994 when the
former general Valentin Varennikov, charged as an accomplice of the
GKChP, recanted his acceptance of amnesty and demanded a resump-
tion of his trial for treason. He took this step after courts had refused to
accept his petition to initiate a criminal case against high-ranking
Communist reformers and liberal politicians for their role in the
breakup of the Soviet Union. Varennikov insisted that since the truth
had not yet come out about the disintegration of the nation, and since
no one was investigating the matter objectively, he would take his
chances in court. Varennikov explained that he had agreed to go along
with the amnesty only because he had wanted to support the Duma and
to avoid entangling his co-defendants in a case that might have ended in
harsh sanctions. As a collaborator with the GKChP but not a member,
Varennikov seemed less likely to be convicted of conspiracy.[47]

At his new hearing before the military collegium of the Russian
Supreme Court, which began in June 1994, General Varennikov argued
that he considered himself morally, but not criminally, guilty for failure
to prevent the breakup of the USSR. Chief among those whom Varen-

nikov considered at fault in the disintegration of the Union was Mikhail Gorbachev. In contrast to his refusal to appear before the Constitutional Court at the trial of the CPSU, this time Gorbachev willingly obeyed a summons to testify. He seemed to take the challenge to his account of the coup as a personal insult. In court, however, he suffered the added indignity of being called a "renegade and a traitor" by the general, who personally cross-examined him.[48]

Before the military tribunal could consider a verdict, the state prosecutor in charge of the revived case surprised the court by asking that the charges against Varennikov be dropped. He admitted that he had found no evidence of criminal intent by the accused, and claimed that he had long thought that the case was weak and the prosecutor's office's own investigation faulty. On August 11, 1994, almost on the eve of the anniversary of the coup, however, the court went ahead and acquitted Varennikov; it found that Gorbachev had not actively opposed the plotters, as evidenced by his willingness to shake hands with them when they left after visiting him in Foros to announce their plans for a state of emergency and by his failure to order his guards to arrest them then. In other words, the judges ignored Gorbachev's claims that he had been a prisoner in Foros.[49] They left the impression that the coup plotters were not criminals at all.

Commemorations of August vs. October

In 1994, on the heels of Varennikov's acquittal, many democrats feared people would conclude that there had been no coup attempt. Hence liberal commentators recalled key images such as tanks in the streets and Ianaev's shaking hands, and argued that without the events of August there would have been no new Russian state and no new freedom. In 1994, for the first time, liberals engaged their opponents' arguments directly. Otto Latisa, an editorial writer for *Izvestiia*, for instance, countered Communists' claim that the GKChP was only following the will of the majority as expressed in the March 1991 referendum in favor of preserving the Union. Support for preserving the boundaries of one's homeland should not be equated with support for the old political system, he contended.[50] Yet, though he and other democrats continued to condemn the GKChP, they now looked back on August 1991 as a time of hopes that were soon to be disappointed.

Meanwhile, President Yeltsin did not even interrupt his Black Sea holiday in August 1994 to address the nation in person. Instead, his administration funded a conference on the lessons of August. Yeltsin sent the participants a brief written address in which he lamented that some people continued to question whether the coup really happened. He praised August as the first revolution in defense of the law in Russia, and he alluded to October only in expressing dismay that three years later some participants in the defense of the White House had renounced their actions. In response to a request from Living Ring, Yeltsin did make August 22 a holiday. He issued a decree declaring it State Flag Day, but did not explain why the flag was the one piece of August to be enshrined or how the day was meant to be marked.[51]

The participants in the 1994 anniversary conference, a mixture of human rights activists, intellectuals, and government officials, all continued to hold on to the idea of August as a turning point, an occasion when the populace had repudiated totalitarianism. But the atmosphere in 1994 was hardly joyful. The reform economist Stanislav Shatalin summed up the feeling of participants when he said that the Varennikov verdict made him feel as if someone had spat in his face. The acquittal provoked spirited calls for more reform of the judicial system and other expressions of concern that the break with the past had been far from complete. Elena Bonner, the widow of Andrei Sakharov, and the democratic activist Lev Ponomarev cast some of the blame for the loss of the democratic spirit of August onto Yeltsin, whom they accused of squandering the opportunity to make a real popular holiday to mark the August victory. Ponomarev also criticized Yeltsin for his growing isolation.[52] Yeltsin's absence from the conference and from the public sphere on this holiday seemed symptomatic of a growing sense of unease, even with people who had supported him in 1991 and in 1993.

Yeltsin withdrew further from public scrutiny in 1995 and 1996, when he marked the anniversaries of August only with short "interviews" with newspapers of his choice. As *Pravda* exposed in 1995, Yeltsin had adopted the practice followed by CPSU general secretaries: he returned written responses to questions submitted ahead of time. In other words, the "interviews" allowed for no give-and-take and were most likely ghost-written by Yeltsin's staff.[53] The president clearly felt a need to be insulated from embarrassing or difficult questions. Moreover, perhaps to distract attention from the many democratic activists who had broken with Yeltsin over Chechnia and other issues, Yeltsin used the 1995 anniversary to argue for a new concept of "democrats"— the prototypical democrat, he argued, was no longer the dedicated demonstrator, the radical opponent of the old regime, but the professional policy maker. He thus downplayed the significance of public demonstrations of support. Indeed, while praising Russian citizens as "ordinary people who dream the same dreams as all normal people in the West," Yeltsin no longer linked the anniversary of August with new policy initiatives; now it stood for the principle of stability and the goal of "normalization" of political life.[54]

Yet it seemed as if the October events had dampened liberals' dreams that Russia might become a "normal" democratic state. It had become difficult to recall August 1991 without reference to October, and October did not inspire joy. Playing up the territorial parallel, one newspaper featured a photograph of anti-Yeltsin graffiti on a wall near the White House next to a picture of the 1994 reunion of those who had been on the barricades in August.[55] Two years later, *Nezavisimaia gazeta* presented August as simply the prologue to a series of coups. Its editor argued that the myth of August as a revolution ending totalitarianism could no longer be believed, so celebrations of the anniversary were absurd. In fact, Tret'iakov argued, the restructuring of politics in October showed that August was not a decisive victory. The October 1993 battle between politicians who had resisted the GKChP together led another editorialist to look back on the whole episode as a strange dream.[56] The romanticism, the mythical quality of August had evaporated. Tat'iana Malkina, the young woman who had exposed the putschists for what they were with her sharp question at the August 1991 press conference, recalled in 1996, perhaps only half in jest, that she had imagined herself as an old woman visiting youth groups to talk about the art of defeating coups. Now, she noted, that scenario seemed quite unlikely. No one would be looking back on August as a shining victory for the Russian people.[57]

Conservatives, by contrast, gained confidence in their interpretations of August and October. They continued to depict August 1991 as a tragedy, principally because it initiated the dissolution of the Soviet empire. Interestingly, like the democrats, the former coup plotters now looked back upon themselves as having been naive in 1991. After their amnesty, the GKChP members claimed they had erred in not using force. Varennikov added that there would be "no naive steps" if another such opportunity presented itself.[58] The question of what exactly happened in August 1991, however, was now essentially moot for the opposition. Given the amnesty and the acquittal, they felt themselves vindicated, and used the anniversaries of August as simply prime occasions to excoriate Yeltsin and his policies.

The rising status of the nationalist-Communist opposition was already evident in August 1994, when, in a major change of pace, opposition forces kicked off the anniversary "celebrations." On August 19 the conservative Communist Union of Officers laid flowers on Marshal Akhromeev's grave and held a press conference at which Varennikov spoke. That afternoon a radical Communist group organized a demonstration of some 2,000 in protest against Yeltsin's military policy.[59] Democrats began their activity only that evening, when a variety of organizations and representatives of the August defenders of the White House gathered on Free Russia Square.

The pattern of commemoration by democratic activists has remained the same as before October 1993: a meeting by defenders at the White House, a rally, and a rock concert. But enthusiasm for demonstrations has clearly waned. The main democratic meeting in 1994 attracted only 200 people, partly because of bad weather, whereas counterdemonstrations by the united opposition the next day gathered a crowd of 2,000 to 3,000. The customary wreath laying at the graves of the three victims was attended only by low-ranking officials, and even the rock concert was poorly attended. In 1995, liberals could not even gather in front of the White House, which was now fenced in for reasons of security. By 1996, the festive side of the program dominated. The rock concert drew the largest crowd and received the most press coverage.[60] Festivities remained, but detached from the original context of a victory celebration.

Canonizing October

Opposition interpretations and rallies have also dominated commemorations of October. Anniversary meetings in Moscow organized by socialist and nationalist groups united under a nonpartisan name—the Committee for the Memory of the Tragic Events of September–October 1993 in Moscow—consistently drew thousands of people in the years after 1993.[61] The commemorations featured a variety of Communist, nationalist, and even fascist symbols, but the dominant images displayed were poster-size reproductions of photographs of victims. Annually, after a parade in which each organization marches behind its own banner, all gather for an Orthodox funeral service at the Memorial Territory, near the White House. In this script, leaders appear together but only the priest speaks, so that any political contradictions are submerged. In general, the opposition has displayed remarkably more unity than the liberals; its leaders have not pointed out each other's mistakes in October or indulged in public recriminations. Thus, in the wake of his strong but unsuccessful presidential campaign in 1996, Ziuganov, who was notably silent during the 1993 crisis, was still awarded the prominent position in the commemorative parade.

The opposition press has treated the October events with great solemnity and pathos. The most common perspective presented on the anniversaries is that of the person drawn by conscience to support the besieged parliament and then brutalized by the police and troops called in by Yeltsin. Communist journalists have used photographs of victims and of the blackened White House to highlight the consequences of Yeltsin's resort to force.[62] The provocative actions of the leaders of the parliamentary camp and the shortsightedness of their offensive on the evening of October 3 are rarely discussed. Though the opposition acknowledges that it lost this particular skirmish to the forces of "counterrevolution," the tragedy is still valued as the moment in which

Relatives of persons killed in October 1993 march on the first anniversary of their loss, Moscow, October 3, 1994. (Photo by S. Pominov. Courtesy of TsMADSN.)

Yeltsin and the democrats were forced to reveal their true nature—dictatorial, lawless, and prone to violence. In this respect, October is seen by the opposition as a much more important turning point than August 1991.[63]

Yeltsin, by contrast, tried to put October in perspective as the culmination of a painful and protracted but successful process of democratic transformation that started in August. In his memoirs he assessed his sentiments on announcing the dissolution of parliament: "Russia was entering a new epoch. We were shrugging off and cleansing the remains of the filth, lies, and falsity accumulated for seventy-odd years. Just a few more shakes and we would all start to breathe more easily and purely." For him the defining image of October was "hysterical demonstrators throwing themselves at unarmed policemen, provoking a horrible massacre." The opposition had forced his hand by attacking Ostankino and the Mayor's office. Therefore, October represented the *opposite* of August: in August nonviolent resistance brought about the withdrawal of troops, whereas in October an aggressive "defense" ended in military suppression. Moreover, Yeltsin argued, since the mutineers failed to win over people either in the capital or in the provinces, October should be seen as a period of popular support for democracy.[64]

On the first anniversary of October, Yeltsin held a press conference where, with a victor's easy grace, he called for the remembrance of all the dead, including those who "turned out to be on the side of those dragging us into the furnace of civil war." For the sake of reconciliation, he now approved of forgiving but not forgetting. He did not refer to his opposition to the spring amnesty, and he told journalists that they did not need to be reminded of the course of events in September–October 1993. What they needed, he implied, was a proper understanding of what occurred—that a "second October Revolution" did not take place, and that civil war was averted thanks to democrats' "strong nerves" and the population's level headedness.[65]

Despite Yeltsin's claim that October 1993 had ultimately been a victory for democracy, the liberal papers' coverage of the anniversaries has been restrained. While defending Yeltsin's decision to meet force with force on October 3, one commentator dwelled on the difference between August and October; in August he felt that everyone was united, but in October he and his neighbors regarded each other with mistrust, and for good reason, since they were divided in their assessments of the defenders of the White House.[66] Struggling to find acceptable images of victory in the rubble of the White House, liberal journalists focused coverage on extremist elements within the opposition, and stressed the "prehistory" of the crisis rather than its ignoble denouement. They also pointed to the crowd that gathered at Moscow's city hall in response to Gaidar's call for help on the night of October 4 and drew a distinction between the "lumpen" elements that supported the opposition and the "thinking people" who supported Yeltsin.[67] Rather than try to unravel what really happened in October, liberal journalists marked the anniversaries by printing the opinions of members of the establishment intelligentsia, most of whom called the October events a tragedy but accepted Yeltsin's interpretation that the opposition had been starting a civil war. Even those who condemned the use of violence to settle conflicts argued that Yeltsin then had little choice but to dismiss the parliament and to answer force with force.[68]

Competing Myths

The image of Yeltsin standing on top of a tank, rallying citizens to defend the constitution against the grim old men of the GKChP, remains in public memory, as does the image of a jubilant crowd trying to pull down the monument to Dzerzhinskii. But these visual memories no longer seem to evoke the sense of victory over Communist rule that many Russians experienced at the time. A 1999 poll on the eighth anniversary of August showed that only 9 percent of Russians remembered the defeat of the coup as a victory of democratic forces over the Communist Party. The more common view was that the conflict had been an ordinary battle for power among the political elite.[69] The Yeltsin administration's preferred version of the October events also lost ground over time. According to surveys and press reports, support for Yeltsin's decisions to dissolve parliament and take a hard line with those who resisted has diminished. A survey published by the liberal *Moskovskii komsomolets* revealed that in 1993, 78 percent of Muscovites had said they were on Yeltsin's side in the October events, but in 1996 only 39 percent claimed to have supported him. Moreover, whereas a poll conducted in November 1993 revealed that 53 percent blamed mainly the Supreme Soviet for the bloodshed in October, three years later 42 percent said it was hard to say which side was in the right.[70]

The October events, the pretrial amnesties of the coup plotters and the leaders of the parliamentary resistance, and the acquittal of Varennikov all influenced popular understandings of August 1991. The geographic and symbolic parallels in the two defenses of the White House put the Yeltsin administration in the unenviable position of seeming to have stepped into its former enemies' shoes. The subsequent impunity of the members of the GKChP and those who had initiated the violence in October 1993 further cleared the way for all sorts of partisan interpretations of August and October to vie for credibility unchecked by neutral or responsible arbitrators. As one St. Petersburg journalist lamented, "Those who thought up this 'amnesty' and allowed it to happen have, first of all, deprived me for the umpteenth time of the possibility of FINDING OUT THE TRUTH."[71]

Though historical contingencies affected collective memories of August, choices about whether and how to commemorate the apparent founding moment of the new regime also shaped popular understandings of the event. By not immediately making the August anniversary a national holiday, Yeltsin lost an opportunity to craft a new democratic ceremonial practice. Why not have made the anniversary of the coup an occasion to rival the anniversary of the Bolshevik Revolution? Fear of heavy-handed propaganda need not have prevented all state support for patriotic rites. Neither brief televised speeches nor demonstrations organized by a small Moscow civic association without permanent funding or official standing could have the impact of nationally orchestrated participatory festivities.

When Yeltsin and his allies finally decided in 1994 that a holiday might help consolidate their version of August as a moment of national liberation and peaceful revolution, they did not pick a symbol or create a ritual that would have enhanced memories of those parts of August with the most popular resonance. Yeltsin chose to focus on a state attribute—the flag, which was more often associated with the increasingly unpopular fact of Russian sovereignty rather than with the heady experience of defeating the old regime. The historical Petrine tricolor invoked continuity with precommunist Russia but did not call up the moving aspects of August—such as the civic nature of the defeat of the GKChP's reincarnated Brezhnevite socialism. Moreover, by not participating personally in popular celebrations of August, Yeltsin sacrificed the emotional link with the nation that he had created when he marched with the crowds to the funerals of the three victims of the coup. Reacting to the president's laissez faire attitude toward commemorative mythmaking, one liberal commentator observed in 1994, "It won't be much of a surprise if on a future anniversary the defenders of the White House decide that victory over the putschists was only their personal holiday. And then people will wonder: is this a holiday at all?"[72] Indeed, each year fewer and fewer citizens have celebrated the defeat of the August coup by participating in public remembrances.

In contrast to Yeltsin's restrained approach to shaping collective memory to reflect his preferred versions of the recent past, Communist opposition leaders recognized the value of investing organizational resources in spreading their version of events. They used multiple arenas—the courtroom, the floor of the legislature, and the street—to propagate countermemories of August and October. Street demonstrations particularly suited the opposition. Through public meetings they made their movement visible, built a sense of solidarity among participants, and graphically demonstrated the regime's lack of hegemony in the public sphere. The format of the protest meeting also accommodated differences within the opposition; from one platform speakers with diverse opinions could join in the general criticism of the existing regime. Opposition politicians' representations of August and October were complemented by sympathetic journalists who wove together individual accounts, photographs, and political commentary into a narrative of betrayal and victimization at the hands of the so-called democrats, Gorbachev, and the West.

Journalists play a major role in keeping the memory of past crises alive in the public imagination. On the opposition side they helped create myths. On the liberal side, no doubt to the chagrin of the president and his team, they spread myths but also held them up to scrutiny over time. Anniversaries have provided occasions for journalists to remonstrate with politicians as regards their lack of commitment to principles of nonviolence. Thus, in the context of Yeltsin's undeclared war in Chechnia, a liberal editorialist wrote in 1996, "Five years ago the president asked forgiveness for not being able to protect three youths from absurd deaths. If he should have to do this today, the biggest difficulty would be that the whole presidential apparat would not be able to tell Yeltsin how many Russians had been killed."[73] In the new context of political pluralism, mythmaking was bound to be subject to contestation, but the Yeltsin administration did little to counter the opposition's memories of the October events.

The battles over the memory of August 1991 and October 1993 show a myriad of political actors searching for positive mythic elements with which to inspire an increasingly jaded and apathetic public. Despite their substantively different interpretations of these key events, politicians across the spectrum have demonstrated some similar interests. First, all wished to claim the mantle of genuine civic support. They used the language of democracy to present themselves as truly popular representatives and as committed to a legal order. Second, both Communists and democrats focused on the victims, praising the dead rather than elevating the leaders. People who feel themselves victimized by the difficulties and unpredictability of transition are no doubt rightly perceived as more likely to empathize with the suffering of other ordinary people. Hence canonization of top leaders—whether Yeltsin, Rutskoi, or Khasbulatov—subsided in the press and in political discourse. Third, both sides drew attention away from the fluid, rapidly shifting alliances in postsoviet politics. After all, it was hard to present a manichean scenario if one was perceived to be fighting one's former partners. Similarities in content, however, were not matched by similarities in efforts. The early and persistent efforts of the opposition to counter liberals' preferred interpretations may have given them a lasting advantage in shaping memories of recent political history.

[4]

Disposing of the Spoils of World War II

In the summer of 1994, demonstrators in Moscow burned the Russian minister of culture in effigy. They were protesting their government's intention to return art and books removed by Soviet troops from occupied Germany at the end of World War II. The so-called trophy art had been taken as reparations for Soviet losses, but never acknowledged or displayed. In the months leading up to the demise of the USSR, after an article by Russian art experts in an American journal revealed the existence of secret caches of Western art, Soviet cultural bureaucrats reluctantly admitted to the existence of secret collections. The new Russian government, by contrast, proved to be eager to rid itself of this embarrassing inheritance by restoring the trophies to their former owners. But in 1994, before a program of returns could be instituted, Communist deputies in the Duma took up the campaign to block any handover of trophies. By 1997 they had gathered enough support to pass a tough law dedicated to keeping World War II spoils, and even to override a presidential veto for the first time in the legislature's history.

The case of trophy art demonstrates how the liberal drive for destalinization lost ground in the mid-1990s to a revamped patriotic ethic. The continuing debate over the fate of trophy art illustrates what sorts of lessons both Russian liberals and increasingly nationalistic Communists were extracting from the national past. In particular, it highlights differences in attitudes toward the nature of Stalinism and its centrality in Soviet/Russian history. While Communist "patriots" converted powerful memories of World War II into currency for present political conflicts, liberals changed their rhetoric, if not always their policies, to respond to aspersions cast on their patriotic credentials. In essence, the controversy surrounding the trophy art illuminates both interpretations of the past and their active deployment in the battle between an increasingly Communist-dominated parliament and an increasingly defensive liberal government.

The Problem

During World War II many works of art were destroyed in the course of military operations and millions of objects were looted, sometimes more than once. Vandalism and looting by individuals occurred in all the armies involved in the conflict. German policy, however, lay behind much of the removal of cultural objects. Hitler and many of his top aides aggressively collected art from the occupied lands. Some works they purchased, often at artificially low prices; some they took from museum collections; and others they confiscated from private collectors. In the East, special collecting brigades accompanied German occupying forces and simply requisitioned books, works of art, and archeological material of interest to German museums and powerful private collectors. Nazi collectors, for the most part, disdained works by Russians, whom they considered an inferior race, but they avidly pursued German and other West European items in Soviet collections.[1]

Even though the Soviets managed to evacuate many treasures from Leningrad and Moscow behind the front lines for safekeeping, Soviet cultural losses during the war were enormous. At the Nuremberg trials, Soviet officials estimated that the Germans had looted 427 museums, damaged over 2,000 religious buildings, and destroyed or expropriated over 180 million books. For many Soviet citizens, the fate of the former tsarist palaces in the environs of Leningrad symbolized the nation's suffering at the hands of the Germans. From the palaces-turned-museums the Germans confiscated the best of the items that had not been evacuated in time—most notably the Catherine Palace's Amber Room, which Soviet curators had deemed too fragile to move but which the Germans transported to Königsberg (Kaliningrad), whence it vanished at the end of the war.[2] The Germans used lesser items from the palaces to furnish their quarters or for raw material—converting antique cabinets into outhouses, for instance. Before retreating in 1944, they vandalized, mined, and even set fire to some palace buildings.[3]

As Allied forces pushed the Germans back, American and British arts units sought to protect historical monuments and cultural treasures from damage by combatants on both sides. Gradually these art specialists were drawn into the effort to untangle competing legal claims to the works they had rescued. Allied officials had to reckon with questions of ownership of individual works, and to decide whether art should be taken from the Germans as compensation. Some American politicians and curators expressed their desire to claim works of art as reparations, and General Lucius Clay, the deputy military governor of the U.S. zone in Germany, supported the idea of keeping German valuables in a sort of "trusteeship" until "the German nation . . . re-earned its right to be considered a nation." But the members of the arts brigades protested vigorously, and ultimately successfully, that such proposals were reminiscent of the Nazis' hypocritical labeling of their confiscatory policies as "safeguarding."[4] For Soviet officials, however, the basic question of reparations was resolved quickly and decisively in favor of seizing cultural objects as compensation for losses.

In 1945, after Allied leaders agreed at the Yalta conference that the Soviet Union might take billions of dollars' worth of compensation from Germany, Stalin formed a "Special Commission on Germany" to oversee the acquisition of trophies of all sorts, from factories to art books. The primary focus for the Soviets, just as for the Germans in their wartime "collecting," was to be on acquiring works or materials related to their own nation, however tenuous such links might be. Often operating with little discretion, Soviet arts brigades gradually discarded the lists that had been drawn up behind the lines and simply began to collect as much as possible. They removed boxcar loads of cultural objects from Germany. Though their haul included such priceless objects as the Pergamon altar and the Sistine Madonna, they took anything that might have been of use to Soviet cultural institutions, including musical instruments and theater props.[5]

In the postwar chaos, the fate of displaced art and archives often became murky. Problems with transportation, security, and storage caused the loss of many items that had fallen into Soviet hands. And curators in the USSR were overwhelmed by the volume of material, especially since much of it came with little documentation. Most significantly, the Soviets did not make public their finds or admit to the Western allies the extent of the reparations extracted from the eastern zone of Germany. Objects that until the 1990s Western experts thought had been lost include the Turgenev library, confiscated first by the Germans in Paris, and the Berlin Museum's collection of Heinrich Schliemann's Trojan artifacts.[6] Meanwhile, Soviet efforts to track down their own lost objects were poorly coordinated. According to Russian scholars who have researched the fate of trophy art, the Soviets were so busy hauling off German possessions that they did not bother to establish a commission to look for missing Soviet objects until 1947, and even then they did not look very hard.[7]

In autumn 1946, workers at the Pushkin Museum of Fine Arts in

Moscow arranged an exhibition of the trophy brigades' finest treasures, including the Sistine Madonna. But on the eve of the opening, the Party officials who had ordered the public display reversed themselves. Only well-connected members of the Soviet political, cultural, and scientific elite received permission to view the displaced artworks. After the one restricted exhibition, museum workers placed most trophy art, books, and furniture in secret storage sites. Works by Cézanne, Renoir, and Degas from the collections of German industrialists, along with papyruses from the Austrian library and the Trojan gold, disappeared into museum vaults. On orders from above, a veil of secrecy was drawn over the displaced art. At the same time, the dispersal of trophy art to museums in the Russian provinces and republican capitals ceased.[8]

After Stalin's death, however, the political leadership reopened the question of what to do with trophy art. In 1955, with no public debate, Nikita Khrushchev, who had become a bold critic of many of Stalin's policies, approved of the return of some 750 items belonging to the Dresden Gallery. Soviet propagandists used the return of art to Dresden to herald the strength of Soviet–East German friendship. They also promoted a heavily dramatized semifictional version of how the Dresden artworks had been "twice saved"—first by the Soviet Army's 164th Trophy Battalion, which rescued them from a secret German shelter in an old mine where they allegedly might have been damaged by American bombers or Nazi saboteurs, and then by talented restorers in Moscow and Leningrad who undid the damage caused by underground storage. "The main element of the myth," according to contemporary analysts, "was the terrible condition of the paintings found in the damp caves. . . . [The paintings were] likened to wounded soldiers and the [Soviet] restoration workshop to a military hospital."[9] Hence the art's extended and unpublicized sojourn in the USSR was explained away as part of the process of saving the paintings.

Over the course of the next few years, the Soviet government approved of the return of many items to its socialist allies. Works that came from private collections or from public institutions located in what was now West Germany, however, were excluded from return. Books and archives of potential scientific or political use also remained in the USSR. Over the opposition of some cultural officials, who thought returns should be based on reciprocity, Khrushchev forged ahead with the handover of more than a million objects to East Germany in 1959. Still many trophies remained in the USSR. The Pushkin Museum alone concealed well over 200,000 objects—including Schlie mann's Trojan gold.[10] Their existence was a well-guarded secret even among museum workers and art historians.

Revelations and Recriminations

Despite the easing of censorship under Gorbachev's policy of glasnost, young art historians who sought to expose the existence of hidden troves of trophy art could not get even the most liberal journals and newspapers of the time to publish their reports. The only account to appear before 1991 limited itself to the less sensational topic of trophy books. Meanwhile, the Central Committee of the CPSU refused to address petitions from some curators and art professionals regarding the return or display of trophy art. It even blocked the efforts of an individual to arrange the return of art objects that he had rescued. As a young army officer, the architect Viktor Baldin had saved old master drawings belonging to the Bremen city art collection from casual looters. He had later deposited his trove with Moscow's Shchusev Museum of Architecture, but had never ceased to petition the Soviet authorities for permission to return the works to Germany.[11]

In 1990, Gorbachev signed a friendship treaty with Germany that included a clause stating that the parties agreed "that lost or unlawfully transferred art treasures which are located in their territory will be returned to their owners or their successors." But Gorbachev and his government did not follow up on the agreement with any gestures of openness regarding Soviet knowledge of the location of trophies. Though Yeltsin, as president of the Russian Republic, did not then have the power to resolve the issue, he responded sympathetically in 1990 to a letter from Baldin seeking help in returning the Bremen drawings. In a sign of what was to come, Yeltsin wrote that such a policy "would be correct and politically advantageous."[12]

Stymied at home, liberal Russian art historians finally took their revelations about trophy art to the foreign press in 1991. In January, Aleksei Rastorguev, a young lecturer at Moscow State University, published an article on trophy art in a Paris Russian-language newspaper. In April two museum specialists, Konstantin Akinsha and Grigorii Kozlov, created a sensation in the international art world with a detailed exposé in the American journal *Artnews*. They offered specific information on the activities of Soviet trophy brigades in occupied Germany and on the return of art in the 1950s. They also repudiated the myth of the rescue of the Dresden Gallery, revealing that the artworks had not been damaged by their storage in a German mine.[13]

Rastorguev, Akinsha, and Kozlov shared an interest in solving what they saw as the problem of what do with trophy art. In a follow-up piece in May, Akinsha suggested several ways trophy art might be repatriated. Among them was Rastorguev's vision of a process of selective returns based on careful evaluation of each object, with only items from private collections and from third countries, as well as pieces of great significance for Germany's cultural heritage, being handed over to their previous owners.[14] Rastorguev decried the view that all of the trophies should be rapidly returned; he called such heedless generosity, which he saw as prevalent in liberal circles, "moral maximalism." Rastorguev recognized, however, that some people would want either to continue the deception or to declare the possession of the trophies to be legal. Yet he predicted that few were likely to back the idea of simply declaring the art Soviet property, since that course would demand more "ideological self-sufficiency," more "confidence in one's rightness," than anyone was currently willing to display.[15]

Indeed, while the initial reaction in democratic circles in the USSR was to call for the handover of all trophy art, state officials and some art professionals reacted less charitably in the months before the August coup attempt. The director of the Pushkin Museum, Irina Antonova, who in her youth had helped receive trophy art as it arrived from the front, accused her subordinate Kozlov of betraying his responsibility to the museum and to the Soviet Union. She expressed fear that the bad publicity in the West would inspire Soviet leaders to "return everything to the Germans free of charge!" She continued to deny knowledge of the whereabouts of the Trojan gold and other lost treasures.[16] At a June 1991 meeting of museum directors, however, Antonova and Soviet Minister of Culture Nikolai Gubenko grudgingly agreed that returns could be made on a reciprocal basis; that is, if Germans produced missing Soviet cultural objects. Later Gubenko affirmed that he meant a one-for-one exchange.[17]

Two months after the defeat of the August coup attempt, Gubenko admitted at a press conference to the existence of secret troves of trophy art, but not to the possession or location of specific items. He wanted to talk about Russian losses during the war, not about the Trojan gold or Bremen drawings. After he pontificated about the creation of a new presidential commission, Russian journalists rebelled. One charged that his evasive and unresponsive replies reminded her of the behavior of an unreconstructed Soviet bureaucrat. Another challenged him to apologize for his ministry's role in concealing the trophy art for decades. Gubenko sarcastically responded: "I should say I'm sorry to those who shot my father down and hanged my mother?"[18] His reminder of the human suffering inflicted by Germany on the USSR effectively ended the debate on that occasion. The tempest offered a glimpse of future conflicts between democratic "moral maximalists" and Communist "patriots," but in late 1991 Gubenko and many other conservative Soviet bureaucrats were about to lose their standing and hence their influence over policy.

Moral Maximalism and Market Pragmatism, 1991–1993

Between 1991 and 1992 the most commonly expressed public sentiment regarding trophy art was shame. Again and again commentators asked why, if the Soviet rulers were so confident of the justice of their claims to German art, they had deprived the world of access to those treasures for so long? After all, as Konstantin Akinsha noted, "There is no such concept as *spetsfond* [secret depository] in any other country in the world. This is our Soviet concept."[19]

The first flurry of articles in the Soviet press featured comparisons designed to elicit shock and dismay from their readers. In his 1990 piece describing the sorry condition of thousands of uncataloged books stored haphazardly in a moldering seventeenth-century church tower, the cultural journalist Evgenii Kuz'min created a picture that contradicted the myth of the "twice saved" Dresden artworks. He replaced the image of the Soviet restoration center as a field hospital with that of the storage center as a "cultural Katyn," where books instead of people lay in "anonymous common graves."[20] Aleksei Rastorguev dubbed the hidden artworks "the last prisoners of war," and likened their fate to that of Raoul Wallenberg, the Swedish diplomat who disappeared while in Soviet custody at the end of the war.[21] With these references to other Stalinist crimes, journalists identified the trophies of war as victims of the Soviet regime. The treatment of trophy art became yet another Soviet sin for which Russians needed to atone before they could enter the common European home with "clean hands."[22]

The return of trophy art was presented as a potential means for both restoring historical justice and improving Russia's relations with the

West. The problem of what to do with trophy art, liberals suggested, might be resolved in a way that signaled the conscious casting off of old totalitarian ways and laid the groundwork for new positive international relations. The return of art to the light of day, and ideally to its rightful owners, would symbolize an end to decades-old hostilities. As one *Izvestiia* writer observed, "The Germany of today is already an entirely different state than the one that was our opponent in that war," and consequently Russia needed "to step at last onto the path of civilized, legal resolution of the issue. And most important, to stop lying, concealing, and pretending all the while that we have everything in order from a legal and moral perspective."[23] Indeed, a critical perspective on the history of trophy art might remind people that both Soviets and Germans had lived and fought under oppressive, sometimes arbitrary regimes. Instead of cursing Germans for their role in the war and refusing to give them any quarter regarding trophies, the art expert Savelii Iamshchikov suggested, "perhaps it is time to understand patriotism a little differently? A more flexible, all-human position, recognizing the right of nations to possess those masterpieces that belong to them, would be helpful to us too." Generous behavior might set a good precedent for the return of Russian treasures.[24]

A new stance toward trophy art could show that Russian values had changed. Kuz'min warned his readers that "attempts to console ourselves that it wasn't us who started it only distract us from the problem that we need to solve ourselves: what are we like today and how are we going to live from now on?"[25] The business-oriented newspaper *Kommersant-Daily* offered an answer: Not like the Bolsheviks. It warned:

> Since the conviction exists that art belonging to private individuals can be a bargaining chip in political disputes, the private and corporate collections now appearing in the country are no more protected than the objects collected by Bremen's industrialists for the municipal [art collection] that turned up in Moscow, or the things collected by Russian industrialists for the family home . . . that ended up in the Hermitage.[26]

Only a policy that respected individual property rights could move Russia forward to a law-based, capitalist state.

Yet, in a practical sense, trophy art also seemed to many liberals to be a good lever to pry concessions out of Western nations. Since few items looted from Russia could be found in public collections in the West, German offers to trade library technology and modern German

literature for antiquarian German books seemed attractive to many liberals, including Mikhail Shvidkoi, Russia's deputy minister of culture.
He framed such exchanges as a matter of conscience and pragmatism.
Material assistance, he emphasized, could help revitalize *Russian* cultural institutions. Indeed, a number of librarians with trophy materials
in their collections were quite prepared in the early 1990s to simply
ship them all back to their home countries.[27] Yeltsin also showed himself quite amenable to the idea of using trophy objects to improve foreign relations. On a 1992 visit to Hungary, as a gesture of goodwill, he
handed over two paintings initially taken by the Nazis from private
Jewish collections in Hungary.[28]

Views on whether to profit from trophy art depended on interpretations of the circumstances surrounding the acquisition of the items.
Those who most vehemently decried Stalinist policies often hesitated
to endorse the acceptance of material rewards for the return of art. Andrei Kovalev, an editorial writer for *Nezavisimaia gazeta*, compared the
situation with that of heirs to a house who open an old trunk and find
objects that they know belong to their neighbors. It would be moral and
a sign of strength to invite the neighbors to reclaim their goods, he argued. "It seems that the war ended a long time ago, and the Federal Republic of Germany was never at war with the Russian Federation. It is a
little late for such settling of accounts." He protested strongly against
the idea of demanding new compensation, especially from nations such
as the Netherlands, which were themselves victims of the Nazis.[29] A
more typical view, however, cited rewards for returns as justice—in
view of Russia's sacrifices to save Europe from fascism, it did not owe
anyone anything![30]

The view of trophy art as an embarrassment to be dealt with expedi-
tiously was reflected in the new treaty on cultural cooperation with
Germany signed by Yeltsin in December 1992. The new agreement
reaffirmed the 1990 USSR-German treaty's commitment to returning
"lost or unlawfully transferred cultural property."[31] Moreover, in 1993,
Minister of Culture Evgenii Sidorov finally announced that the Russians had Schliemann's Trojan gold, and his ministry coordinated plans
to return items to coincide with Yeltsin's meetings with foreign dignitaries.[32] At the urging of art experts, a new Russian state commission
immediately set to work compiling information on Russian losses and
holdings. It began negotiations with German, French, and Dutch representatives, among others, for the return of art and archives. Plans were
drawn up for the return to Bremen of artworks salvaged (some would

say looted) by Viktor Baldin. As part of the agreement, Bremen would donate money and technical assistance to the ongoing restoration of Russian churches in Novgorod. The French meanwhile consented to pay for the Russians to microfilm a selection of files of their choice from French archives before their return.[33] Hence it seemed that the problem of trophy art was going to be resolved in a manner in keeping with the spirit of destalinization and the reality of economic need.

Patriot Games, 1994–1997

Plans for the return of art and archives to West European countries stalled, however, in 1994, when the activities of the state restitution commission attracted the suspicion of Yeltsin's Communist and nationalist opponents. During May and June 1994, emboldened nationalists went on the offensive against the Russian government, particularly Minister of Culture Sidorov, whom they accused of "servility" toward the West for his work to facilitate the return of trophies. The government restitution commission, they added, was in the business only of giving away cultural treasures and not of reclaiming Russian objects. Their supporters demonstrated outside the Ministry of Culture and even burned Sidorov in effigy. More important, the Duma summoned Sidorov and a representative of the State Archives administration to account for the ongoing return of archive materials to France. Nationalist and Communist parties had done well in the December 1993 elections. Whereas the two main liberal parties together mustered only 20 percent of seats, Vladimir Zhirinovsky's virulently nationalist LDPR captured 14 percent of seats in the Duma and the revived Communist Party (KPRF) and its Agrarian allies won 11 and 7 percent, respectively. Now Duma deputies insisted that only they could set a legal basis for any returns.[34]

The dispute in the parliament centered on whether the return of archives under a 1992 accord with France equaled the selling off (razbazarivanie) of Russian national treasures or the return of inalienable French national property. The well-known nationalist deputies Aleksandr Nevzorov and Sergei Baburin grilled the state representatives on the extent of Russian losses, and both liberal and conservative deputies expressed concern about what they perceived as "miserly" compensation from the French. Under pressure, Minister Sidorov defended both his patriotic credentials and the deal with France by arguing, "You should know what we will receive in exchange, what we are being offered, and decide what we love—Russia or our love for Russia. These are different things." His claim to true patriotism and his pragmatic, materialistic argument provoked an emotional response from a KPRF deputy, who focused instead on Russia's symbolic and irreplaceable losses, demanding to know, "Who will return the Amber Room to us? Who will return to us the fifty years spent on the restoration of the Peterhof palaces, where the restorers are still at work . . . ? Why do we owe anyone anything?"[35] Patriotism grounded in a liberal future clashed with patriotism grounded in a heroic Soviet past.

After the uproar over the return of archives, deputies in the Federation Council prepared a bill with the bold title "On the Right of Ownership to Cultural Treasures Transferred to the Territory of the Russian Federation as a Result of the Second World War." Two things were immediately clear: the authors of the bill intended to keep trophy objects in Russia, and they rejected any criticism of those who arranged for the "transfer" of trophies at the end of the war. The 1994 legislation barely addressed the question of how to regain lost Russian items. Its primary goal was to prevent further "illegal" removal of treasures from Russia; its framers wanted no more "goodwill gestures." Citing the peace treaties of 1947, acts of the Allied Control Commission, and orders of the Soviet military command in occupied Germany, the lawmakers justified the seizure of cultural treasures as "partial compensation" for Russian losses.[36] By their reckoning, the practice of taking restitution was normal and legal; hence later treaties regarding "unlawfully transferred" objects did not apply to cultural trophies.

The draft legislation mandated that all trophy collections, with very few exceptions, were to become Russian property. Any art or archives that might contribute to a revival of militarism in Germany or that might serve the state interests of the Russian Federation would not be returned. Even objects from other states occupied by the Germans would become Russian property if those states had failed to file claims against Russia in a timely fashion—that is, during the period set out in the peace treaties that ended the war, with February 1950 as the latest date. Moreover, Russia would entertain requests for returns only from religious organizations, private charities, or individuals who had lost their property because of "active battle against Nazism (fascism)" or because of "racial, religious, or national attributes." Claimants would have twelve months (later extended to eighteen months) to get their states to appeal on their behalf. Furthermore, they would have to show that Germany had not already compensated them for their losses, and would have to wait for the Russian parliament to pass a federal law approving each return. As a final indignity, the drafters stipulated that successful claimants must reimburse Russia for preservation, restoration, storage, and even transport of their items.

The Ministry of Culture, President Yeltsin, and liberal deputies all lobbied against sweeping claims to trophy art. In 1994, four liberal deputies offered an alternative draft law aimed at resolving disputes over past spoils of war and setting out rules in case of future armed conflicts. The drafters offered as their goal the unobjectionable but uninspiring formulation "the rebirth and development of Russia's cultural property as a component of the cultural property of all humankind." Throughout the bill, they highlighted Russia's place in a larger community and its international interests. For instance, they argued for a role for international institutions in mediating disputes over trophies, and took the Geneva and Hague conventions as the legal basis for determining the fate of displaced treasures.[37] They also distinguished between the property of Germany and its wartime allies and the property of Russian allies and neutral states. Property of the neutral states and of those that had belonged to the anti-Hitler coalition was not subject to seizure or confiscation. The exempt property included works such as the Netherlands' Koenigs collection—a collection of fifteenth-to-nineteenth-century European drawings that included works by Tintoretto, Rubens, Rembrandt, Dürer, and Tiepolo—acquired by Germans through deals in occupied countries. The Allies had decided in 1943 that any such transactions were conducted under duress and hence not binding. Only war criminals were to be excluded from claiming property.

Wishing to return trophy art but wanting to uphold the USSR's right to material compensation, the authors of the alternative legislation stipulated that Russia would return cultural objects only upon receipt of new material compensation. They treated the artworks as temporary hostages to secure the compensation that Germany, as the aggressor, was obliged to pay. Thus they endorsed the principle of reciprocity, but did not set impossible conditions such as a one-for-one exchange of lost Russian items for German items. Liberal deputies saw Russia as facing a choice between self-righteous isolationism and affirmation of its bonds with the international community. Hence they sought to leave the door open for negotiations with the West.[38] Moral maximalism yielded to market pragmatism, but not to ultrapatriotism.

Neither the law "On the Right of Ownership" nor the liberal alternative passed the Duma on its first reading in June 1995. In a roll-call vote, the "patriotic" draft, however, received more than twice as many votes as the liberal draft. The Communists increased their representation in the legislature through the December 1995 elections, and in the summer of 1996, on the eve of the presidential elections, the new Duma put a revised version of the conservative legislation to a vote. This time the draft law passed overwhelmingly, but now the Federation Council, which included many regional politicians aligned with Yeltsin, rejected the bill so as not to provide the Communist leader, Gennadii Ziuganov, with a policy victory to boast about during the ongoing presidential race.[39] Only in spring 1997, as NATO prepared to begin membership negotiations with Poland, Hungary, and the Czech Republic—all states liberated by the USSR in World War II and its former Cold War allies—did the legislation finally pass in both houses.

Though retitled "On Cultural Treasures Displaced to the Soviet Union as a Result of the Second World War and Located on the Territory of the Russian Federation," the final law had not changed substantially from its first draft. It had not been amended to comply with requests from the Russian government and the Our Home Is Russia faction to draw a distinction between Allied and enemy property, to remove the statute of limitations on the rights of individual owners, and to create a less onerous procedure for returns. Nationalist deputies made only one serious concession—a provision allowing Russian libraries to trade duplicate books for other literature.[40]

To understand why the harsh law was ultimately adopted and the liberal variant so rapidly dismissed, one must examine the arguments raised by nationalists and Communists with special attention to their appeals to collective memory. Their basic attitude toward trophy art rested on a distinction between German and Soviet roles in the conduct of World War II. Communists and nationalists contended that Germany, as the aggressor in the war, had no moral or legal claim to spoils. The Germans were guilty of stealing cultural treasures from occupied lands and of deliberately seeking to annihilate Slavic culture. Soviet authorities in collecting trophies of all sorts, by contrast, were exercising their legal rights as victims of aggression to compensatory restitution.[41] Since the Soviets had the "right" to restitution, it was "inadmissible to put Germany and Russia (USSR) on an equal footing."[42] That the trophies had been acquired by force did not matter—the Soviets had simply followed the time-honored tradition of Napoleon and other military victors.[43] Couching similar reasoning in emotional terms, Communist deputies claimed that "Russia has been robbed," but harshly rejected any suggestion of Russian wrongdoing. They rebuked a liberal deputy who protested the complex procedure of returns by asking how a Polish peasant whose icon had been stolen could show that the theft was due to his struggle against Nazism. The USSR did not "steal."[44]

The self-described patriots recalled the war years with unrestrained pride as a time when Soviets displayed bravery and prowess in defending their nation against invaders. They valorized the wartime efforts of all citizens, including members of the trophy brigades, curators, and restorers. They always cited the unwavering belief of veterans of trophy brigades that the art should not simply be handed over to the Germans. In this regard, they could look to Irina Antonova, head of Moscow's Pushkin Museum, who continued to propound the myth of the rescue of the Dresden Gallery and to use the "field hospital" metaphor. As for the later veil of secrecy, she referred to herself and her fellow museum workers as "hostages to many erroneous decisions."[45] Similarly, on the occasion of its first display of trophy art, the Hermitage's director, Mikhail Piotrovskii—whose father had welcomed trophy art into that museum's collections—told employees: "We can be proud of ourselves and our work. We saved the paintings and we kept our secret." Though he called secrecy "a sin," Piotrovskii credited "the sequestering of these paintings for decades" with the "[retention] of their original appearance, with no need for the kind of overly energetic restoration that can alter a work."[46]

Communists put Soviet practices into the context of the USSR's wartime efforts, suggesting that the Soviet Union had suffered and sacrificed more than the other Allies. The author of the catalog accompanying the Hermitage's "Unknown Masterpieces" exhibit of trophy art relativized Soviet acquisitions by reminding the public that Russians were not the only ones scouring Germany for art treasures after the war. He pointed to the work of American art brigades and their delay in returning some objects to German control. While admitting that "American officials, when taking custody of museum objects, generally did not remove them from Germany," he justified the desire of Soviet officials and cultural leaders' for compensation by pointing to their cultural losses under German occupation—an experience that Americans obviously did not share.[47] More strident patriots, in fact, accused Americans of having acquired the lion's share of art objects looted from Soviet territory. Expressing mistrust reminiscent of Cold War attitudes, Antonova and others insisted that Germany had not turned over all

Russian items, and charged the Germans with having sold art to private collectors in the United States.[48]

Many nationalists saw the timing of Germany's demands for the return of trophies as suspicious. Rather than acknowledge that German claims came in response to Russian revelations about secret caches of trophy art in 1991, they charged that Germany was reacting to Russia's weakened international position, and was seeking to reverse, in effect, the outcome of World War II. They also labeled Germany's negotiating stance on the trophy art issue "aggressive," hinting that Germany had not changed its ways over the past five decades. Moreover, they falsely claimed that Russia had never gotten any of its treasures back from the West, and they pointed to Germany's willingness to pay a hefty ransom to recover religious treasures looted from the town of Quedlinburg by an American soldier, but not for Russian trophies, as signs of Germany's low opinion of Russia's bargaining power.[49]

Russian democrats' apparent catering to German wishes seemed like evidence that Russia had accepted its loss of superpower status. One nationalist deputy compared the liberals' readiness to give away displaced art with the Bolsheviks' shameful surrender of property and population in the Brest-Litovsk pact at the end of World War I—except that nowadays, he hoped, the people could protest and stop the flow of art overseas.[50] The outspoken émigré art expert Vladimir Teteriatnikov even called the return of Russian property a way "to 'punish' the Russian people for daring to win the war against Germany." He railed: "If Russia gives away its property just like that, then that will in and of itself confirm Hitler's opinion of the Russian nation as substandard [nepolnotsennoi]."[51]

In light of the nationalists' perceptions of geopolitical relations, the head of the Duma's upper house, Egor Stroev, promoted the law "On the Right of Ownership" as a fitting means to mark the fiftieth anniversary of victory in World War II. The law, he argued, "protects Russia from all kinds of encroachments and defends her national achievements." By affirming Russian claims to trophy art, deputies would align their behavior with that of defenders of the fatherland.[52] The battle over trophy art was a "spiritual Stalingrad." Nikolai Gubenko, the last USSR minister of culture, now a KPRF deputy in the Duma, used this comparison to rally his fellow parliamentarians behind the law "On the Right of Ownership," warning, "The history of Russia preserves the memory of heroes and traitors. Let each of you after this vote say with a clear conscience: 'We are pure before Russia in this difficult time.' The mission of those thousands of youths lying in graves beside the Volga is complete." Although he suggested that there were some "traitors" in parliament's ranks, Gubenko harked back to a time of extraordinary national unity.[53] In effect, he offered his colleagues the opportunity to form once again a common patriotic front behind the leadership of the Communist Party.

The Communists invoked positive, uplifting memories of victory, not embarrassing allusions to Stalin-era repressions. In fact, in their deployment of collective memories of the war, Stalin, the strong leader, became the unspoken hero and Khrushchev the villain. They depicted Khrushchev as arbitrary, rash, and indifferent to legal norms of justice. Rather than recognize his efforts to curb many of the illegal practices common under Stalin, Communists lambasted Khrushchev for his flamboyant, domineering style. They lumped together Khrushchev's transfer of the Crimea from Russia to Ukraine with his massive return of trophy art to East Germany, both of which they interpreted as thoughtless squandering of Russia's national resources. Today's liberalizers, especially Yeltsin, were portrayed as similarly prone to heedless "goodwill gestures." Thus the Communists tried to convince the public that the liberals were the ones lacking in legal culture.[54]

Finally, some members of the anti-return camp used the issue of access to art to highlight what they perceived as the strengths of the old political system. When he explained why the Hermitage's first exhibition of trophy art was titled "Unknown Masterpieces," for instance, the show's official chronicler noted that the public's unfamiliarity with these works was often due to the practices of prewar dealers and collectors. "Dealers were interested in getting good prices, too, and sometimes this tended to keep certain works in the shadows. A clever dealer, having got his hands (and cheaply) on a masterpiece that the public has not yet learned to appreciate, can hold on to it, even hide it away, hoping for a more favorable market in the future." He also cited the practices of private owners who collected for "personal pleasure" rather than to enrich the nation. Admittedly, the main reason for unfamiliarity with the works in the exhibition was that Soviet museums had hidden them for fifty years; but now that they had freed the paintings from secret storage, the same museums were making them accessible to all—something that might not happen if the works were returned to their previous owners.[55]

Lastly, many Communists and nationalists rejected policies that reflected "market pragmatism." They frequently accused government officials of selling off the nation's treasures and even insinuated that government servants were reaping personal benefits. They saw their new law, by contrast, as a populist measure, one that restored art to the Soviet/Russian people.[56] Nationalist and Communist politicians made supporting it a litmus test of patriotism. The KPRF's Gubenko challenged the head of Our Home Is Russia: "I ask: where is your 'home,' respected party of power—in Holland, in Germany, or in Russia, where the fascists executed your grandfather?"[57] The Communists and their nationalist allies insisted on roll-call votes for their trophy art bills, so as to force liberals to reveal their alien capitalist values and their true sympathies with the West.

Liberals responded to these increasingly personal and nasty attacks in several ways. Besides lobbying against the law "On the Right of Ownership," they hedged on earlier support for the quick return of trophies. By 1994 the art expert Savelii Iamshchikov, for instance, had adopted a more nuanced stance on returns: Russia should first exhibit and study works, and perhaps it was not such a bad idea to make the heirs of private collections buy back their items, with the money thus earned going to museums.[58] Mainly, democratic cultural officials continued to hold out hope for a practical solution to disputes over trophy art. If the legislature allowed "civilized negotiations," then Ministry of Culture officials could satisfy the interests of all parties. If the Germans could not return lost Russian objects, for instance, let them come up with suitable items for exchange. Why not swap artworks that Russian curators did not really want for what they did want, such as Soviet art of the 1960s or early Italian works?[59]

Since the Communists had bound the topic of trophy art to the history of World War II, Deputy Culture Minister Shvidkoi finally responded in those terms. In a 1996 essay he ascribed to his father, a war veteran, the view that while Russians did not owe Germany anything, they did not fight the war for the purpose of rounding out Soviet museum collections. Yet Shvidkoi also did not want to offend veterans of trophy brigades or curators of secret depositories. Elsewhere he asserted: "We lived in a country in which not only individual museum holdings but also entire cities did not officially exist, and the museum directors are not to be blamed for this." Thus he managed to blame the Soviet system without reproaching individuals.[60] Shvidkoi acknowledged the importance of the war in collective memory and argued that this shared memory of tragedy and rejoicing was too precious to be sacrificed to present-day political divisions.

Having rebuked the so-called patriots for exploiting memories of the war in current political battles, Shvidkoi nevertheless concluded with an indirect appeal for antistalinist thinking in the name of war veterans: "Those who cried and laughed on Red Square on May 9, 1945, were certain that a new—wonderful and just—life had arrived. Perhaps it would be worth trying a half century after the war not to deceive their hopes." In other words, veterans dreamed of more freedom than a Communist regime would ever give them. The trophy art issue, Shvidkoi implied, offered Russians a chance to invest in a better, more liberal future.[61]

Lastly, liberals turned to episodes from the era of Soviet rule to discredit their Communist opponents. Shvidkoi wryly observed: "The same *Pravda* that welcomed the return of the Dresden Gallery [to East Germany in 1955] today accuses me of not observing the state's interests." And Gubenko, who now led the charge against returns, was minister of culture under Gorbachev when the 1990 Friendship Treaty with Germany was signed; moreover, as minister, he had even turned over some trophy manuscripts to the Germans.[62] Kozlov and Akinsha, who earned the greatest wrath of conservatives, had the most scathing response to the freezing of the restitution process. They contended that fewer items were lost to the Germans than were sold secretly in the 1930s by the Bolsheviks to raise hard currency: the Leningrad palaces lost 139,615 items to the Bolsheviks compared to 116,346 in the war. Moreover, they charged, Soviet curators never even sorted out the property that they did reclaim or wrote off objects that they knew to have been destroyed, thus creating flawed lists of items that they wanted recovered from Germany.[63]

The Limits of Destalinization

In spring 1997, the law setting out the Russian Federation's right to displaced art finally passed both houses of parliament. Yeltsin quickly vetoed the law; but parliament, in a tremendous show of unity, mustered sufficient votes to override the veto. Nevertheless, Yeltsin twice more returned the law unsigned—first he disputed the Federation Council's use of a postal ballot, then he protested the Duma's practice of allowing deputies to vote for absent colleagues by using their electronic voting cards. In 1998 the Constitutional Court rejected Yeltsin's procedural complaints, but indicated that it would not be averse to an appeal based on the provisions of the law. After a new protest by the administration, the Constitutional Court finally decided in July 1999 to let the law's tough provisions stand, but forced the parliament to distinguish in their application between individuals and states and between former allies and aggressors. Individuals and former allies would receive some privileges denied to former aggressor states in attempting to reclaim their lost treasures.[64]

The stalemate over trophy art represented far more than just the executive-legislative friction characteristic of postsoviet Russian politics. It revealed two perspectives on patriotism grounded in very different views of the national past. Ironically, liberals, who devoted so much attention to Soviet history in the 1980s, failed to anticipate the objections that would arise from a humble posture toward Germany on the matter of returning cultural spoils of World War II. Mikhail Shvidkoi now admits that when he first arrived to work at the Ministry of Culture in the spring of 1993, he did not really understand the ramifications of the prevailing impulse to hand over the trophies with great alacrity.[65] As demonstrated here, the initial stance on trophy art taken by the Yeltsin government and many other liberals reflected perestroika-era antistalinism. Liberals' gut reaction to learning that the Soviet leadership had concealed its cultural trophies was embarrassment and remorse.

Though the idea that trophies had to be restored to their previous owners prevailed in liberal circles until 1994, this "moral maximalism" was gradually tempered by the sense that financial hardship justified accepting compensation for returned spoils of war. Moreover, in the early 1990s, the limits of destalinization as justification for policy decisions began to surface. The question arose to what extent the present-day Russian government should have to make amends for the bad behavior of its Soviet predecessor. It also became clear that for many Russians, Stalinism did not taint all state actions of that era. People wanted to hold on to a sense of positive patriotism, and victory in World War II provided a rare touchstone for such feelings. As one official in the Ministry of Culture admitted, the parliament's law on displaced cultural treasures did in fact reflect a common mood and represented "visible evidence of the injuries of the past war in popular memory."[66] By the end of the parliamentary debates, a few liberals had begun to work out their own patriotic version of the war, one that stressed veterans' desire for peace and freedom.

For the Communist-nationalist bloc the trophy art issue was less complicated. They based their stance toward restitution not on memories of an arbitrary Stalinist system but on the Soviet triumph over Nazi Germany. They put the Soviet Union's dual status as victim of and victor in World War II at the center of their vision of national history. The spectacle of wealthy Germany asking the newly impoverished Russian state to return gratis what had been taken as compensation enraged them. After all, the Soviet Union, led by the Communist Party and the Russian nation, had defeated Germany in a just war, so how could it be that Germans but not Russians were living in prosperity and security? If the new Russian government acquiesced in German demands for the return of trophy art, nationalists and Communists argued, it would demonstrate decisively that Russia had forfeited its superpower status. Hence, in the context of the reunification of Germany, the disintegration of the Soviet empire, and the expansion of NATO, trophy art became a powerful symbolic prize for Russian and Soviet patriots.

The "ideological self-sufficiency" and "confidence in one's rightness" that Aleksei Rastorguev found lacking in 1991 had reappeared in the Communist camp by 1994. By keeping trophy art, "patriots" were able to deny the Western nations something that they desperately wanted. Trophy art provided the perfect means for Russia to show that it had preserved its sovereignty and its sense of national self-worth. In modern times, works of high art have become evidence of their owners' level of civilization, internationally recognized status symbols.[67] In this spirit, according to nationalists and Communists, the display of cultural trophies should have been an occasion for national pride, not self-flagellation. Russian patriotism, then, became equated with hanging on to resources accumulated by Soviet leaders, honoring World War II veterans, and saying no to the West. Not accidentally, nationalist trophy art legislation lumped the rich nations of the West together regardless of their status in World War II. With the wealthy Western countries united in NATO, it was easy for Russian hard-liners to forget old alliances even as they kept alive their preferred wartime memories, such as the high level of national unity inspired by outside aggression.

Communist politicians used the issue of trophy art not only to make a statement in international affairs but also to put their domestic rivals on the defensive. Beginning in 1994, they returned to the matter repeatedly to highlight their own nationalist credentials and to underscore liberals' weak sense of pride in past national achievements. Untarnished memories of victory in World War II proved to be an excellent rallying point for Communist patriots. By defending trophy art, they were able to redeem a warmly remembered moment from the scorn heaped by antistalinists on a whole era. As we shall see, democrats would struggle to try to find similar positive bases for a liberal Russian patriotism.

Recasting the Commemorative Calendar

During the Soviet period, participation in holiday celebrations was sometimes coerced and sometimes by necessity covert. From the earliest days of Bolshevik rule, Party leaders sought to harness all kinds of cultural activities, including public festivities, to serve their new regime. In accordance with their perceptions of ideological orthodoxy, Communist Party propagandists supported or discouraged certain holidays. In particular, they promoted the commemoration of anniversaries of revolutionary events and tried to prevent the celebration of religious festivals. In view of the highly ideological nature of the holiday calendar under Soviet rule, the defeat of the August coup inspired fears that new politicians might deprive Russians of their familiar opportunities to gather around the holiday table.[1] The new government did not take away old holidays, but instead elevated the status of some religious holidays, created its own commemorative holidays, and waffled over whether to ignore or co-opt old Soviet rituals and celebrations. The state still plays a role in sanctioning and marking holidays, but nowadays Russians can openly celebrate Easter or May Day or both.

Yet, despite holidays' natural appeal as breaks from the routine of everyday life and often as chances for a day off from work, a 1998 poll actually found 21 percent of Muscovites in agreement with the statement that Russia had too many holidays. When asked which holidays they considered superfluous, the largest number of respondents—23 percent—chose Russian Independence Day, one of the new Yeltsin-era holidays. While almost no one was willing to give up Christmas, Easter, or Women's Day, 14 percent were ready to live without the anniversary of the October Revolution and 11 percent without Constitution Day. The popularity of commemorative holidays, with the exception of Victory Day, was uniformly low.[2]

Ideally, celebrations of distinct moments in the national past, as well as of other sorts of annual holidays, help to define a community. In modern societies, the holiday calendar and its rituals normally provide both a fixed structure for marking the passage of time and a regular form for reminding people of their national heritage. Religious and seasonal holidays break up the routine passage of time in an annual cycle, while commemorative holidays, as David Cressy has noted, serve as "guiding landmarks" and generally give "expression to a mythic and patriotic sense of history."[3]

Commemorative rites, though rooted in an unchanging past, are by nature dynamic. Given that they are forums for redefining or affirming collective links, official national celebrations must almost certainly reflect changes in political systems and in national borders, especially in the context of sweeping political change, when commemorative rituals present authorities with the tantalizing prospect of "solidify[ing] their power by constructing modes of communication and edification . . . to help citizens understand the relationships between government and the people as well as people and history."[4] In other words, new rulers can use symbols and rituals to "create a legitimizing genealogy" for their regime, a supportive context for new authoritative institutions and practices.[5]

Commemorative activities, however, are meant not only to convey understandings of past events but to foster a sense of community among those who share those experiences or memories. Any attempt by the state to mobilize citizens voluntarily also opens the possibility for embarrassment if citizens either actively resist the official plans or display indifference. Hence state-sponsored celebrations may end up revealing a lack of authority or lack of consensus regarding what should be remembered from the past and how. Conflict over how to celebrate the past often makes commemorative holidays into sites for "memory work" and the production of alternative versions of history.[6]

An investigation of the creation and reception of commemorative holidays provides insights into not only how specific events are being recalled but also how they are being mobilized by states or citizens to cultivate legitimacy myths and to foster social solidarity. Demonstrations, festivities, and interpretive texts are sometimes created by planners, sometimes spontaneously initiated from below, and often the result of interaction between masses and elites. Hence, celebrations may be examined for shifts in agency.

Given my book's focus on the political use of history, I do not address festive occasions—including increasingly prominent religious holidays—that do not mark episodes from Russian/Soviet history. Moreover, in keeping with an interest in politics at the national level, I analyze celebrations held in Moscow and "memory-work" in national politics and in the central media.

Remembering the (Counter)revolution of 1917

The first major holiday to fall after the hard-line Communists' failure to reassert their control over the USSR in August 1991 was the seventy-fourth anniversary of the October Revolution, which is actually cele-brated on November 7 because of the change from the Gregorian to the Julian calendar after the Revolution. As noted in Chapter 2, Yeltsin marked this anniversary of the Bolsheviks' seizure of power in 1917 by banning the Communist Party. November 7, however, remained an of-ficial holiday, though neither the central government nor the Moscow city authorities planned any organized celebration.[7]

Once the most sacred date in the Soviet commemorative calendar, the anniversary of the October Revolution had always been marked publicly and extravagantly by the Communist regime. Holiday celebra-tions were important political and cultural events under Soviet rule. In the aftermath of the Revolution, the Bolsheviks had turned to dramatic mass festivals to increase their political legitimacy. James von Geldern has suggested that they consciously sought to follow in the footsteps of the French revolutionaries by creating dramas in which "time was reset inside the festive circle to show the revolution, and those moments in it that organizers chose to emphasize, as a new beginning to history."[8] The Bolsheviks and their allies in the artistic community hoped these vivid theatricals would not only forge a new set of symbols and myths but also unite citizens behind a vision of the shape society might take. Elements of spontaneity in public spectacles, however, soon gave way to the general trend in Soviet politics toward centralization, standardi-zation, and "sobriety."[9]

Over time, the management of rituals in the USSR became a matter more for ideologists than for artists, and festivities for the anniversary of the Revolution gave way to solemn parades in which the state demonstrated its achievements. Regardless of growing public cynicism toward ritual displays, Party leaders continued throughout the late So-viet era to use holidays as occasions to transmit their preferred values and myths. By eliciting mass participation in rituals that affirmed the authority of Communist Party rule, the state demonstrated its power over its citizens and maintained a seemingly impenetrable facade of social harmony. Whereas the Bolsheviks' early attempts at mass spectacles aimed at providing models for society, the more static rituals of the era of stagnation presented models of society.[10] The former painted a picture of a bright future, the latter of a bright present.

After the collapse of Soviet power, would-be celebrants of its origin were at a loss for direction. No longer could they mark the anniversary of the Revolution simply with a celebration of the achievements of communism. The people who gathered spontaneously at the Lenin monument in Moscow's October Square on the morning of November 7, 1991, according to a *Pravda* correspondent, were anxious and quarrelsome. The boisterous crowd, estimated by journalists at 10,000, ended up both protesting and celebrating. They cheered anti-Gorbachev and anti-Yeltsin speeches, sang "The Internationale" and the popular militaristic anthem "Arise, Great Country," and marched to Red Square to pay tribute to Lenin.

Without much guidance, the crowd sought reassurance in the rituals and physical relics of Soviet power. The demonstrators could identify some scapegoats for the Communist Party's sudden fall from grace, but their nostalgia for the past lacked a narrative base that would have translated the memories of the Revolution into lessons for present actions. Even aspiring leaders, such as Gennadii Ziuganov, fell back on vague predictions of a resurgence of communist ideology and organizations, rather than propounding a new interpretation of the Revolution with relevance for the present.[11]

By contrast, democratic activists and liberal journalists took advantage of the anniversary of the October Revolution to express their conviction that socialism had become irrelevant in modern Russia. They were certain that communism had become an anachronism in the aftermath of August. Reveling in their new political freedom, anticommunist civic activists turned traditional commemorations of the victory of October 1917 on their head by mourning the victims of "Red genocide." In Moscow a coalition of democratic organizations marked a "day of remembrance of the innumerable victims of seventy years of civil war in our country" by marching from the Lubianka, where three months earlier they had toppled the statue of Dzerzhinskii, to the site of the former cathedral of Christ the Saviour. A few thousand people gathered to pray for Red, White, and Green victims of the Civil War. In St. Petersburg, a similar ceremony dedicated to the victims of Commu-

nist repression was held at one of the city's churches, while fewer than
1,000 people gathered at the cruiser *Aurora* to honor the Revolution.[12]

The pattern of dueling rituals to mark the November 7 anniversary
continued in 1992. Democratic meetings at the Lubianka and the site of
the former cathedral of Christ the Saviour, however, attracted smaller
crowds than in 1991. By collectively remembering and mourning the
victims of Communist persecution and the Russian civil war, these
civic activists created ceremonies that stood in sharp contrast to the
highly regimented official celebrations of the glories of the Revolution
held under the old regime. The disparities between new democratic and
old Communist practices, however, were diminished by the fact that
Communist loyalists, who had regrouped considerably by 1992, also es-
chewed stale, rehearsed holiday demonstrations.

In Moscow, socialist organizations mustered an estimated 20,000
people on the anniversary of the Revolution to listen to militant
speeches and to vent their anger at the Yeltsin regime.[13] *Pravda* retold
the dramatic myths of the Revolution to inspire socialists, and assured
readers in a banner headline that "people today are not lined up in
columns, but October remains with the people."[14] In other words,
Communist values and memories had survived 1991, even if formal rituals had not. The anniversary of the October Revolution had become an
occasion for an embattled political movement to express solidarity and
to return to prerevolutionary protest traditions.

The Communist press also used the 1992 anniversary of October to
try to promote the idea that the Communist Party's loss of political
power did not invalidate Marx's theory of the inevitability of socialism.
In an interesting twist, *Pravda* printed a hypothetical account of the
hundredth anniversary of the Revolution. From the perspective of the
year 2017, the newspaper's writers looked back on 1991–92 as the low
point in Soviet history. In this fantasy, these years witnessed only the
brief triumph of the forces of reaction. The revised narrative of Soviet
history, then, cast the present weak position of the Party and its ideology as an aberration in a tale of constant progress. Moreover, like other
coverage, this piece made Gorbachev and Yeltsin into scapegoats, depicting them as traitors at worst and hypocrites at best.[15] Communist
editorials divided past leaders into either revolutionaries or counterrev-
olutionaries, and hence encouraged polarized politics and a manichean
understanding of the past.

Liberal journalists, not surprisingly, offered a very different interpretation of the October Revolution. But, although anticommunist rheto-

ric resurfaced in the media every year on the anniversary of the Bolsheviks' seizure of power, civic counterdemonstrations disappeared from
Moscow streets after 1992. After the resurgence of the KPRF in the December 1993 parliamentary elections, Communists dominated public
space on November 7.[16] In fact, in 1994 the Communists' march ended
up at Lubianka Square, where the democrats had celebrated their defeat
of Soviet rule as embodied by their removal of Dzerzhinskii's monument from that site in August 1991.

Drawing thousands of participants—between 10,000 and 20,000 annually since 1994—the Communists have raised both the status of the
holiday among the faithful and public awareness of their reborn organizations by staging ever more elaborate rituals. In 1995, for instance,
KPRF leaders placed wreaths at Lenin's tomb, the grave of the unknown
soldier, and the new monument to Marshal Georgii Zhukov.[17] Here
they cleverly used symbolic actions to reweave the torn fabric of Soviet
history by linking the Revolution with victory in World War II. Moreover, although focusing on electoral strategies for recapturing power,
even moderate Communists recast themselves in the position of the
original Bolsheviks, struggling once again to defend the interests of the
workers against their oppressors. Hence the October Revolution remained a core event in Communist mythology, and its anniversary
served as an important occasion for representing the socialist model of
an ideal society.[18]

A strange situation developed in post-1991 Russia: November 7 was
officially a day off from work but not a "holiday" otherwise observed
by the state. To the annoyance of liberals, "the Soviet part of the Russian people" continued to greet it with pleasure.[19] No one advocated
forgetting the anniversary of the Revolution, given its undeniable historical significance. And after the resurgence of the KPRF in 1993, it
seemed unlikely that politicians would risk alienating a large constituency by attempting to strike the day from the national commemorative calendar. If it could not be dropped, then what, if anything, could
be done to make November 7 a national holiday? For Communists the
answer was clear—only a return to socialism could restore their holiday to its former prestige and celebratory mood. Anticommunists, of
course, wanted people to see the anniversary as a cause to mourn. In
1996 Yeltsin tried a different tactic. In his first official act since under-
going a quintuple bypass operation, Yeltsin renamed the October holiday the Day of Reconciliation and Accord and announced a program for
a Year of Reconciliation.

To patch up—or paper over—the intractable division over how to remember the (counter)revolution, Yeltsin decreed, among other a competition for a monument to commemorate "victims of revolution, civil war, and political repressions," removal from state buildings of art that violated the constitutional principle of political pluralism, and the creation of awards for peaceful conflict resolution.[20] Yeltsin's decree could be interpreted as a pluralist approach to the past—granting, for instance, the status of equal victims to people of all political persuasions—but it might also be seen as profoundly uncritical, in the sense that it embraced all perspectives on the past without acknowledging the contradictions inherent in different views. After all, though earlier democratic meetings marked the anniversary of the Revolution by remembering victims of the Civil War and repression, they did so in a partisan fashion with the purpose of condemning Bolshevism. Were democrats and Communists now to mark the day together? The prime minister's Our Home Is Russia party tried to present some grounds for reconciliation by recalling the parade on November 7, 1941, when soldiers marched from Red Square directly to the front.[21] But this singular patriotic memory of the anniversary of the Revolution did not hold much relevance in 1996, when internal political divisions rather than an external foe threatened the country.

Political actors and commentators from all camps scorned Yeltsin's attempt to use the anniversary of the Revolution as a symbol of unity. In a scathing parody of the president's decree, the iconoclastic editor of the liberal but aptly named *Nezavisimaia gazeta* (Independent Newspaper), Vitalii Tret'iakov, highlighted the way Yeltsin's plan stripped the past of meaning. Tret'iakov's "decree" proposed, among other things, "to change the name of Revolution Square to Accord Square, Red Square to Tricolor Square, New Square to Old Square, and Slavic Square [the former Old Square] to the Square of Proletarian Internationalism . . . to rename the Federation Council the Presiding Senate and the Security Council the Politburo."[22] In other words, one could concoct a mixture of prerevolutionary, revolutionary, and democratic names, but the result would be laughable.

The democratic leaders' hasty effort to neutralize their opponents' holiday was too transparent to succeed. Indeed, Communist commentators totally rejected Yeltsin's gesture. Ziuganov immediately responded, "It's useless to reconcile people by decree." The KPRF Central Committee took the president's ukase as proof that democrats "do not have the power to erase from popular memory the events of which several generations of our compatriots were proud and are proud."[23] Ignoring Yeltsin's overture, the KPRF and other socialist groups continued to use marches and meetings—once the sole prerogative of the ruling regime—to show their strength and to summon up revolutionary sentiments among their adherents. They preserved the outward form of the parade, but transformed what had once been a formal, routine display of official power into a vibrant exhibition of popular might and resistance.

Victory Day

Officially, the anniversary of the October Revolution was the USSR's national day, but May 9, the anniversary of victory in World War II, held that status in most people's hearts. Since 1945, when crowds spontaneously gathered in city centers and workplaces to share the news of Germany's unconditional surrender, Victory Day has been a day of intense emotion. Stalin demoted it to a workday soon after the war's end, but people continued to mark the anniversary by mourning and celebrating with friends and relatives. In the 1970s, Leonid Brezhnev restored and expanded the holiday celebrations in an attempt to capitalize on popular reverence for those who fought in the war. Affection for veterans, he hoped, could be shared by the CPSU, under whose leadership the war had been won. Despite the creation of elaborate official rites, many citizens preferred to spend Victory Day at informal gatherings with fellow veterans in city parks or with relatives around the kitchen table.[24] Regardless of the injection of official patriotism into celebrations, Victory Day retained a deep personal meaning for members of the war generation and their descendants.

Victory Day's very popularity, however, made it a target of political appropriation during the final years of perestroika. Overall, the Soviet leaders and their supporters sought to make the holiday reinforce a model of a multinational, unified, socialist society that was eroding. Hence the CPSU Central Committee's 1991 message to veterans praised them for having fought without regard for their "comrades' nationality," and urged them to work with younger people to "eliminate interethnic enmity."[25] Liberals, by contrast, had already linked commemoration of the war with criticism of both the Stalinist regime and the current Communist government. They questioned whether the huge losses in the war were inevitable or whether a different leader or a different political system could have prevented them. They encouraged people to think critically about what might have been, and to try to evaluate the past dispassionately—not simply to "change the pluses to minuses." From their perspective, relinquishing old myths, even sacred ones, provided a path forward "out of the terrible past to (no, not a bright) a difficult but *normal* future."[26] For conservative Communists, however, such challenges to standard historiography represented a threat to the nation's patriotic heritage.[27]

After the end of the USSR, liberals faced a problem on Victory Day: how to adapt old patriotic rituals and myths to suit a new democratic Russia. The reform-minded newspaper *Izvestiia* continued to attack Soviet historiography of World War II, but also sought out new inspiring wartime images. In its 1992 Victory Day issue, for instance, *Izvestiia* presented a profile of a World War II veteran who seemed to embody a new interpretation of Russian patriotism. The veteran, Gennadii De-menchuk, was the son of an "enemy of the people." A native of the martyred city of Stalingrad, he joined the army during the war under a false name to hide the fact that he was only twelve years old. De-menchuk's unit helped liberate Belgrade, Budapest, and Vienna. After the war, Demenchuk resumed his own name and worked as a sailor, factory worker, poet, and journalist. He had revealed his wartime con-tributions only when he needed proof of service to obtain the tiny sup-plemental pension available to veterans.[28] Demenchuk represented all of the soldiers who fought and triumphed in spite of Stalin and the con-ditions created by collectivization, hasty industrialization, and the purges.

For his part, Boris Yeltsin amended Bolshevik celebrations of Victory Day by ending the tradition of military parades on Red Square. Instead, in 1992 he laid a wreath at the tomb of the unknown soldier. Then, pay-ing no attention to Communist protesters who tried to block his en-trance, he went to Gorky Park to mingle with the veterans who gath-ered there annually. Thus Yeltsin paid homage to the ordinary fighting man and elevated the status of informal, popular celebrations.[29] Other top government officials participated in a "peace parade" sponsored by Russian and foreign commercial concerns. The parade included foreign representatives and survivors of Nazi concentration camps, and ended in front of the Russian White House. The parade was meant to start a new nonmilitaristic tradition that simultaneously reaffirmed Russia's membership in Europe. Hence, in a myriad of ways, state officials' cele-brations in 1992 signaled Russia's abandonment of the CPSU's dogmatic, pompous ceremonial rites and its evolution toward a more peaceful future.

Communist journalists, however, equated low-key official celebrations in 1992 with abandonment of veterans. They deplored the lack of holiday decorations in Moscow's streets and lamented the "too festive" peace parade, where a German band had marched in front of Russian participants. Even familiar gatherings of veterans looked strange to them against the backdrop of "cooperative kiosks selling American cigarettes, beer in cans, and other foreign goods at prices out of veterans' reach even if they had saved up all year."[30] Communist loyalists felt alienated by the absence of traditional state ceremonies and by the new versions of Soviet history. They specifically rejected the theory that Russians had fought hard during the war out of fear of Stalin and the secret police. They accused the democrats of presenting only negative pictures of the Soviet past, and hence of disparaging the national victory in World War II and of killing the spirit of patriotism. They claimed, for instance, that one could find young people who said, "If we hadn't beaten Hitler, we'd live like [normal] people today!" The emulation of the West promoted by the so-called democrats, in other words, had led the young to disrespect previous generations and their noble sacrifices.[31]

Divisions over how to remember World War II properly were exacerbated in 1993 and subsequent years by political splits reflected in dueling commemorations of May 9. Starting in 1993, Moscow witnessed competing ceremonies on Victory Day. Yeltsin's government took part in events at the Victory Park complex at Poklonnaia gora (the Hill of Prostrations), one of Mayor Luzhkov's pet projects. The large park with its massive central square accommodated festive and solemn ceremonies at the same time. Veterans could meet with members of their former units by markers erected for that purpose, join their families in listening to official speeches and attending concerts, stroll among military relics, and picnic in the park's grounds. The complex's stages could be controlled by officials; in 1993, guards turned away Rutskoi and Khasbulatov, both of whom had angered Yeltsin by abandoning the reform camp. These opposition leaders did lay wreaths at the grave of the unknown soldier by the Kremlin, but separately from Yeltsin. Together with Chief Justice Zorkin of the Constitutional Court, Rutskoi and Khasbulatov also visited Moscow's Gorky Park to mingle with veterans—as Yeltsin had done in 1992—to emphasize their populist leanings.[32]

Ruslan Khasbulatov (left) and Aleksandr Rutskoi (right) lay wreaths at the grave of the unknown soldier on Victory Day, Moscow, May 9, 1993. (Photo by V. Marin'o. Courtesy of
TsMADSN.)

Blocked from participating in the central state festivities, the leaders
of the political opposition organized a Victory Day rally in downtown
Moscow in 1993. The city government, hoping to limit protests after a
bloody conflict had erupted during May Day demonstrations, forced
Communist and nationalist groups to celebrate together. Despite fears
of violence, the 1993 meeting attracted more than 5,000 people; by the
next year the number had tripled. The necessary cooperation among opposition groups made their rallies resemble political primaries, each
speaker trying to outdo his predecessor, but it also increased turnout.[33]
The geographical division of celebrations in the capital forced citizens
who wished to join in mass celebrations of Victory Day to choose between partisan sponsors. Those who opted to join with the opposition
found themselves participating in a demonstration that was really a political protest against the current authorities.

In what would become an annual refrain, the democratic press
blamed the opposition for constructing alternative rituals that ended up
dividing veterans. A commentator for a Moscow city paper admitted
that no one had a monopoly on memories of the war, but lambasted

those who would introduce "hate and enmity, parades in columns, noisy demonstrations, malice, slogans, and curses" into the "day of common memory."[34] Liberal newspapers touted festive and "domestic" alternatives. One offered a story about three veterans' plans for the day—one was going to meet up with other neighborhood veterans for a festive meal, another planned to share old photos of his wartime service with his family, and a third would travel to Minsk to visit his sister, who had lived through the occupation of Belorussia.[35]

Liberals also tried to dispel any nostalgia for the old Soviet-style celebrations by recalling the pomposity of official events under the old regime. For twenty years, they reminded readers, commemorations had focused on Stalin rather than on the contributions of ordinary soldiers. Then, under Brezhnev, people's real memories of the war had again been challenged by a distorted version of history that exaggerated the significance of the battle in which the general secretary had fought. The notion that current commemorations were genuinely populist was intended to appeal to veterans' pride in their own actions and also to reinforce the democrats' preferred version of victory as having come in spite of Stalin and the Communist Party.

As competition between democrats and Communists over patriotic credentials heated up, however, democrats began to reconsider their earlier experimentation with untraditional ways of marking Victory Day. If they abandoned the center of the capital on May 9, they were handing their political foes a space that carried connotations of authority. By the fiftieth anniversary of victory in 1995, the Yeltsin administration seemed to have grasped the merits of encouraging a positive patriotism; it invested considerable financial and diplomatic resources in marking the 1995 jubilee anniversary with showy military parades. To accommodate foreign guests who did not want to honor troops involved in Russia's military action in Chechnia, they even conducted separate military parades—one consisting of veterans, the other of active units. Both the venue of Red Square and the presence of foreign dignitaries added to the authority of the ceremonies.

Besides reviving the display of military might, the Russian government rehabilitated Soviet symbols perceived to be close to veterans' hearts. In 1995 they allowed the red victory banner with its five-pointed yellow star to be hung alongside the Russian tricolor. In 1996 Yeltsin went even further to integrate Soviet symbols and myths into Victory Day rituals: his military parade featured the flag that flew over the Reichstag, and in his address he said, "All the country now clearly sees the continuity of times contained in our symbols, the proud spirit of the motherland in the unity of generations, in each of us."[36]

Despite Yeltsin's proclamation of patriotic continuity with the Soviet period and his revival of old authoritative political rituals and symbols, he and other liberals retained their untraditional perspective that the Soviet Union had won the war in spite of, not because of, Stalin. Though by 1994 liberals had begun to tone down reminders of the horrors of war and to avoid explicit critiques of wartime policies, they continued to recall the USSR's defeats as well as its victories on the battlefields of World War II. And they traced the roots of Russia's present woes back to the totalitarian system, which they argued had begun in 1917 and had been inadvertently strengthened by the USSR's victory in the war.[37]

The new patriotic mix, however, did not always ring true. A *Nezavisimaia gazeta* correspondent complained of the contradictory messages sent by the 1995 ceremonies:

> . . . the synthesis of great power status [*derzhavinstva*] and democracy clearly did not succeed. The ritual of the first parade of the "democratic epoch": the leader on the mausoleum, the minister of defense inspecting the columns of soldiers from an open car to a loud "hurrah"—[this scene] was totally in accord with the scenarios of Soviet times. The red banners with hammers and sickles supplanted the tricolor, and Soviet marches and songs sounded out more often than the Russian hymn.[38]

In other words, the ceremonies were now too Soviet, and they still did not achieve their goal of uniting all Russian citizens. Indeed, political opponents of the Yeltsin regime, although pleased for veterans' sakes with the return of the red flag to the official celebrations, ridiculed democrats for hanging garlands over Lenin's name on his tomb. They diagnosed this gesture as a feeble attempt to pretend that the "horrors" of the past five years had not occurred. But not even veterans, argued *Pravda,* could forget that the joy of Victory Day was tarnished by the end of the USSR and the decline of the economy. Having attacked the Russian leadership for its revisionist history, opposition activists painted themselves as true Soviet patriots and called the democrats traitors. Ziuganov even directly charged Yeltsin, Gorbachev, and the democrats with doing what Hitler could not do—destroying the USSR.[39] Moreover, the opposition persisted with its new tradition of a protest

Gennadii Ziuganov (left) listens to Valentin Varennikov (center), former general and supporter of the GKChP, speak at the opposition's alternative Victory Day rally, Moscow, May 9, 1995. (Photo by S. Pominov. Courtesy of TsMADSN.)

march down Moscow's main street. And the alternative observations have annually attracted several thousand participants, including the leaders of the major Communist and nationalist civic organizations.

Russian Independence Day

Along with attempts to revise the status or content of old holidays, democratic reformers altered the commemorative calendar by adding new memorial dates, foremost a day to honor Russia's independence. Although one might have expected that a celebration of independence would be linked either to the defeat of the August 1991 coup attempt or to the official collapse of the USSR in December 1991, the holiday honoring the new state commemorated an earlier event—the adoption of the declaration of state sovereignty on June 12, 1990. On that day, by a vote of 907 to 13, the deputies of the Supreme Soviet of the RSFSR followed the example of several other republican legislatures and declared sovereignty. Their decision allowed the Russian parliament to wrest greater power from the central Soviet Party-state apparatus. Democratic reformers, led by Boris Yeltsin, hoped to use their increased powers to weaken Gorbachev's authority and speed the pace of reforms in Russia. Other deputies were swayed by the opportunity to enhance their own institution, and hence raise the status of their positions. Also many shared the belief that Russia had been slighted by the central government. After all, the Russian Republic lacked a layer of political and cultural institutions that had been granted to other territorial units. A year later, in 1991, the Russian Supreme Soviet made June 12 a nonworking day to commemorate state sovereignty, but also to facilitate the first election to fill the newly created post of president of the RSFSR—a contest won by Boris Yeltsin.[40]

June 12 almost immediately became a controversial holiday of dubious popularity. In 1992 Yeltsin dubbed it Free Russia Day, and democratic deputies sought to have it recognized as a genuine holiday. They met with considerable opposition, however, from deputies who regretted the total collapse of the old Soviet Union or who simply disliked Yeltsin. Nationalists and Communists saw the June date as marking two fateful steps toward the dissolution of the USSR and the subsequent squandering of its resources—namely, the declaration of sovereignty and Yeltsin's election as president. Yeltsin countered these charges in his first anniversary address by blaming the collapse of the USSR on the August coup attempt and the incompetence of former leaders.[41]

But even those who had not changed their minds about the merits of sovereignty could question the aptness of celebrating June 12. Was it, after all, a national or a presidential anniversary? In 1992, deputies lobbying for recognition of June 12 as a genuine holiday touted its association with the legislature's act. But the president later added to the uncertainty surrounding the date's meaning by jokingly referring to the June 12 holiday as "my jubilee."[42] Perhaps, as Yeltsin himself suggested in 1992, people could use the June 12 anniversary to reflect on both the sovereignty vote and the more memorable defeat of the August coup, as both were landmarks on Russia's path to freedom. Indeed, a photo essay for the occasion in 1992 spanned the vote on sovereignty, demonstrations in Moscow in March 1991 in support of the Russian legislature, Yeltsin's election, and the defeat of the August coup attempt, while an editorial in the same government paper traced Yeltsin's career from perestroika to the present.[43] It seemed that the holiday could best be understood as commemorating a series of linked events culminating in

August 1991; but if so, was June 12 really the most significant date for Russia?

Tellingly, whereas some politicians associated June 12 with Yeltsin's election and others with state sovereignty, many ordinary people had no idea of the date's significance. Every year since 1991, the press played up the public's unfamiliarity with what was being commemorated. In 1993, journalists for *Rossiiskaia gazeta* found no banners or posters marking the holiday in Moscow on the eve of June 12 and no one who could be distracted from personal troubles to contemplate the occasion of Russian independence. Even in 1997, a *Moskovskii komsomolets* street poll of fifteen Muscovites failed to turn up anyone who knew the meaning of the holiday. And when told of the holiday's history, three respondents still asked, "Independence of Russia—from whom?"[44] The liberal journalists had no easy answer to this question.

In fact, Yeltsin's critics latched onto Russians' ambivalent associations with independence to subvert the meaning of the holiday. The democratic commentator Vitalii Tret'iakov argued in 1994 that the term "independence" was inaccurate as applied to Russia; former colonies had independence days but former colonizers did not. Thus he drew attention to the absurdity of Russia, the power behind the USSR and before that behind the Russian Empire, "suddenly declar[ing] itself free from its own territories, its own colonies, from its own government that it created."[45] In common with many conservative Communists, Tret'iakov could see May 9 as an independence day of sorts, since it marked liberation from an occupying force; but he interpreted June 12 only as the start of the collapse of a strong state.

Communists and nationalists employed other variations on the independence theme as well to challenge and ridicule the Yeltsin government. They called June 12 the anniversary of "the authorities' independence from the people," and they used the anniversary to express the idea that Russia, which was always dominant in the USSR, had since 1991 subordinated itself to foreign lending institutions—a charge echoed by ordinary people as well.[46] Most typical, however, was the idea reflected in the comment of a participant in an opposition protest on June 12, 1994, who angrily asked: "From whom did Russians become independent? From Ukraine, Belorussia, Kazakhstan? . . . From our relatives who live there?"[47]

In view of the lack of public understanding of or enthusiasm for the June 12 holiday, Yeltsin's 1994 decision to make it the official national holiday of the Russian Federation surprised many people. One liberal paper observed, "Five years ago any school child could answer a question about the main attributes of the state—flag, heraldry, hymn, and major holiday. Today the same question would give most adults, including the state bureaucrats responsible for protocol issues, difficulties."[48] Other commentators began to compare June 12 unfavorably with Victory Day, a day of popular patriotism and great emotional resonance. Even the democratic press tended to condemn Independence Day with faint praise, remarking, for instance, that at least for the new Russian holiday the authorities did not herd people into mass demonstrations or respond to jokes about state holidays with jail sentences.[49] Overall, June 12 became an occasion for intellectuals and politicians to contemplate the new state's failure to create a popular founding myth.

The June 12 holiday suffered not only from its obscure origins but also from a general absence of cause for celebration. In 1992 Yeltsin could hope to counter the unfestive mood by promising that this year would be the hardest, but that, having swallowed the bitter pill of reform, Russians could expect economic health in the long run. By 1995, however, the head of the presidential administration struggled to explain why Russians were still "passing through the most difficult period." What was there to celebrate about five years of independence except the alleged "normalization" of the political system?[50] The Russian government might wish people to get a holiday message about what society could be like in the future, but journalists and political opponents persisted in looking at June 12 as an occasion for assessing the new state as it was.[51]

Yeltsin could not remain indifferent to people's profound disdain for Russian State Sovereignty Day. Thus in 1997 he attempted to assuage popular alienation by renaming his own holiday, henceforth to be known as Russia Day. Announcing this change, he observed, "As president, I would like [June 12] to be a special day. [To be remembered] not as the day when a document was signed, an important event but one far removed from the lives of ordinary people, but rather to be accepted as a common holiday. As the day of our country—Russia."[52] Although he did not say so, by removing the word "independence" Yeltsin also stripped the day of its association with sovereignty. Now people could be encouraged to think of the nation's centuries-old history on June 12. Yet once again, as with November 7, Yeltsin was bound to discover that a name change in pursuit of neutrality did little to affect perceptions of the holiday.

Indeed, on the ritual front, prospects for Russia Day as a meaningful occasion looked bleak. From 1993 on, the political opposition used June

12 for routine anti-Yeltsin rallies. For the majority of Russians, June 12 was a day off from work but not a holiday. Celebrations of June 12 across Russia have thus far consistently lacked a coherent theme. The nation's capital has hosted small street fairs and concerts in public parks. And a national newspaper's roundup of celebrations across Russia revealed that cities in 1996 marked the day with a mix of general festivities—concerts, carnivals in parks, and free admission to museums. But officials often combined the day with some local anniversary or linked it to celebration of some larger event, such as the 300th anniversary of the Russian navy in 1997.[53] The diversity and small scale of festive practices seem less indicative of a resurgence of local identities than of confusion over how to make the date meaningful at all.

In the late 1990s, one could see the government's growing desire to make patriotic connections but no consensus on how to do so. A suggestion to raise the stature of the holiday by marking it, as November 7 had once been marked, with a military parade was not embraced. Nor was a relevant symbol found to define the holiday. On the fifth anniversary of Russian sovereignty, the main government newspaper resorted to featuring a photograph of an enormous Russian tricolor flag being borne through the streets by a crowd rejoicing at the defeat of the August coup. A picture of August at least resonated with the idea of independence, and the editors would have been hard pressed to find a more recent image of a genuinely popular celebration.[54]

After August 1991, the Russian government had rarely reached out to citizens. Indeed, only in 1996, when the date coincided with the final stages of the presidential election race, did Yeltsin join the public in some June 12 festivities—he appeared in Moscow at a "Vote or Lose" concert for young people, attended by a half million people. The partisan nature of his activities on that occasion meant, however, that it "did not become a means for consolidation of society, did not become a day for seeking shared values and unity, but was turned into a day of political struggle and an occasion for pure propaganda."[55] Even Yeltsin's supporters admitted that June 12 would not become a full-fledged state holiday until it was marked by some family customs or traditions.[56]

Constitution Day

Yeltsin's second attempt to create a popular holiday commemorating the establishment of a new Russian state met a similarly rocky reception. In 1994 Yeltsin needed to issue a special decree to make December 12, the anniversary of the referendum in 1993 in which the new Russian constitution was adopted, a nonworking holiday. Parliamentary deputies had refused to endorse Yeltsin's suggestion of a new Constitution Day. For many of them, the December 1993 elections were inextricably linked in their memories with the forcible dissolution of the previous Russian legislature that October. Recalling the circumstances behind the adoption of the Yeltsin constitution, they voted against giving December 12 the status of an official annual holiday.[57] Hence the day has been a vacation day since 1994 only thanks to an annual presidential order.

Political opposition to celebrating the new constitution stemmed from more than a general dislike for the Yeltsin regime. First, many people believed that the Yeltsin government padded the 1993 vote tally by several million votes to reach the minimum level of participation—50 percent of registered voters—to make the referendum binding. To their minds, the constitution had been imposed illegitimately. Second, especially within the legislature, there was a strong sentiment that the new constitution had resolved the battle over the separation of powers too strongly in the executive's favor. Third, the objection was often raised that the constitution was frequently not enforced, and therefore did not really improve the situation of the ordinary citizen.[58]

The president and his administration, however, defended both the constitution and the holiday in the name of a new spirit of the rule of law. They stressed the democratic nature of the referendum by which it was approved, arguing that the vote had made it a sort of social contract voluntarily entered into by the Russian people. Yet they recognized that for many citizens the constitution remained only an abstraction. While admitting that the constitution had not been fully implemented, they noted that the parliament had failed to adopt the laws necessary to carry out some of its provisions.[59] For instance, the constitution permitted alternative military service, but the Duma had not provided for any alternative. Nevertheless, democrats held out the constitution as an appealing model of what society should be and could be like. In fact, in the late 1990s they even went on the offensive to compare the "declarative-decorative" constitutions of the Soviet era with the new one, which had at least been implemented to the extent of allowing freedom of speech and of association. In his holiday address in 1998, Yeltsin reminded listeners that the old constitution had permitted persecution of religious believers and one-party rule.[60] But the tradition of a presiden-

tial address on December 12 was not complemented by any other celebrations. Constitution Day was not marked by festivities even in the
capital.

Divided Holidays

A review of the new Russian state's commemorative calendar starkly
reveals that much of the blame for the unpopularity of historically
based holidays lies with the government. Russian leaders' efforts to
commemorate the past in general and to enshrine new holidays in particular seem extremely laissez faire and poorly planned. Commemorative holidays, with their capacity to serve as either models of or models
for society, offer new political leaders the means to try both to
strengthen their grounding in the past and to promote their visions of
an attractive national future. But such opportunities to revive or revise
collective memories and public rituals must be seized.

The democrats' lack of resolution in forging traditions through holiday
celebrations may be attributed in part to the crises of identity prevalent
across the political spectrum in Russia, as well as to a desire to avoid the
heavy-handed manipulation of festivities practiced by the old regime.[61]
Whatever the reason for the new authorities' initial reluctance to develop
or support commemorative practices, the result was a wasted opportunity in the wake of the defeat of the coup to create a new populist holiday
celebrating their triumph and marking what many people at the time perceived as the real turning point in the struggle against Communist rule.

The new regime passed over the dramatic events of August, which
might have created the basis for a new populist myth, and chose to
mark as its main political holidays the legislature's accord on one document and the adoption by popular vote of another. Voting is unques-
tionably an important part of democratic practice, but since neither of
those votes aroused tremendous public excitement at the time, neither
could easily function as the core of a dramatic myth. Moreover, the
main holiday of the new state, Independence Day, remained unfamiliar
to most citizens. Among editorial writers and other opinion makers, it
served to recall Russian history since 1990 and so inspired mostly
gloomy thoughts about the hardships of the economic transition. Constitution Day at least provided a pretext for thinking about the future
consequences of legal reform, and thus had the potential to generate
some optimism—but it received even less state attention than June 12.

In addition to their problematic content, new state-invented Russian holidays suffered from a lack of participatory opportunities. Russia witnessed some voluntary return of citizens to the public sphere during perestroika, when street meetings gradually became an accepted form of political expression and real political demonstrations sometimes disrupted choreographed holiday "demonstrations." Having encroached on urban spaces once monopolized by the state for its self-expression, citizens used the familiar forms—marches and meetings. Once Yeltsin's regime took control, however, the opportunity appeared to change or co-opt state-sponsored ceremonial traditions as well. The prospect arose for new forms of festivities and commemoration, ones that might combine state support with voluntary civic participation and allow for a mixture of planned activities and spontaneity. But the Russian state rarely brought its celebrations into accessible public squares.

Admittedly, liberals faced a problem with old forms of public commemoration. In the postsoviet context, mass demonstrations sparked two common associations: protests against the regime and highly regimented, involuntary displays of support for the Soviet regime, neither of which seemed appropriate for celebration in a liberal democracy. But new traditions that mixed civic activity and government participation, such as Yeltsin's meeting with veterans in Gorky Park, might have been invented and sustained. One could imagine, for instance, a joint reenactment of the August 1991 defense of the White House. Instead, the authorities have invited citizens to mark Independence Day and Constitution Day as utterly passive audiences for television or radio broadcasts of official speeches. Democratic civic groups have continued to hold public gatherings on what is now State Flag Day. They also mark October 30, once the unofficial holiday of Soviet dissidents, now a working holiday dedicated to remembrance of victims of repression.[62] But in neither of these cases have resource-poor organizations benefited from infusions of state assistance or attention to spread awareness of the new holidays' existence and to raise their status.

Journalists and intellectuals have employed the media on holidays to communicate collective memories of important events in the transition from communism to a new more liberal state. Yet without some ritual component, new holidays cannot create solidary or transformative experiences that might promote a sense of national unity and belonging.

By 1995, however, one could see signs that Yeltsin and some of his colleagues had finally come to crave a set of traditions that would resonate with the public and contribute to a positive sense of patriotism. To this end, the authorities turned their attention to older commemorative holidays. The prize in the battle for patriotic credentials became the fiftieth anniversary of Victory Day. In the case of Victory Day, one could see a slow but steady shift from state officials' participation in low-key, informal celebrations toward a return to state-run, hierarchical, structured events. Anxious in particular not to let the fiftieth anniversary of the end of World War II fall entirely into the hands of his political opponents, Yeltsin set out to woo the support of older generations, even if he had to show tolerance of old Soviet symbols to do so. While he co-opted the form of Soviet military parades, however, the narrative of war now contained a critical component—the idea that victory came in spite of, not because of, Stalin's leadership. Although Yeltsin and his team made concessions to the popularity of Soviet symbols associated with World War II, they consistently promoted a new, coherent, liberal version of the war to replace the Brezhnevite one. Given the popularity of the holiday, however, it is not yet clear to what extent the large crowds that have gathered at Poklonnaia gora in Moscow on Victory Day since 1993 have been attracted by the new political message rather than by the nonpolitical aspects of the festivities.

The negotiation of new symbolic and ritual practices for the commemoration of World War II showed the new Russian regime grappling with the problem of how to lay claim to popular symbols and how to pick and choose precedents that would support its particular vision. By 1995, the liberals had realized that they could not simply jettison the past outright, and they found some merit in co-opting and reworking old rituals and myths.[63] At least on the day for remembering the people's sacrifices in World War II, they willed that the tricolor and the red banner could coexist.

Although the combination of some old symbols and practices with a new antistalinist script helped the government defuse tensions around Victory Day, the same cannot be said of Yeltsin's attempt to redefine the anniversary of the October Revolution by renaming it. Recycling of the past in the form of clumsy renaming of old holidays did not change the content of commemorations. Public holidays need scripts and rituals to become effective means of communication. Moreover, the new reality of hot contestation over how to remember the recent Soviet past remained, as is evident in the persistence and scale of the alternative Victory Day meetings in the Russian capital.

Although the commemorative calendar in Russia lost its coherence after the end of Soviet rule, it did not lose its political salience. On the contrary, with the relaxation of one-party rule and the continued polarization of political forces, the commemorative calendar became increasingly contested and partisan. The relative openness—and emptiness—of the public sphere also opened the door for nongovernmental actors to play significant roles in filling the need for communal activities, even by challenging new or old ceremonial practices. Indeed, socialist organizations, frequently with the cooperation of nationalist allies, recognized and capitalized on the potential of public rituals to communicate values.

Like Soviet planners before them, today's advocates of socialism in Russia grasped the importance of "cultural management" for the establishment of ideological hegemony. Though the end of the Communist Party's monopoly on public space and open speech changed the conditions for organizing rituals and favored forms of action different from those popular under Brezhnev, Communists still found a way to use commemorative occasions to rally supporters and to convey political messages. Now they organized protest marches instead of triumphal parades. Not only did they dominate public celebrations of "red days," but their counter demonstrations often outstripped other gatherings on "democratic" anniversaries.

The highly partisan nature of opposition to organized holiday activities, however, has its drawbacks as well. Holiday celebrations in the form of political demonstrations may be considered another factor in the overall public distaste for commemorative holidays. While protest meetings certainly increase the solidarity of people committed to the same political ends, they may alienate those interested in more neutral festive activities. On Victory Day in Moscow in 1996, for instance, one could see many families with children at Poklonnaia gora, but only a few adolescents in Young Pioneer uniforms attended the opposition's march and meeting. The critical reception by all political actors of Yeltsin's call to make November 7 a day of reconciliation, however, left little hope that common ground would soon be found in the arena of commemorative holidays.

Perhaps then national accord, like popular celebrations, will focus on other sorts of holidays. Newly sanctioned religious dates and consumerist holidays, often imported from the West, are competing with each other and with commemorative days for the public's attention in Russia today. When asked which they actually celebrate (otmechat'), Muscovites revealed to pollsters their disdain for new commemorative holidays and their fondness for secular festivals such as New Year's and International Women's Day, marked by 99 and 82 percent, respectively. Participation in religious holidays also outstripped celebration of old "Red days." Just over half marked Easter, but only 24 and 20 percent engaged in some celebration of November 7 and May 1. Although some people marked religious holidays by attending church services, Russians seemed to have a clear preference for holidays that are celebrated by exchanging gifts and gathering in the home. The Russian Orthodox Church may be reaping the rewards of its substantial efforts to reacquaint people with the meaning and tradition of church festivals. But a poll also revealed that far from all of those who intended to mark Easter could explain its biblical basis, and that many associated it with the start of spring or saw it as an "expression of national tradition."[64] As a setting for demonstrating affinity for Russian traditions, Christmas and Easter services attracted Yeltsin and other politicians. The restoration of religious freedom, however, is only one of the accomplishments of democratization, and church holidays alone are insufficient to create the legitimizing genealogy needed by a new regime. Nor can holidays celebrated primarily in the private sphere provide much of the sense of a common national past so necessary to hold a country together.

Remaking the Capital's Landscape

S ince the mid-1990s, the Russian capital has resembled a construction site. Driven by both market reforms and the change
in political regime, commercial and symbolic building projects
have sprung up across Moscow. Unlike holiday parades and demonstrations, which only fleetingly transform a city's surface, the construction,
destruction, and renovation of pieces of the built landscape have the potential to alter the city's visage over the long run. In fact, monumental
ventures often appeal to political actors for their capacity to project images of authority and to perpetuate an interpretation of national
identity. Moscow's energetic Mayor Iurii Luzhkov understood that public art and civic architecture, especially in the national capital, provide
natural means for the expression of patriotism. He realized that by
shaping his city's image, he could simultaneously convey both his concern for national heritage and his aspirations for the future.

In the wake of political upheaval, new rulers typically seek to occupy or destroy the sacred spaces of their predecessors. Boris Yeltsin
rushed to occupy the historic Kremlin complex even before Mikhail
Gorbachev had quit it. The seizure of the capital presents an opportunity for newcomers to show their strength; its subsequent alteration
may allow them to reshape the representation of power in the popular
imagination. The importance of the external form of the state lies in
the fact that, as Brian Ladd observes in his history of Berlin, "memories
often cleave to the physical settings of events." Consequently, "how
these structures are seen, treated, and remembered sheds light on a collective identity that is more felt than articulated."[1] In other words,
through the preservation or destruction of the built environment, as
well as through the construction of new monuments and government
buildings, would-be opinion makers can shape collective memory. In
the case of Moscow after the end of Soviet rule, the power to make decisions about place names, public art, use of public space, and recycling

or construction of state structures lay partly with federal authorities and partly with city officials.

The earliest changes made by liberal reformers in the capital's symbolic landscape concerned the names of city streets. Place names are a traditional medium for representing bits of the past, and Communist Party rulers had frequently used them to enshrine an array of socialist values and to elevate a pantheon of political leaders. in 1990 democrats in the city government struck out at Soviet rule and at the same time pleased Russian nationalists by restoring prerevolutionary street names in Moscow's historic city center. Symbolic alteration of the city text was a surrogate for the real change they lacked the power to effect, but also a sign of gradually shifting power relations.[2] Once more marked transformations of the cityscape become possible, the low-profile and technically onerous process of changing street names lost its appeal.[3] But initiative in altering the capital's appearance remained with city authorities. For Mayor Luzhkov, the key arenas became monumental art and the reconstruction of historical landmarks. By the year 2000, the Russian capital boasted numerous new symbolic constructions, most of them due to his activism.

A long-time city functionary, Iurii Luzhkov was elevated in 1990 to the position of deputy mayor under Moscow's first democratically elected head, Gavriil Popov. Together he and Popov promoted economic liberalization and supported democrats among the central Russian leadership. After Popov resigned in June 1992, Luzhkov took over as Moscow's mayor, and four years later he won election in his own right with an astonishing 90 percent of the vote. Luzhkov declared himself to be "nonideological" and touted his management skills as the key to his success. Nevertheless, Luzhkov recognized the importance of bread and circuses. The self-proclaimed economic pragmatist, in fact, expended considerable resources to mold the face of the city to express a distinctive version of Russian national identity. In the absence of initiative from central authorities, Moscow's mayor imprinted his own patriotic ideas on the capital's facade. Hence the altered Moscow cityscape reveals one liberal reformer's version of how to turn the past to the service of the present.

I investigate monumental sculpture in Moscow's public spaces and the treatment of historical landmarks, two aspects of Moscow's cityscape that have undergone tremendous change at the behest of politicians since 1991. The choice of historical sites to restore or recreate naturally embodies a judgment about what elements of the national past are important for people today. Commemorative monuments, too, represent evaluations of history. The construction of such monuments and the preservation of landmarks, then, offer great insight into what is being remembered, how, and by whom.

The City as Pantheon

By immortalizing certain historical individuals or events in stone or metal, those who make or commission monuments can attempt to propagate an interpretation of the past, to shape collective memory, and to contribute to a sense of national identity. As one scholar of monumental art notes:

> Since "the nation" is a cultural and political construct, its symbolic representation in ceremonies, monuments and images makes it a palpable object, comprehensible to a population that has to imagine itself as a unified community. Symbolic representations of the nation, such as monuments . . . give substance to abstract concepts and enable the spectators to identify themselves with this large and remote entity. Moreover, each particular representation is also a statement about the nature of the nation.[4]

As students of Soviet history know well, however, monuments that represent the beliefs of the ruling elite may depend on that elite's continued hold on power for their own existence. Shifts in political power not only may determine the fates of specific objects, but may also affect the conditions for appreciating and making art.

In the USSR, the decline of state censorship under Gorbachev permitted criticism of Socialist Realism as the official artistic style. Furthermore, by allowing nonstate organizations to emerge and to promote their own interests, the authorities opened up monumental art to new and competing visions of national and group identity. How did the new rulers of Russia and Moscow deal with their monumental inheritance and what kind of new works of public art did they sponsor?

Unlike its revolutionary predecessor, the new Russian government neither rushed to destroy the old regime's monuments nor hastened to replace its symbols.[5] When Muscovites celebrated the failure of the Communist hard-liners' coup attempt in August 1991 by seeking to topple the monument to Feliks Dzerzhinskii in front of KGB headquarters, the city government, fearing for the safety of the crowd, brought in a crane to take down the statue. The authorities also removed nearby smaller monuments to the Bolshevik leaders Iakov Sverdlov and Mikhail Kalinin. But the crowd's energy waned before authorities were forced to remove any of the other large socialist monuments, such as the mammoth figure of Lenin in October Square.[6]

Subsequently, Moscow city authorities showed themselves opposed to the wholesale destruction of Soviet monuments. They even protected the pedestal where Dzerzhinskii had stood from a small group of demonstrators who tried to plant a cross atop it the day after the putsch was defeated. In this case, they referred to the pedestal's "historic value"—before the Revolution it had held a monument to a tsarist general. The cultural historian Mikhail Yampolsky heralded the result, declaring: "The emptiness above the pedestal begins to radiate time; the pedestal itself becomes a monument."[7] But in Moscow tidiness triumphed, and eventually the pedestal rejoined Dzerzhinskii in the "statue graveyard" created on the grassy verge of the sculpture garden at the Central House of Artists.

Apparently in response to a chance remark by a television commentator, the city authorities adopted the idea of placing representative monuments of the old regime together in a park.[8] Such a solution partially satisfied calls for preservation based on an appreciation of socialist artworks' aesthetic value. Even on the heels of the coup attempt, some liberals classified the tearing down of monuments as vandalism. Though they recognized in the attack on representations of the old regime a popular desire "to deepen the process that began at the walls of the White House,"[9] liberals found amnesia unattractive. They did not want to imitate Nikita Khrushchev, who simply erased his disgraced predecessor's image from public space. Hence the Moscow City Council chose to reduce the number of memorials to Lenin but to keep him as part of the landscape. The massive statue of Lenin in October Square (now Kaluga Square) remains, but the statue of him in the Kremlin was finally transferred out of Moscow in 1995.[10] The lack of destruction may be seen as a sign of tolerance of different political views, indifference, or acceptance of the past as common history. Arguably, democrats in the federal and city governments wanted people to remember the Soviet era but not to feel nostalgia for it.

Of course, destruction of monuments to the old regime is only one way to use public art to send a message about a change in regime. The inventors of *sotsart* (a sort of pop art that takes off on Soviet rather than capitalist icons), Vitalii Komar and Aleksandr Melamid, advocated re-configuring Soviet monuments to subvert their original meanings. In 1992 the two artists, who were living in emigration, issued a call for proposals to "save Russia's Socialist Realist monuments" by "trans-form[ing] them through art into history lessons." The statue of Dz-erzhinskii in Lubianka Square, they suggested, could have been "sup-plement[ed] with bronze figures of the courageous individuals who climbed onto its shoulders and wrapped a noose around its neck on that historic day last August." Similarly, instead of tearing down a monu-ment to Lenin, one could, for instance, add "a huge pigeon" to its head.[11]

Despite the numerous clever and witty suggestions for recycling old monumental propaganda elicited by Komar and Melamid, no such works, or indeed any new modern pieces of public art, grace Moscow's streets. Yeltsin's government gave little material support to the kind of conceptual art championed by nonconformist artists. Moreover, the new Russian federal government did not commission any monuments to commemorate its triumph or subvert any old ones. Yet Moscow is home to numerous new monuments. In the absence of federal initia-tives for new monumental propaganda, Mayor Iurii Luzhkov stepped in to transform the face of the capital. An examination of two grand proj-ects in which he was directly involved—the Central Victory Monu-ment at Poklonnaia gora and the 60-meter-high statue of Peter the Great—as well as of a number of smaller monuments that have been in-stalled with his support, reveals how Luzhkov and special interest groups serving as "moral entrepreneurs" in gathering resources and building consensus behind artistic projects have attempted in their own way to overcome the symbolic poverty of the late Soviet period and to give shape to a new Russian patriotism.

Luzhkov's first venture into the sphere of monumental propaganda came in the early 1990s when he took on the task of overseeing the completion of a memorial complex celebrating the Soviet victory in World War II. Despite the centrality of this event in poststalinist Com-munist legitimacy myths, until 1995 the capital of the USSR lacked a large-scale victory monument. As early as 1957, land at Poklonnaia gora, near Moscow's historic center, had been set aside for a museum and a memorial. An early design competition, however, failed to pro-duce a winner, and the whole project languished until Brezhnev made the construction of World War II memorials an important part of the state's program for instilling patriotism in its youth. In 1979 another competition was held to come up with a design for Moscow. The result of this closed competition fully embodied the spirit and style of the times.

The memorial complex would have had as its center a museum that conveyed an ideologically sound narrative of the war and enshrined its officially recognized heroes. A "Parade Avenue" lined with fountains featuring 1,418 jets of water—one for each day of the war—would lead up to a large sculpture in front of the museum. As described by the American historian Nina Tumarkin, the monumental centerpiece by Nikolai Tomskii was to be "a seventy-meter-high, wavy banner of red granite with a huge bas-relief of Lenin's familiar three-quarter profile." The banner was to "be held aloft by a group of diminutive Soviet people crowded onto a tall pedestal." This design focused on a sacred relic of the war, the victory banner raised by Soviet soldiers over the Reichstag in Berlin. This design, Tumarkin noted, with "its small figures dwarfed by the Lenin banner, hardly seemed to commemorate the victory of the Soviet *people*."[12] It did, however, evoke the leadership role of the Communist Party and a spirit of Leninism.

When perestroika began, the landscaping of the site, but not the actual construction of the monument, was already under way. With this opening for constructive input, in 1986 the artistic community initiated a new debate on the form of a central memorial. Several new design competitions, including two open ones, between 1986 and 1991, produced a plethora of designs relying on stale imagery and familiar gargantuan forms. One architect mournfully concluded, "We are not capable of thinking up a truly worthy monument to an event that gave us all the chance to live, and to live not in slavery."[13] Despite the predominance of Socialist Realist entries, some designs reflected the emergence of a Russian nationalism that drew on religious traditions. Indeed, the top two entries in the 1988–89 rounds of the competition aimed to reproduce a feeling of being in a church, although one was more insistent than the other on its identification with the Russian Orthodox Church in particular.

Tat'iana Nekrasova led a group of young artists in the creation of a structure made up of golden arches sheltering sculptural figures of a grieving mother and a young sentry. The well-known sculptor Viacheslav Klykov proposed a churchlike bell tower topped by the figure of a woman holding branches in her outstretched arms. Neither Nekrasova nor Klykov came close to Tomskii's unabashed and politicized triumphalism: both used the image of a woman to pay tribute to the suffering of civilians and provided space for the living to mourn their dead. They also drew on the ancient Russian tradition of erecting churches to mark military victories. But while Nekrasova rejected the notion that her "shrine" was per se a "Russian church," the Slavophile Klykov admitted that he saw the Orthodox Church "as a unifying force" in Russian history, and presumably in the future as well.[14]

Klykov's project won the active support of the anti-Semitic and virulently nationalist Pamiat' group, which spread the rumor that Nekrasova was Jewish. In the midst of the subsequent outcry, the jury announced in December 1989 that it could not choose between the two finalists, and so another contest was organized in 1991. This time the Ministry of Culture settled on a monument of a woman holding a child. But this design was also not realized after protests from, among others, the Council of Veterans, who did not think that a statue of a "single mother" captured the gravity and dignity of their feat.[15]

In the absence of consensus on a monumental centerpiece for the Victory Park complex, only work on the museum and the landscaping had begun when Mayor Luzhkov took an interest in the project in 1993. Luzhkov worked out a schedule for completion of the grounds and museum, and approved the construction of a Russian Orthodox memorial chapel in the park. Finally, he decided to complete the ensemble without any more contests. He simply commissioned his friend the sculptor Zurab Tsereteli to design a monument that would fit the allotted spot.[16] The result was an unusual combination of a simple geometric form and various sculptural figures.

Completed for the fiftieth anniversary of the Soviet victory, the monument consists of an obelisk modeled after a bayonet and topped by a figure of Nike, the Greek goddess of victory, who in turn is flanked by two angels blowing trumpets. Bas reliefs outlining a traditional narrative of the war from Brest in 1941 to the 1945 victory salute in Moscow decorate the obelisk's base. At the foot of the obelisk stands a large figure of Moscow's patron saint, George the Victory Bearer, on horseback, with lance upraised as he slays a dragon. The dragon lies on a base marked with swastikas and other Nazi attributes. Hence Tsereteli used a traditional classical form—the obelisk—and realistic sculptural figures to create a vertical monument that conveys the spirit of military triumph. He deliberately avoided standard Soviet symbolism, however, and instead mixed several Christian and pagan images historically connected with the theme of victory.

Artistically, Tsereteli's composition has several shortcomings. First

Detail of Zurab Tsereteli's central victory monument at Poklonnaia gora, Moscow, 1996. (Photo by Kathleen E. Smith.)

of all, the figure of Nike is difficult to make out from the viewer's per-spective. The fine details of Tsereteli's figurative work simply cannot be seen from the foot of the 1,418-meter pedestal. This distorted pro-portionality led to several derogatory nicknames, including "the grass-hopper on a needle." Second, the figure of St. George with its delicate lance seems incongruous with the slabs of dragon at his feet. Visitors complained that it looked as if he were slicing up a sausage. Finally, the reliefs carved into the base of the obelisk have been described as "crude . . . ponderous, boring in their composition, and monotonous, having been repeated three times on three sides [of the obelisk]."[17] Per-haps critical review by a jury of experts might have prevented some of these aesthetic problems.

More important from the perspective of commemoration, however, were the perceptions of the monument's symbolic content. The monu-ment sent a clear message that what was important to remember about the war was not popular suffering or individual sacrifice, but rather the pride that came with triumph. Though Tsereteli's design does not fit all the precepts of Socialist Realism, it is still very much in the heroic mode common to Soviet war memorials. It also meets the traditional international physical standards for victory monuments—"vertical pre-eminence, grandness of size and lightness of color"—but falls short in "national symbolism."[18] The goddess Nike is foreign to Russia; and St. George, though formerly and now once again the subject of Moscow heraldry, was alien to most citizens of the nation that fought the war, the officially atheist USSR. Indeed, both of these symbolic elements drew criticism precisely because ordinary Soviet soldiers might never have heard of them.[19]

Early complaints in the popular press, in fact, focused on the appro-priateness of the monument's interpretation of the essence of collective memory of the war. Although some citizens preferred an uplifting ver-sion of the war, many others found fault with the triumphal nature of the proposed monumental complex. They equated unabashed celebra-tion with elitism. As one Muscovite wrote in response to an article in *Izvestiia*, "There's no respect for the sorrow, deaths, hardships of the war. From the very beginning, this was conceived of as a monument to the generals' war. The goal was to draw attention to the CPSU, its lead-ership [*verkhushka*], and to hide the truth about the people's [*narodnoi*] tragedy."[20] This letter represented more than a common criticism of public art for its association with elite interests. It also reproached those who would sanitize collective memories of the war, who pre-

ferred the uncritical, uplifting Soviet narrative of victory to one that included the stories of POWs and punishment battalions. A formal ceremonial monument could not capture the horror of war or the suffering
of those whom it touched on the frontlines and on the home front.
Hence Tsereteli's obelisk, argued one commentator, would be better
suited to commemorate victory in a war of aggression than in a war for
survival.[21]

It seemed that the controversy clinging to the wartime leadership,
especially to Stalin, heightened the desire for a populist monument.
Elsewhere war memorials have downplayed societal discord over war
and its costs by "honoring the individuals who fought rather than the
country's lost cause."[22] Indeed, two Russian critics who disagreed on
whether the Poklonnaia gora monument should commemorate sorrow
or glory both argued for a memorial that embraced the perspective of
the foot soldier. One expressed his desire to see the figure of Vasilii
Terkin, the simple soldier made famous by Aleksandr Tvardovskii in
his humorous poems, riding with other soldiers on the back of a tank as
they returned from the front; the other proposed a trio of sculptural figures depicting a "soldier-victor, a woman worker, an adolescent jour-
neyman."[23] Another populist suggestion came from a woman who admired the way the American Vietnam Veterans Memorial preserved
family memories. She advocated collecting the once common memorial plaques created by Soviet institutions to honor their war dead by
name and making them part of the monument.[24] A populist memorial
might have reinforced the liberal attitude toward individual rights
promised by democratic politicians.

Ironically, however, Tsereteli's one effort to address the terrible
human losses involved in World War II was spurned by his powerful patron after it become the subject of criticism in the media. The piece in
question was a free-standing sculpture consisting of figures of frail,
emaciated men, women, and children toppling like dominos. Tsereteli
installed this work, titled *The Tragedy of the Peoples* and dedicated to
the victims of fascist genocide, on the main avenue of the park. A liberal art critic who generally disliked Tsereteli's work praised this one
because of its sorrowful theme. She noted that it reminded viewers of
the fate of both civilians murdered at Babi Yar and Russians who died in
German prison camps or in Stalin's labor camps after the war. After all,
she argued, World War II should be remembered not only on May 9 but
also on June 22, the anniversary of the Nazi invasion.[25]

Residents of the region whose children used the Poklonnaia gora complex as their neighborhood park, however, complained about the gloom of the monument and about the removal of some kiosks to make way for more construction. They were joined in their disparagement of the *Tragedy of the Peoples* by the frequently caustic editor of *Nezavisimaia gazeta*, who turned his daily column into a forum for criticizing Tsereteli's work and this sculpture in particular.[26] He and others claimed that this composition had originally been intended for Israel, implying that Israel had a monopoly on memory of concentration camp victims.

Without raising the issue of anti-Semitism, one of Poklonnaia gora's designers rebuked the neighbors for their selfishness. He accused them of preferring commercial kiosks to a reminder of the terrible losses in the early days of the war, of putting private preferences "above the historical values of several generations."[27] Luzhkov, however, apparently agreed with the assessment of *Tragedy of the Peoples* as depressing and not in keeping with the design of the park; he ordered it moved to a site invisible to casual visitors to the Victory Park—at the rear of the museum, by the service entrance. Now the park lived up to its name, recalling the conclusion of the war rather than its process.

An analysis of Luzhkov's first monumental project for Moscow would not be complete without consideration of the religious buildings included in Victory Park. The complex features a Russian Orthodox church, which stands in the foreground of the main monument and museum, as well as a synagogue and a mosque. Built with city funds, the Orthodox church, dedicated to St. George, opened in time for the fiftieth anniversary of Victory Day. The mosque and synagogue, which opened in 1997 and 1998 respectively, were funded largely by their religious communities. The banking and media tycoon Vladimir Gusinskii led Jewish organizations in raising money for the synagogue, while Muslim communities across Russia gave their own money and solicited donations from Muslim states to pay for a shrine to their war dead.[28] These places of prayer offer visitors a chance to reflect on their personal losses. Each provides a warm, intimate space in contrast to the gigantic museum and obelisk that dominate the park.

On the one hand, the inclusion of three religious traditions in the Victory Park complex was an unprecedented display of pluralism and tolerance; on the other hand, the funding, positions, and even styles of these buildings made clear their unequal status. The church was located on the central avenue, on the highest ground in the park. Its dedication to St. George mirrored both the official victory monument and the Moscow city coat of arms. The mosque, with its tall minaret, was visible from the road on one side of the park. Its designers chose an architectural style—red bricks with white trim and a copper turret—to reflect the city authorities' preference for a building that fitted in with Moscow architecture.[29] The mosque, in other words, had to show its Russianess to outside observers. Meanwhile, the synagogue, a low building of modern design surrounded by trees, stood in a distant corner of the park and was nearly invisible. Only a sculpture of a menorah by its entrance identified it as a Jewish place of remembrance. Despite their marginal locations, the mosque and the synagogue attracted protest from Russian nationalists. Luzhkov, however, did not back down on his commitment to permitting the Jewish and Muslim communities to honor their veterans. At the dedication of the synagogue, he and Yeltsin both spoke out against contemporary manifestations of fascism in Russia.[30]

Luzhkov's second foray into monument making, like his first, honored a military theme, featured a Russian hero, and executed a design by Tsereteli. After a hastily organized competition for a design to commemorate the 300th anniversary of the Russian navy in 1996, approval went to Tsereteli's proposal for a 60-meter-high statue of Peter the Great at the helm of a sailing ship. Dressed in an old fashioned costume, holding a scroll in one hand and the helm with the other, Peter stands on the embankment of the Moscow River on a piece of wasteland adjacent to the Central House of Artists. The enormous statue stands just across the river from the Kremlin and the rebuilt Cathedral of Christ the Saviour. According to Tsereteli, the document in Peter's hand represents the plan for the Russian state and the ship the tsar steers indicates Russia's new course. Tsereteli promoted the monument as contributing to the "firm foundation of the glorious historical deeds of our forefathers," which must underpin Russia's progress.[31] Peter the Great, then, embodies both state-building and reform imperatives. Thus, in paying tribute to this tsar, Luzhkov grounded himself in Russia's heritage and found a precedent for a modernization program that drew heavily on Western technology and investment.

Unlike Nike, Tsereteli's Peter the Great provoked an outcry less for its symbolic content than for its style and creator. Opposition to Peter came from several sources. The monument was seen as evidence of Tsereteli's dominance of the Moscow art scene, which aroused so much resentment that other artists referred to him as "Luzhkov's court sculptor." Both citizens and critics deplored the secretive process that pro-

Tsereteli's monument to Peter I overshadows the Cathedral of Christ the Saviour, March 29, 1998. (Photo by V. Marin'o. Courtesy of TsMADSN.)

duced the monument. Why had there been a closed design contest and no public review? Critics suspected that Tsereteli's Peter I was merely a recycled version of his monument to Christopher Columbus, which the sculptor had failed to sell to a Western city to mark the 500th anniversary of the discovery of America. The monument's aesthetics, too, drew criticism. Besides its gargantuan proportions—wits to called it "Gulliver"—Peter, like Nike, was sculpted with detail indistinguishable from the viewer's perspective. Lastly, the monument's location was deemed inappropriate. Why, asked commentators, place a statue of Peter the Great in Moscow, a city that the tsar himself disdained, and on an insignificant body of water unsuitable for a grand naval vessel?[32] A Tsereteli supporter defended the choice of Moscow, as it was there that Peter won his political battles to establish his "window on the West" and other modernizing initiatives.[33] Nevertheless, in the popular imagination, Peter the Great was inextricably linked to the city he had created, St. Petersburg.

After Marat Gelman, the owner of a modern art gallery, initiated a noisy campaign for a referendum on whether the colossal monument should be dismantled, the hue and cry around the monument and around Luzhkov's heavy-handed management style forced the mayor to act. Put off by the expense of conducting a citywide referendum, Luzhkov nonetheless agreed to commission research on city residents' opinions of the monument and to appoint a special commission of experts to determine the monument's fate. Tsereteli's supporters meanwhile used the press to defend Peter I and to publicize the cost—estimated in the millions of dollars—of removing the monument. To the dismay of Tsereteli's vocal critics, pollsters found that approximately half of Muscovites liked or were at least indifferent to the monument, and that few of the others wished to have the city bear the additional expense of dismantling the massive bronze.[34] A radical Marxist group tried to blow up the Peter monument to protest the liberal media's campaign to bury Lenin, but the statue survives.[35] Nevertheless, the controversy raised Russians' consciousness of the closely guarded process by which public art was being approved in "democratic" Moscow.

Despite Tsereteli's apparent monopoly on monumental commissions in Moscow, sculptures by other artists have been unveiled there since 1991. After Tsereteli, the most prominent sculptor in postsoviet Moscow is Viacheslav Klykov, an artist working in the realist tradition and a leader in the ultranationalist movement. A list of his projects for

Moscow alone since 1989 demonstrates the range of nationalists' interests in the imperial past, Orthodoxy, and Russian military and cultural traditions. In 1990 Klykov placed a monument to Grand Duchess Elizaveta Fedorovna in the courtyard of the Marfo-Mariinskaia convent, which she had founded. A member of the Romanov royal family who had become a nun and devoted herself to charitable works after socialist revolutionaries assassinated her husband, the governor general of Moscow, in 1905, the grand duchess was murdered by the Bolsheviks in 1918. Klykov next erected a monument to the Russian saints Cyril and Methodius in central Moscow in 1993. His model of the founders of the Cyrillic alphabet became the accepted location for Orthodox Church officials to celebrate Slavic Literacy Day (May 24), a holiday popular with nationalists since it was first celebrated in Russia in 1985.[36] Klykov's most famous work, an equestrian monument to the World War II hero Marshal Georgii Zhukov, was placed on Manezh Square, near the Kremlin.

Like Tsereteli, however, Klykov had one notable failure. Luzhkov firmly rebuffed Klykov's efforts to erect a statue to Nicholas II in the Kremlin or on the central Borovitskaia Square. The last Russian tsar was the subject of controversy even among nationalists, some of whom blamed him for the collapse of the autocracy. Though Klykov lost the battle for a position in the symbolic heart of the Russian state, he attracted a representative of the presidential administration, as well as the local bishop, to the dedication of his monument to Nicholas II in 1996 in the village of Tainskoe, where the tsars had often stopped to rest on their journeys to Moscow. Both this statue and a second Klykov monument to Nicholas II in the Moscow-region town of Podolsk, however, have since been destroyed by vandals who claimed to be members of a radical revolutionary group.[37]

Klykov's traditional, realistic monumental style suited his mission of fostering public pride in Russia's military, cultural, and religious heritage. His work, while not exciting, was well executed and intimate in style and proportions. With the exception of Nicholas II, Klykov unerringly identified heroic subjects of broad patriotic appeal. Although his monument to Marshal Zhukov was a state commission, many of his other works have been donated to the city. Klykov successfully raised funds from nationalist groups and garnered support within the hierarchy of the Orthodox Church. His influential supporters helped him get permission from the city government to place his work in prominent sites.

The cases of Klykov and Tsereteli show that the simplest way to get a piece of public art installed in Russia after 1991 was to donate it to a city or to get a unilateral decision in its favor from a city's mayor.[38] Demonstrated ability to please the public or to impress art critics did not determine which pieces of monumental art were erected. As one art expert observed, "The shining moment of urban planning democracy turned out to be short-lived."[39] Public hearings and open design competitions once again vanished. The power to make public art, like the power to do many other things in postsoviet Russia, lay in access to private money or to the executive branch of government. As a consequence of the increased importance of financial and political patronage, the dominance of a few sculptors in the field of monumental art was out of all proportion to the artistic merits of their works. But even they had to tolerate the whims of their political patrons.

Luzhkov's preferences clearly ran to grandiose, realistic monumental works depicting figures from the Russian past or honoring Russian military, religious, or cultural achievements. His artistic taste so closely resembled that of his Soviet predecessors that new heroes seemed to take their places effortlessly among the old. The monumental art patronized by Luzhkov served as a vehicle for reconnecting selectively with Russia's heritage. Monuments, like street names, offered opportunities to honor personages or discrete events without necessarily constructing a coherent, credible narrative version of history. Moscow's mayor took advantage of this characteristic of public art to avoid summoning up controversial or tragic recollections of Russian/Soviet history. Yeltsin, by contrast, occasionally supported the use of public art to signal a deliberate break with the past. Most notably, he donated some of his book royalties to Ernst Neizvestny's modernistic memorial in Magadan to victims of Stalin's purges, and helped obtain federal funds to allow its completion on the eve of the 1996 presidential election.[40] But, over all, Yeltsin did not exercise his influence to tackle either old or new monumental propaganda. Luzhkov, for his part, confidently employed the Russian capital as a platform for expressing pride in, not remorse over, the national past.

The City as Heritage Theme Park

Luzhkov's interest in propagating positive images of Russian history manifested itself not only in the commemoration of heroes and heroic events through the medium of monumental sculpture. Luzhkov also actively promoted the preservation and re-creation of historical landmarks in Moscow. Beginning in 1992, he helped oversee the reconstruction of the Kazan Cathedral on Red Square. Under his patronage, the city further restored an earlier version of Red Square's visage by rebuilding the Iverskie gates in 1995. But the mayor's most ambitious and physically striking effort to resurrect a piece of Moscow's lost architectural past was the re-creation from scratch of the massive nineteenth-century Cathedral of Christ the Saviour. In all of these cases, city funds flowed to projects that created copies of works of Russian architecture that had been deliberately destroyed under Stalin. The cost of these symbolic gestures raises several questions about the self-proclaimed "pragmatic manager" Luzhkov: What does historical preservation mean to the mayor? What message is he trying to send about himself and his domain with his choice of objects and the manner of their restoration?

Originally conceived by Tsar Alexander I in 1812 as a tribute to God for his help in the Russians' defeat of Napoleon, the church dedicated to Christ the Saviour was built by his successor, Nicholas I, who chose the architect Konstantin Ton to design a cathedral in the "Russian style." Ton drew for inspiration on the five cupola Kremlin churches, but at 102 meters high, his cathedral towered over the nearby Kremlin. The Cathedral of Christ the Saviour's interior space was divided between the church area and a gallery housing memorial plaques listing the fallen officers and major battles of the War of 1812. In keeping with Nicholas's dictate that the decor promote his belief in the distinctiveness of the Russian people, interior murals and exterior sculptural compositions included depictions of episodes from Russian history that showed God's special kindness to the Russian autocracy over the centuries.[41] Hampered in part by delays in the allocation of money from the imperial treasury, the construction of Ton's cathedral took forty-four years. Despite the currently prevailing myth that the cost of the Cathedral of Christ the Saviour was met by small contributions, the state provided the overwhelming majority of funds.[42]

The original cathedral held several meanings and served a variety of functions simultaneously. For the primary agents behind its construction, the cathedral sent a message of gratitude to God and reinforced the notion that the Russian people had a special destiny. Its grandeur and scale also reminded foreign visitors of the might of the Russian state and of its triumph over Western invaders. The Orthodox Church used the church for daily contact with its parishioners, and enjoyed the awe inspired by the huge cathedral and its opulent decorations. For the few surviving veterans and for the many descendants of soldiers in the War of 1812, the Cathedral of Christ the Saviour commemorated their specific sacrifices. And for visitors during Russia's later military campaigns it was a place to seek divine intercession or to register their personal losses. Finally, the addition of a monument to Alexander III and plans for statues of Alexander I and Nicholas I for their services in presiding over its construction arguably made the cathedral a monument to its political sponsors as well as to a specific military victory.

The Bolsheviks' desire to rid Russia of its traditional religions, combined with their need to enshrine their own heroes, led to the destruction of the Cathedral of Christ the Saviour. In 1918 they smashed the monument to Alexander III located on the church's terrace. The cathedral itself continued to function as an Orthodox church for several more years, but its profile made it a prime target for antireligious city planners, who described it as a monument to militarism and national chauvinism. Meanwhile, several architects lobbied to have the cathedral's prime location selected for the planned Palace of Soviets, a monumental structure that would commemorate Lenin and the creation of the USSR. In December 1931, having dismantled some of the church's bas reliefs and removed fragments of its most famous murals, workers used explosives to reduce the church to rubble. Soon thereafter, its site was in fact earmarked for the Palace of Soviets.[43] The Soviet government intended to erect the building in two years, but the design competition stretched out until the spring of 1933, and soon World War II made resources too scarce to permit construction to proceed. In 1960 the government finally abandoned plans for the Palace of Soviets and instead opened a large outdoor swimming pool on the site where the church once stood.[44]

Luzhkov was not the first to raise the idea of rebuilding the martyred cathedral, nor can he even be numbered among early promoters of historical preservation. Long before perestroika, Russian nationalists of various stripes had embraced the cause of saving Russia's endangered patrimony. Indeed, support for historically significant buildings was one of the few catalysts of civic activism in the USSR before 1989. To defend decaying estates and abandoned churches was in effect to criticize the Soviet regime, which had done so much to transform the landscape by destroying or neglecting the architectural legacies of the imperial period and by devastating traditional Russian village life with inept

policies. Yet some scholars, history buffs, and writers risked offending
the government because they saw conservation of Russian architecture
and the natural landscape as means of expressing love for their native
land and culture. The writer Vladimir Soloukhin, for instance, supported historical preservation and environmentalism as stepping-stones
to a revitalization of religion and patriotism in Russia.[45]

Perestroika emboldened some preservationists to articulate the patriotic rationale for their efforts more openly. For instance, a 1989 article in a prominent architectural journal welcomed the plan put forward by a voluntary society of preservationists, and newly endorsed by
Communist Party authorities, to rebuild the Kazan Cathedral, originally erected to commemorate Russia's liberation from foreign occupation in 1612. The article's author hailed the planned duplicate as "a
symbol of the return of living memory about the valor and unity of our
forefathers in the salvation of Russia."[46] Since the Cathedral of Christ
the Saviour also held the distinction of being both a war memorial and
a place of worship, its rebuilding could similarly be cast in patriotic
terms. Moreover, the cathedral's dramatic dynamiting to make way for
a Soviet project made it a particular martyr in the eyes of believers and
of others who were critical of Soviet rule. They compared the event
both to the Bolsheviks' brutal murder of the Russian royal family and to
the crucifixion of Christ.[47] Thus, not surprisingly, as early as 1988–89
several Russian intellectuals raised more or less simultaneously the
idea of rebuilding the cathedral.

Most notably, the sculptor Vladimir Mokrousov proposed that the
dispute over how to commemorate World War II in Moscow could be
resolved by rebuilding the cathedral alone or together with a new,
smaller cathedral dedicated to St. George "as a memorial to two fatherland wars." When his model of the Cathedral of Christ the Saviour was
exhibited in 1988, it attracted other like-minded people. A community
of believers formed and began to seek the return of the sacred space
where the cathedral once stood and to collect funds toward its reconstruction. In 1990 the Russian Orthodox Church officially recognized a
group of the faithful who held the more modest short-term goal of
building a chapel on the site of the former cathedral.[48] All of the be-
liever-activists conceived of the reconstruction as an act of repentance.
They insisted that it was primarily an Orthodox church dedicated to
the Resurrection and only secondarily a historical monument or architectural landmark.

A second civic initiative to rebuild came from Russian nationalists working through the newspaper *Literaturnaia Rossiia.* Initially, however, they made the case for re-creating the cathedral as a monument to military sacrifice. They stressed its significance as a monument to the War of 1812, and recalled that visitors to Moscow had once felt morally obliged to pay their respects at the cathedral.[49] Although *Literaturnaia Rossiia's* first publication carefully argued that the Cathedral of Christ the Saviour was a fully international memorial because it was not Russian but "Christian" in character and dedicated to a victory of the multinational Russian empire, the newspaper soon began to feature the views of more extreme nationalists.

Drawing on the myth of its populist origins, nationalists averred that the construction of the cathedral represented a time in Russian history when people were united in their religious faith and loyalty to a powerful state. Reconstruction of the church therefore offered Russians the opportunity to reassert themselves in the present as religious subjects of a strong state. The extreme nationalists, who regarded all of Russian history in the light of a perceived battle between Russia and the West, also saw the Cathedral of Christ the Saviour as a martyr from the beginning of its existence. Several contributors blamed Jews, namely the main Moscow city planner, Lazar Kaganovich, and the Palace of Soviets' architect, Boris Iofan, for its destruction. Nationalists even attributed the criticism of Ton's architecture by his contemporaries to the church's Russian, as opposed to classical, style. Similarly, they touted a new Cathedral of Christ the Saviour as a bulwark against Western capitalism and Western artistic taste. Indeed, nationalists saw a real threat in Western businessmen, who they claimed sought to preserve the swimming pool and to develop a complex of shops and exercise facilities around it.[50]

In 1989, with *Literaturnaia Rossiia's* assistance, religious, military, and literary social organizations united in a single foundation to promote the resurrection of the Cathedral of Christ the Saviour. The foundation's governing board included both proponents of a positive, relatively inclusive nationalism such as Soloukhin and virulent nationalists such as the dissident mathematician Igor' Shafarevich and the monarchist sculptor Klykov.[51] As Russia entered the post-perestroika years, however, the nationalists' dream of rebuilding the cathedral seemed impossible. Despite their best attempts to raise funds for the project, religious believers and nationalist intellectuals had made little progress. Meanwhile, though political reform had made it possible for religious communities to reclaim their former places of worship, the

Russian Orthodox Church lacked the funds to repair all of its surviving buildings, let alone to build new ones. Market-oriented reforms, moreover, required historical preservation to be considered in light of economic factors. It often fell to government authorities to weigh the competing interests of developers in modifying or tearing down old structures, of citizens and experts in preserving cultural relics, and of localities in attracting tourist dollars with historic districts.[52]

Yet, undeterred by the potential costs, Mayor Luzhkov, acting with the endorsement of President Boris Yeltsin and the cooperation of Patriarch Aleksii, announced in 1994 with great fanfare that the Cathedral of Christ the Saviour would be rebuilt with donations from private citizens and businesses on its original site and in its original form. Moreover, using the concrete foundation of the Palace of Soviets, engineers would add floors below street level to house offices for the patriarch, a parking garage for hundreds of cars, and a conference hall with seats for over 1,000. A new social council and fund-raising apparatus under the mayor's office would replace the older civic groups that had thus far managed the collection of donations. The composition of the new council demonstrated the mayor's seriousness and his interest in supporting some form of Russian patriotism: it was dominated by municipal bureaucrats and professional construction engineers, but included also three members of the creative elite well known for their Russian nationalist sentiments—the writers Valentin Rasputin and Vladimir Soloukhin and the painter Il'ia Glazunov.[53]

After adopting the idea of reconstructing the cathedral in 1994, Luzhkov invested considerable time, attention, and political and financial resources in the project. He reviewed the plans, visited the site, chastised the builders, and exhorted donors. The cost of the cathedral was estimated to run over $400 million, and fund-raising is an ongoing struggle. Officially, the city government offered tax breaks to organizations involved in its construction. Unofficially, Luzhkov used his position to coax and coerce donations from private and state-run businesses. The administrator of the Christ the Saviour Fund admitted that good relations with city government helped in the solicitation of corporate contributions. After all, the mayor's office still controlled access to much of the office space in Moscow.[54]

Moreover, despite denials, the Cathedral of Christ the Saviour Council also asked for and received federal subsidies, including tax breaks for big donors. During the 1995 budget debate, a close Yeltsin adviser even

(Left to right) Patriarch Aleksii II, President Boris Yeltsin, and Mayor Iurii Luzhkov at the dedication of the Cathedral of Christ the Saviour, September 3, 1997. (Photo by V. Marin'o. Courtesy of TsMADSN.)

called the cathedral set-aside one of two "sacred subsidies" that could not be reduced—the other was the Victory Fund to provide special veterans' benefits for the fiftieth anniversary of victory in World War II. The amount of so-called nonbudget revenues directed to the construction project from the city's coffers remains a well-guarded secret, but one city legislator who investigated the question estimated that during the construction phase only 10 percent of daily expenditures at the site were paid for by charitable donations.[55]

The Cathedral of Christ the Saviour clearly appealed to religious believers and Russian nationalists because of its original symbolism, but what did it mean to the self-proclaimed "economic pragmatist" Luzhkov and the "democratic" Yeltsin? In view of Russia's dire economic situation, the decision to devote significant state money to the creation from scratch of a copy of a historic building required explanation. The pragmatic response to financial quibbles was plainly stated by Luzhkov's deputy, Vladimir Resin. Though Jewish himself, Resin deemed Ton's cathedral a "world-class achievement," and argued:

First, man does not live by bread alone. Second, surely the situation with housing wasn't better when they first built this cathedral. And it was quite bad when they blew it up. And who blew it up? Our relatives, our grandfathers. Together we bear full moral responsibility. . . . We didn't ask the believers when that was done. And the church is being built from donations and nonbudgetary sources. . . . So what's better? A nonbudget cathedral or a budget swimming pool [or] fifty homes?[56]

The mayor, like the tsars before him, was tending to the nation's moral and spiritual life. Indeed, Luzhkov contended that Russians would be no better than complacent cattle if spiritual, cultural, and moral development did not accompany economic progress. Echoing the mayor, Yeltsin justified the state's interest in what had been a pipe dream of small Russian nationalist groups by explaining: "It is a Russian national sacred place and must be reborn. With it, it will be easier to find the path to social accord, the creation of goodness, and a life in which there will be less room for sin."[57] Thus the mayor and the president attempted to link larger civic goals to religious and nationalist values. They did not, however, embrace the more extreme nationalists who had initiated the drive to rebuild the cathedral.

During perestroika, the Cathedral of Christ the Saviour did not lack admirers among the liberal intelligentsia. Like nationalists of all sorts, they perceived the cathedral as a victim of Stalinism. But liberal commentators had tended to focus on the tragedy of the cathedral's destruction. One architect rejected Mokrousov's plan to build a copy of the cathedral in favor of another design from the victory monument competition—one that would have commemorated the loss of the cathedral by placing a small chapel devoted to repentance in the center of a towering metal skeleton that outlined the dimensions of the original cathedral. Such a project would have reminded viewers of Soviet history and provided a place for believers to pray without the costly and perhaps technically impossible process of duplicating the old cathedral.[58]

Once Luzhkov began to plan the reconstruction in earnest, some liberals raised the argument that reproducing the cathedral would send the false signal that the traces of the Communist period could be quickly erased. Covering up the sins of the past, they argued, was not the same as atoning for them. Moreover, many liberals, unlike Russian nationalists, saw the destruction of the Cathedral of Christ the Saviour as just one of many outrages committed by the Soviet regime against people of all nationalities and religions. Contradicting Luzhkov and Yeltsin, they reasoned that singling out for state support a monument to a particular religious faith could hardly unite all citizens of a multi-ethnic, multidenominational Russia.[59]

Another complaint applied to Luzhkov's other preservation projects as well. Those committed to saving Russia's architectural heritage deplored the choice to invest in a replica of a historic building rather than in the conservation and restoration of surviving landmarks. They also bemoaned Luzhkov's "improvements" to the original, such as the cathedral's concrete shell and underground office/garage complex. Though Luzhkov cited the merits of elevators and a modern ventilation system for the cathedral's durability and comfort, these changes clearly marked the reborn church as a *novodel'* (new model). As the art historian Aleksei Komech noted, Luzhkov adopted principles of restoration that valued appearance and facade over authenticity and interior.[60] With his pragmatic outlook, the mayor did not see why a historic building should not be altered to meet the needs of modern users; and those in the administration of the cathedral project who were too wedded to historical accuracy found themselves encouraged or forced to leave. From a religious point of view, of course, it is not the age or appearance of a church but rather the activity that it hosts that matters; but for those who value historical artifacts, authenticity has a value of its own.[61]

Luzhkov's fondness for inserting representations of Russian heritage into the urban landscape can be seen in numerous other city-sponsored construction projects, as well as in the influence exerted by city planning bureaucrats over private building ventures. Architects for major commercial projects—whether banks, offices, or hotels—have felt pressure to make their designs adhere to a nebulous idea of historic "Moscow style." Moscow is home to a mix of architectural styles, but eclecticism has not opened the door to creativity. Conformity to Moscow style has most often meant adding small towers after the model of the Kremlin or echoing the design of Orthodox churches. As one critic wryly observed: "To draft blueprints of a building in Moscow taller than three stories and without a turret—this is the equivalent of applying for an exit visa during the years of stagnation, [this is] to officially declare oneself a dissident."[62] As a result of the mayor's preferences, modern materials mix with old forms and commerce must coexist with heritage.

The underground shopping complex at Manezh Square, a Luzhkov pet project, epitomizes the possible combination of shopping, entertainment, and history. Built at the expense of a large expanse of public space, a popular site for political demonstrations in the late 1980s, the city-financed Manezh mall created a new capitalist environment with historical touches. Zurab Tsereteli provided ornamentation so that each underground level might convey the taste of a different century. His metalwork motifs in the mall's corridors and the elevator buttons labeled by "century," however, hardly disguised the typically Western content of the boutiques and restaurants that could afford the complex's steep rents. Genuine history in the form of centuries-old artifacts uncovered by archeologists in the few months they were allowed to explore the construction site were relegated to a small museum in one wing of the complex, allotted 400 square meters of space rather than the 3,000 promised.[63]

Although the idea of an underground shopping center had originally seemed to be an ideal means of housing commerce discreetly within the historic center, Luzhkov permitted Tsereteli to decorate the outside of the mall as well. As a result, the now familiar figure of St. George slaying the dragon tops a semitransparent abbreviated globe that serves as a skylight for the underground complex. On the side of the shopping center closest to the Kremlin, a series of fairy-tale creatures—the old man with the golden fish, a bear, a duck, and so forth—now perch in a small canal created by temporarily releasing the Neglinnaia stream from its underground conduit. The landscaping and statues attract spectators, especially children, whose gaiety amid the fountains seems at odds with the solemnity of the tomb of the unknown soldier sheltered under the nearby Kremlin wall.

Luzhkov's investments in shiny replicas of historical landmarks and his interest in forcing new buildings to include historical motifs show the mayor to be a fan of Moscow's heritage, but not of its history. Luzhkov sought to popularize the Russian past, but most often not by recalling specific events or even clearly defined time periods. He would have Russians embrace a vague folkloric concept of their roots—one that included castles and churches, tsars and soldiers.[64] Gritty social history and balanced interpretations of past policies have no place in his vision of the national capital. When dilapidated buildings threatened to mar gentrification projects, Luzhkov showed no qualms about disregarding laws protecting landmarks.[65] The appearance of history in tidy and imposing forms was sufficient to represent Russia's past. In short, Luzhkov's ideal Moscow more closely resembled a historical theme park than a museum.

Patriotism in One City

Unlike many other liberal politicians, Iurii Luzhkov realized early on in the formation of the new Russian state that the population might be receptive to a patriotism based on respect for the national past. By honoring past feats, he reinforced a sense of some positive continuity. With the reconstruction of the Cathedral of Christ the Saviour he a created a link between the prerevolutionary and postsoviet periods. By pitching the restoration of a piece of the nineteenth-century landscape as part of a package of modern economic and political reforms, Luzhkov suggested that such "development" was more a return to traditions interrupted by communism than an imitation of Western ways. In a sense, Luzhkov used heritage, as is common elsewhere, to offset the sense of alienation often produced by major social changes.

Proponents of recreating or preserving cultural heritage everywhere point to heritage's potential to foster feelings of common cause and of rootedness in historic traditions. But, as David Lowenthal points out, the downside of heritage is that it can just as easily "glamorize narrow nationalism." Unlike history, which "tells all who will listen what has happened and how things came to be as they are," Luzhkov's replica of the Cathedral of Christ the Saviour, like other bits of heritage, "passes on exclusive myths of origin and continuance, endowing a select group with prestige and common purpose."[66] Despite Luzhkov's claims to ideological neutrality, his symbolic gestures carried meaning. Indeed, it is naive to think that the past can be reproduced or presented in some purely objective fashion. As the head of the cathedral's fund-raising organization admitted, Christ the Saviour "will become a monument to us, to those living today, a monument to our times."[67] If the new symbolic constructions are monuments to Luzhkov and his times, then what do they imply about the new regime?

The Cathedral of Christ the Saviour, Poklonnaia gora, and other grandiose additions to Moscow's built landscape are monuments to their builder—Iurii Luzhkov. His close personal involvement in these projects ensured that he received credit for their realization. Moreover, although he sought projects that would please the people, Luzhkov

The reconstructed Cathedral of Christ the Saviour. (Photo by Kathleen E. Smith.)

clearly did not value civic participation in urban planning. He pushed aside the volunteers who had begun to raise funds for the Cathedral of Christ the Saviour and he sidestepped open competitions in his choice of a victory monument. Luzhkov tolerated no obstacles to the rapid completion of his complex construction projects. By building his model of the Cathedral of Christ the Saviour in just a few years, Luzhkov demonstrated that he was more capable than either the tsars, who labored for decades on the original, or the Bolsheviks, who never came close to completing their substitute showplace. His imperious management style and presumptuous use of city funds, however, irked many liberals. They also felt uncomfortable with the symbolic content of Luzhkov's projects.

In assessing the content and style of Luzhkov's monumental achievements, one Russian critic concluded that Luzhkov was bent on "realizing the imperial idea."[68] The mayor's choices both of heroes from the past to be honored and of an appropriate monument to World War II reflected traditional artistic tastes and a patriotism that exalted military successes and embraced forceful political leaders. The mayor seemed nostalgic for an idealized distant past, when Russians were united around faith in their state and and in their church. Though not raised in a religious family, Luzhkov saw the Russian Orthodox Church as an important, though not the sole, source of values. According to him, city government should orient itself on "religion together with culture, family traditions, sport, and morality."[69] He saw no problem with including places of worship at Poklonnaia gora or with state funding for memorial shrines.

While remembering positive aspects of Russian heritage, often in festive and celebratory ways, Luzhkov opted to "forget" gloomy and controversial facets of Russian history. His victory monument celebrates the triumph itself, not the human suffering that lay behind it. Through monumental propaganda, he attempted to dispel the image of Russia and Russians as victims. In fact, although he did not ignore the Communists' destruction of the Cathedral of Christ the Saviour, he generally stressed the merits of its reconstruction rather than its tragic past. The cathedral's grandeur was more important to Luzhkov than its history.

By the mid-1990s, Luzhkov's reputation as a builder had helped to elevate him to national prominence. Luzhkov had literally and figuratively proved himself to be a constructive leader. Whereas Luzhkov won reelection handily in 1996, St. Petersburg's liberal mayor, Anatolii

Sobchak, who criticized Luzhkov for running around construction sites in a cloth cap rather than sitting in an office signing important decrees, lost his reelection bid to his deputy, who adopted Luzhkov's self-description of "economic pragmatist."[70] Although the provision of bread and circuses had won the hearts of many Muscovites, however, Luzhkov's path was not free of criticism. As we have seen, many liberals worried about the artistic and social consequences of Luzhkov's heavy-handed management of urban planning. Besides their concern over the lack of civic participation, they expressed alarm that Luzhkov's brand of patriotism seemed to mean glorifying military sacrifice, excluding religious minorities, and raising monuments to the nation's leaders rather than to its citizens.

Luzhkov's symbolic choices undoubtedly demonstrated a deep commitment to a strong Russian state. Yet, although the patriotic touchstones that Luzhkov provided had the potential to support illiberal nationalism, he himself did not exploit them for such ends. Moreover, Luzhkov did not combine his elevation of heroic figures and military feats with the crafting of a narrative account of Russian history complete with explicit lessons for the future. Hence, one can see Luzhkov's successful identification of popular historical symbols as leaving open the door to more sophisticated ideologues—of various political stripes—to refine and exploit his themes by linking them more explicitly to their values.

Campaigning on the Past in the 1996 Presidential Race

In the 1996 Russian presidential race, the incumbent, Boris Yeltsin, squared off against Gennadii Ziuganov, the head of the Communist Party of the Russian Federation (KPRF). At every campaign stop, Ziuganov stressed that he was the candidate not just of one political party but of a bloc of nationalist and socialist associations. The ideal nature of this coalition was represented at the final rally for his Union of Popular Patriotic Forces by the juxtaposition of red Soviet flags with banners bearing traditional Russian Orthodox depictions of Christ, Mary, and St. George. Instead of countering his opponent's invocation of Soviet and prerevolutionary myths and heroes with a positive patriotic vision, Yeltsin ultimately turned to antistalinist themes from the perestroika era. "The Communist Party hasn't changed its name and it won't change its methods," warned posters in the final weeks before the runoff election between Yeltsin and Ziuganov. By reviving unpleasant memories of the Soviet past, Yeltsin and his allies hoped both to rouse disaffected voters and to weaken the coalition of nationalists and Communists.

Campaigning for elective office is a type of political activity in which symbols, though not necessarily historical references, play an important role. In his book on the changing symbolic politics of the Italian Communist Party after 1989, David Kertzer notes:

> For many political analysts, there is the "real" stuff of politics and then there are the effluvia of political life: symbols, ceremonies, flag-waving, and baby-kissing. In this view, those observers who are sophisticated enough to peer through the surface . . . are able to see that what explains political action are such hard-nosed matters as financial interest and the jostling for personal gain.[1]

"The Communist Party hasn't changed its name and it won't change its methods," warns an election poster, July 1996. (Author's collection.)

Obviously voters are motivated by complex reasoning that includes perceptions of their short-term economic interests, the candidates' personalities, and many other factors, but Kertzer contends that symbols in fact lie at the base of political authority. Hence names and myths matter both in individual decision making and in the formation of collective identities. Therefore, while an examination of politicians' use of historical references during election campaigns cannot entirely account for either voters' choices or the culture of political organizations, it nevertheless illuminates both the process and the results of the ongoing renegotiation of political identities in Russia.[2] The behavior of the most popular presidential contenders in 1996, Gennadii Ziuganov and Boris Yeltsin, raises interesting analytic puzzles of great relevance to the ongoing study of Russian politics.[3] How had the Communist Party leader woven together Russian nationalism, with strong affinities for the prerevolutionary period, and nostalgia for Soviet socialism? And what did it mean for Yeltsin to have to turn to an antisoviet platform to win reelection?

The Experience of Parliamentary Elections

To understand the mobilization of symbolic capital in 1996, we must briefly consider the image-making efforts of the main contenders in the two national electoral campaigns preceding the presidential race. Half of the positions in the lower house of the new Russian legislature are filled by proportional representation on a national basis, the other half by winner-take-all voting in single-mandate districts. The focus here is on the national competition for party-list seats.[4] Parties and political movements generally work hard to form a public image that conveys to viewers some sense of the organization's identity. Without such communication, voters would be unable to distinguish between contenders. In well-established party systems, the electorate may take basic differences between parties for granted, leaving candidates to elucidate finer policy differences. Defining, let alone representing, interests, however, proved to be an enormous challenge for Russian proto-parties during the perestroika years.[5]

In the political, social, and economic chaos in Russia after 1991, identity crises continued to plague organizations and individuals. Not surprisingly, then, personality rather than program often served as the clearest distinction between Russian parties. But the attractiveness of an individual leader rarely provides sufficient glue to hold an association together, let alone to rouse the lasting enthusiasm of the public at large. Political organizations, therefore, not only have to define themselves for activists and members but also have to build bonds with citizens by mobilizing common cultural referents, especially shared memories. What symbols did Russian electoral associations find to offer voters, and perhaps more important for future races, did parties manage to fit themselves into appealing narratives of national history?

After his unconstitutional dissolution of the Russian Supreme Soviet in September 1993 and the ensuing bloody conflict, Yeltsin worked rapidly to organize elections for a new legislature and a plebiscite on a new constitution. Given the extraordinary tension surrounding this election and the procedural irregularity of voting for delegates to an institution at the same time as for the constitution that might legalize its existence, Yeltsin decreed that those deputies elected in 1993 would sit for only two years, instead of the projected four-year norm. The majority of political organizations, despite the negative feelings generated by the violence used by both sides in the October events, agreed to participate in the December elections, and some of Yeltsin's restrictions on political activity and publishing were eased in time for the largest opposition party, the KPRF, to campaign with some support from the main socialist newspaper, *Pravda*.[6] The next elections took place on schedule in December 1995.

Postsoviet parliamentary elections have been characterized by a profusion of political organizations competing for party-list seats in the Duma and a predominance of formally "independent" candidates running for single-mandate spots. In both 1993 and 1995 neither the liberal nor the Communist camp could agree to unite in a large bloc. Hence dozens of organizations competed in elections, but most failed to gather the 5 percent of overall votes necessary to qualify for any of the party-list slots. Yeltsin did attempt to encourage a two-party system in 1995 by working behind the scenes to create two centrist organizations—Our Home Is Russia (led by Prime Minister Viktor Chernomyrdin) and the Bloc of Ivan Rybkin (headed by the former Speaker of the Duma, a moderate Communist), but these artificially created parties struggled to create social networks.

Moreover, although some associations, such as the Agrarian Party, represented real interest groups, most organizations had only vague programs and unclear ideologies. Many groups tried to survive on the popularity of individual candidates. In 1995 there was a definite trend toward blocs that proffered general slogans and flowery statements of principles, made unsupported promises of paths to prosperity, and were headed by some sort of representative triumvirate—for instance, one military leader, one cultural figure, one economist.[7] The importance of mustering at least a few famous names was reinforced by the fact that official ballots for party-list seats included only the name of the organization, its top three candidates, and an official symbol to identify each competing association.

In terms of basic identifying marks, Communist parties of various temperaments had access to a set of clearly recognizable symbols. Competing socialist associations modified the old hammer-and-sickle motif used by the CPSU to indicate the changes that had been introduced in their own organizations, as well as to highlight the differences among them. In January 1995 Gennadii Ziuganov's KPRF added the outline of a book as the background to a rather delicate drawing of a hammer and sickle. The book stood for the inclusion of intellectuals and white-collar workers, who now made up a fair portion of the party's leadership. The less threatening-looking hammer and sickle could be seen as appropriate for an organization that had abandoned revolutionary methods for electoral politics. The more militant Communist groups, which in advance of the 1995 elections formed an alliance called Communists–Working Russia–For the Soviet Union, made the Soviet Army's five-pointed star the backdrop for the traditional hammer and sickle in their official symbol.

The KPRF's main ally in the 1993 Duma, the Agrarian Party, used as its symbol a sheaf of wheat—which various Soviet republics had incorporated in their emblems as testimony to their rich agricultural resources—bound with a ribbon bearing a small hammer and sickle. In 1995 a bloc that included the head of the reformed official trade union umbrella organization used a stylized version of its initials (ST in Russian) to create a hammer-and-sickle logo in which a small triangle atop the sickle transformed it into a rocket in flight. Thus a variety of socialist parties used widely known iconic elements of Soviet imagery to signal to voters their basic location on the political spectrum, and yet simultaneously tweaked these familiar forms to provide further information about whom or what they sought to represent.

A glance at the 1995 ballot reveals that democratic and centrist organizations generally opted either for no electoral symbol or for some neutral, modern sign that rarely held any political meaning. The centrist Women of Russia, for instance, chose a sunflower, and the pro-reform Common Cause and Forward, Russia! came up with a squirrel and a hedgehog, respectively. Others chose symbols that evoked their names, but only a few had any link to the substance of the party's program. While the ecological association Cedar and the Beer Lovers' Party wisely opted for simple representations of their names—a tree and a mug of beer—to remind voters of their preferences, the Bloc of Ivan Rybkin and Iabloko picked symbols that fitted their names—a fish (ryba)[8] for the former and an apple (iabloko) for the latter. In the best of circumstances, the apple and the fish reminded viewers of the parties' names. But since the names themselves were drawn from the surnames of the parties' leaders (a combination of the initials of Iavlinskii, Boldyrev, and Lukin inspired "Iabloko") rather than from some programmatic distinction, the emotionally neutral fish and apple stirred up no ideological associations. Iabloko used television advertisements to try to drum up positive associations with its "brand name"; one spot showed Isaac Newton being inspired by being struck by a falling apple. But the party did not find a way to link the apple with its liberal policy stances.[9]

More evocative than the apple or the fish but laden with a potentially negative connotation was the "roof" symbol employed by Our Home Is Russia. The "party of power" tried to turn its name into a patriotic logo by putting a tricolored triangle atop a square constructed of the two short words "our home." Billboards featured its leader, Prime Minister Viktor Chernomyrdin, making a roof shape with his hands. But since "roof" had become a synonym for mafia protection rackets, this advertising strategy led to numerous jokes at the expense of Our Home Is Russia.

Other electoral associations created no visual symbols. Aleksandr Lebed's Congress of Russian Societies, the blocs of Stanislav Govorukhin and Panfilova-Gurev-Lysenko, and, in 1995, Russia's Democratic Choice[10] used their names, initials, or no symbol at all to represent themselves on the ballot. Their advertising featured their leaders but no visual shorthand to capture some aspect of their ideology or program. Oddly, even the colorful and creative Vladimir Zhirinovsky, despite his exuberant Russian nationalism, also coined no symbol. His inappropriately named Liberal Democratic Party of Russia simply used its initials in place of some patriotic logo on the party-list ballot.

The lack of historically rooted or even meaningful contemporary symbolism in the logos of the pro-reform and centrist parties, however, did not mean that they campaigned without any references to the national past. But the main liberal contenders—Russia's Democratic Choice, Iabloko, and Forward, Russia!—ran explicitly forward-looking campaigns. The liberal parties all warned of the possibility of a Bolshevik revanche, yet concentrated on selling their own capacity to lead Russia into the twenty-first century. In view of their interest in promoting themselves as economic reformers, liberals saw relevant national history as really beginning in 1989–91. They analyzed the period of experimentation with market mechanisms and democracy in order to extract lessons for better policies to achieve the same goals. In particular, Russia's Democratic Choice, well aware of the public's suspicion of the role played by its leader, Egor Gaidar, in the painful economic changes in Russia, recognized the need to delve into the intricacies of recent events to justify its role in market reforms.

By 1995 the focus on recent history gave liberals less cause to demonize the Communist opposition, which after all had shown itself capable of playing by parliamentary rules over the past two years. Hence, in a pamphlet for voters, Gaidar admitted that the current Communists did not want to return the country to 1937 or even 1953; their aim, he said, was to return to 1989–91, a time when semi-reformed socialism had reached a dead end and was unable to develop further in any direction.[11] Iabloko, meanwhile, attempted to broaden its electoral base by appealing to the Communist Party's natural audience, those whose standards of living had dropped significantly since the 1980s. To this end, Iabloko largely refrained from attacking the KPRF and stressed its own commitment to social justice. One of its posters declared: "We're not fighting communism, we're fighting poverty."[12] Only Forward, Russia! made a strong anticommunist pitch with a billboard announcing that victims of civil war, collectivization, and repression would not vote for Ziuganov.[13] Not only did liberals make few efforts to tar their socialist opponents with the brush of the past, they did not promote themselves as heirs to the dissident tradition—the exception being the biographical campaign literature put out by individual candidates who had been active in the human rights movement.[14]

While many blocs could opt to concentrate on either their opposition to current social evils or their roots, the new "party of power," Our Home Is Russia, had no such choice. A brand-new alliance, formed to try to capture the support of centrist voters in the 1995 election, the bloc headed by Prime Minister Chernomyrdin could not criticize the status quo, since it represented the current government. The bloc used a rooster as a symbol of its Russian roots, but the main image that it

sought to project was not of plain folk but of a group of highly compe-
tent professional politicians. Both Chernomydin and his popular supporter Mayor Iurii Luzhkov had cultivated reputations as strong, pragmatic managers, not ideologues—hence their slogan, "Our Home—on
the sound foundation of responsibility and experience." Despite their
choice of a patriotic name for their coalition, Our Home Is Russia's
leaders did not follow in the steps of the nationalist demagogue Zhirinovsky, who frequently indulged in lengthy discourses on Russia's traditions and historical mission. Instead, they presented themselves as
representatives of happy, prosperous Russians: photos of clean-cut
young people with their smiling elders graced their rather insipid and
forgettable posters.

The concept of a deliberately nonideological party was promoted
also by the economist Boris Fedorov's Forward, Russia! All of Fedorov's
literature stressed that his party served common interests, and that
Russians should not be divided. Under the slogan "We are not left or
right, we are normal—like you," Fedorov urged, "First, we need to
reach a worthy standard of living, and then we can decide what to call
things."[15] Both Chernomyrdin's and Fedorov's parties presented slick
advertising campaigns that held out the promise of Western lifestyles
without actually touting them as such. Our Home Is Russia and Forward, Russia! called themselves patriotic parties, but did not spell out
what their love for their homeland meant in terms of policy choices.
Nor did they ground themselves in national history by pointing to historical figures or traditions that they admired.

The KPRF, too, in 1995 promised an improved standard of living and
increased law and order, but unlike its rivals, it drew heavily on national history—both Soviet and Russian—in its electoral platform. Indeed, in contrast to its official program, the KPRF's election theses
barely referred to Marxist-Leninist theory. The tract titled *For our Soviet Motherland* tackled both recent and distant history in an attempt
to ground the policies of the renewed Communist Party. Recent history
served to explain why citizens dissatisfied with the present should vote
for the KPRF; Soviet history reminded Party loyalists of continuity between the CPSU and the KPRF; and prerevolutionary Russian history
was deployed in an effort to link Communist principles with older
moral values.[16]

By 1995 the CPSU's heirs were far better prepared to deal with the
question of how they had lost power than they had been at the Constitutional Court hearing three years earlier. Two arguments raised in

1992 had been refined for public consumption. The first consisted of the theory that Western forces had conspired to weaken the USSR, just as they were now assaulting Russia. Communists pointed to instances of economic and cultural imperialism, which they blamed for giving Russians an inferiority complex and inciting them to tear down their own institutions in a vain attempt to imitate the West. They called upon Russians to take inspiration from past battles against the Teuton and Mongol invasions, and from the experiences of rebuilding a shattered nation in 1917 and 1945. Second, KPRF leaders disavowed Gorbachev and Yeltsin, whose reforms they saw as self-destructive. Reviving the idea presented in 1992 that there had always been two parties within the CPSU, one of traitors and one of principled idealists, Ziuganov explained that a pure core had emerged from the travails of the past few years. Those who had joined the Party to further their careers had left, and in their stead had gathered the spiritual heirs of the cosmonauts, hero workers, and cultural and scientific giants of the Soviet era.[17]

Having renounced any responsibility for perestroika, the leaders of the KPRF tried to cultivate nostalgia for the postwar and Brezhnev periods of Soviet rule. Their weekly insert in *Pravda* featured a special column headed "A Name from the List," which provided heroic biographies of KPRF candidates. They presented their nominees as grateful beneficiaries of the opportunities for social mobility provided by the old system. Deputy Alevtina Aparina, for instance, had been born on the eve of World War II and grown up fatherless in a rural village, but thanks to the Soviet system, she was able to get a higher education. Having "preserved in her heart gratitude toward the toilers of the countryside," she had labored as a regional Party secretary to alleviate the hard lives of the people until her work was disrupted by the events of August 1991—not by the coup attempt but by the sealing of CPSU offices across Russia.[18]

Citing shrinking production, worsening health statistics, and a declining birth rate, KPRF propagandists stressed how bad things had become since perestroika started. Any negative reference to the Soviet past, such as the Civil War, was paired with a current woe, such as increased deaths from violent crime.[19] Such comparisons allowed the KPRF to rebuff criticism of CPSU policy rather than just deny accountability for the mistakes of the past.

In promising to take the best from the past, the KPRF's leaders looked back beyond the Soviet period to find older Russian values that fitted with Communist ones. The KPRF's electoral platform made frequent references to Russia's ancient past, citing its history as a strong state with a rich cultural heritage.[20] The KPRF promised to follow the lead of past statesmen and to rebuild the nation in keeping with the positive moral features embodied by the Russian and Soviet peoples over the centuries. It warned voters of the error of trying to start "with a clean page" instead of drawing on national traditions.[21] In praising these traditions, the KPRF did not explain what exactly they meant for the present, but its leaders made it clear that for the reformed Communist Party relevant history started long before 1989.

The 1993 and 1995, parliamentary elections, in sum, were characterized by a multitude of competing parties, often with similar slogans and indistinguishable programs. Even professional designers and image makers complained about clients who could not explain what sort of impression they wanted to convey to voters.[22] Most parties ended up promoting their leaders—they devoted their free television time to monologues by the people who headed their lists, and they featured those same faces on their leaflets and posters. With the exception of the colorful Zhirinovsky, however, the personalities presented to the voters held little charm. Liberals and centrists trying to exude professionalism as they promised a "normal life" could rarely find catchy means of selling stability.

The KPRF and other left-wing parties, however, wooed voters with fiery rhetoric and vivid images of the people's suffering in the present. Moreover, they faced up to what might have been considered the stigma of their past, and both mined it for heroic stories and used it to promote links to older values such as statism. By modifying old names and symbols, the KPRF could promote both continuity and change. It could attract loyalists and yet promise not to repeat the errors that had led to the demise of the CPSU. The realization that the KPRF might well put together a dominant coalition in the Duma in 1995 even spurred Yeltsin to intervene. Two days before the elections, he went on television and in what one commentator called his "most striking and sharpest anticommunist appeal since August 1991" called on voters not to be misled by parties promising a return to the past. He denounced the planned economy, the threat to private property, and plans to restore the USSR. He implored disaffected young people to think about their future and asked older people who recalled "what real hunger, real fear, and real mass repressions are" to explain them to younger generations.[23] Despite Yeltsin's last-minute warning, however, the KPRF won 22 percent of the party-list vote in 1995—10 percent more than in 1993—and the hard-line Communists–Working Russia–For the Soviet Union won 4.5 percent, nearly enough to overcome the 5 percent barrier to representation in the Duma.[24]

The KPRF candidate for president in 1996, therefore, could draw on the organizational resources and the propaganda base built up over the course of two parliamentary campaigns. His party had been refining its version of Russian/Soviet history to appeal to noncommunist patriots, but needed to capture more antireform voters to win the presidential race. Hence the stage was set in 1996 for further fine-tuning of socialist symbolic politics. The democrats, by contrast, had accumulated few organizational resources and seemed little inclined to cohesion. Moreover, the campaigns constructed by liberal parties had featured little in the way of vivid imagery or historical narratives. While many democrats had presented a vision of the future in which the Russian standard of living matched that of the West, they had not grounded their programs in the Russian experience; that is, they had not shown how Russia was suited to market democracy. They were unprepared to counter the KPRF's patriotic claims with similar positive historical referents that would serve their own cause.

Running against the Past

Yeltsin began the campaign season of 1996 as the underdog. His popularity figures were measured in the single digits, far below those of his main competitors. Challengers to the incumbent president included not only the leader of the revived Russian Communist Party but also the liberal economist Grigorii Iavlinskii, the eccentric nationalist Vladimir Zhirinovsky, the stern, somewhat mysterious former general Aleksandr Lebed, and even Yeltsin's old rival Mikhail Gorbachev. All of these politicians were poised to attack Yeltsin's economic record. Each also had already begun to craft a distinct appeal to the dissatisfied citizens of Russia

The Communists and their nationalist allies focused on the decline in the general standard of living and in industrial production; Iavlinskii stood ready to woo democrats with his stance against the Chechen war; Zhirinovsky trumpeted his familiar theme of loss of empire; Lebed spoke out sharply against crime and corruption; and Gorbachev presented himself as a genuine social democrat. Meanwhile, the Yeltsin team spent the early spring of 1996 in disarray, divided on basic questions of strategy. Only in March did the president formally appoint a set of campaign advisers. Yet before long, Zhirinovsky's campaign sputtered when resources ran out and the attempt to give the candidate a more serious image failed. Liberals, except for the most stalwart human rights activists, abandoned Iavlinskii in favor of Yeltsin as the candidate most capable of beating Ziuganov. Gorbachev was scorned by voters angry about the collapse of the USSR, leaving only Lebed as a viable third candidate. Much of the credit for this change of circumstances must be given to Yeltsin and his advisers.

Starting in his home region of Sverdlovsk in February, Yeltsin began a preelection marathon of trips across Russia. With tree plantings, meetings with voters, speeches to students, and appearances on concert stages, Yeltsin proved himself a fit campaigner. He laughed off references to his health and rumors of a serious drinking problem. Yeltsin also showed no qualms about exploiting his position as president. He plundered the state coffers to shower each region that he visited with credits and grants. Yeltsin's constant activities in front of the television cameras raised his profile and his rating with the public. His campaign advisers, meanwhile, acquired further resources for his promotion when behind-the-scenes negotiations with media barons and oligarchs secured their cooperation and financial support for a massive propaganda campaign on the president's behalf.[25]

Initially Yeltsin followed the advice of those in his inner circle who argued against an anticommunist strategy. In April 1996, Sergei Filatov, his former chief of staff turned campaign organizer, urged him to present himself as a "consolidating" force, uniting a divided society. Another campaign official stressed that the president had a responsibility to hold himself above divisive party politics, and averred in May that "Yeltsin can't conduct an anticommunist campaign, and won't conduct one, precisely because he is the president of all Russia."[26] The results of this strategy can be seen in Yeltsin's early speeches and slogans. Billboards proclaiming "Yeltsin is our president" and "Yeltsin is the president of all Russia" proliferated. Moreover, the president told his supporters in April, "We have ceased to see the world in terms of red and white. Before our eyes it became multicolored, vivid, and bright."[27] Yeltsin's promise of a better future encompassed everyone. Soon, however, both Yeltsin's official and unofficial campaigns began to feature efforts to mobilize divisive collective memories to the president's advantage.

Despite the forward-looking campaign envisioned by his advisers, Yeltsin's most discussed set of advertisements made striking use of black-and-white images taken occasionally from archives but most often from ordinary people's photo albums.[28] Billboards featured enlarged group portraits of young people taken in the 1940s and 1950s and more recent photos of veterans. The smiling faces of today's grandparents were accompanied by the simple handwritten text: "I believe, I love, I hope" and Yeltsin's signature. Television clips from the same series featured old family snapshots and voice-overs recalling the good and bad of the past, followed by a contemporary shot of the speaker explaining why, despite the difficulties of the present, he or she would vote for Yeltsin. One pensioner's words seemed calculated to elicit grudging nods from the unenthusiastic: "Among those who are running, I don't see a figure who is that much better than Yeltsin."[29]

A similar set of print ads presented transcriptions of comments made by callers to a pro-Yeltsin hotline. Here too support for the president was conveyed in plain language. Carefully choosing excerpts that focused on the hardships of the past and hopes for the future, the ads' designers skimmed over the problems of the present day, problems that might easily be ascribed to Yeltsin's administration. The pro-Yeltsin

Poster from the Yeltsin campaign's "I believe, I love, I hope" series. (Author's collection.)

scrapbook advertisements differed sharply from earlier Duma spots in neither highlighting the candidate nor promising prosperity. Analysts admitted that the humble images of plain citizens evoked more compassion and attention than representations of state power. One even compared them with a miniseries—an apt comparison, since these short clips, packed with tribulations and joys, had the power of family sagas.[30] The populist form of oral history presented in the "telephone of trust" print ads and in the black-and-white "I believe, I love, I hope" series cleverly downplayed the general resentment and mistrust of politicians.

The unadorned personal histories collected by the Yeltsin campaign also contrasted sharply with the official faceless version of the past long propagated by Soviet history textbooks. Although the short clips did not provide complex narratives of the past, they did convey definite interpretations. In one, a woman presented the Soviet restrictions on worship as a cause to value the postcommunist period. Moreover, these ads often directly challenged the nostalgia for the Brezhnev era promoted by the KPRF. Here people recalled the hardships and frustrations of the years of stagnation. One caller to the Yeltsin hotline, for example, reminisced about how her energetic husband had been stymied by the lack of entrepreneurial options.[31]

Another set of visually striking and textually succinct ads for Yeltsin were aimed at Russian youth. "Vote or Lose" posters carried no other text; they simply displayed one object under the word "Vote" and a contrasting item under "Lose." One juxtaposed a globe with a coil of barbed wire. These posters were part of a larger campaign, fashioned loosely on an American model, that purported to be a neutral voter mobilization drive. The source of the funding for the rock concerts that formed the centerpiece of this project, however, remained unclear. Moreover, despite their claims not to be backing any single candidate, the organizers of the "Vote or Lose" concerts gave a platform only to musical stars who were ready to speak out on Yeltsin's behalf. The musicians' widely displayed slogan was "Yeltsin is our president."[32] And more than once they welcomed the president himself onto their stages, giving journalists a fine opportunity to photograph the candidate looking hale and hearty as he danced to rock music.

The paired objects in the "Vote or Lose" posters were calculated to draw on differences between life before and after the end of the Soviet system: a denim jacket versus a prisoner's striped coat, a person's feet

"Vote or Lose" poster from Yeltsin's 1996 election campaign. (Photo by Kathleen E. Smith.)

shod in sneakers versus the bronze legs of a statue. Here Western consumer goods, all but unavailable before perestroika, stood next to objects evoking two of the most disliked aspects of Soviet life: the gulag and the cult of the leader. The symbols of consumer consumption were bound to resonate with modern youth. Moreover, by showing relatively affordable items of clothing, the advertisements' designers minimized the possibility of provoking resentment of the new rich, which might have worked to Ziuganov's advantage. The "Vote or Lose" posters reminded young people also of the sorts of freedom—to travel, to speak out, to enjoy foreign cultures—that their parents had not had. Without actually using political symbols, the ads drew a sharp contrast between the ideological monopoly of the past and the freedom of the present, and hence contributed to the Yeltsin team's emerging theme that this election constituted a choice between polar-opposite political systems, not just between personalities or policies.

Yeltsin and those who supported his bid for the presidency worked hard to remind all voters of the hardships and restrictions of the Brezhnev era. After welcoming Yeltsin to his home in the Krasnoiarsk region of Siberia, the Russian writer Viktor Astaf'ev told journalists that his memory of that time focused on lines—lines "for stockings, for boots, for coal, for firewood, for milk and bread. . . . My wife always had writing on her palm [numbers recording her place in a queue]."[33] Posters put out before the second round, sometimes anonymously, stirred up similar negative recollections. One showed black-and-white photos of empty shops above color shots of well-filled shelves in clean, bright supermarkets. "Think and Choose," read the text.[34] Others more bluntly promised the return of ration cards, lines, and shortages if voters did not make the right choice. In answer to fears that the Communist Party leader would benefit from low voter turnout, one sign even warned those who might be tempted to spend election day at their dachas and vegetable plots: "Gardeners: If you don't go to the polls, others will decide for you. But you'll have to stand in line yourself. Communists + power = shortages."

The Yeltsin campaign's use of images from the past was not limited to reminders of stagnation. The same Filatov who had discouraged anticommunist campaigning in April was telling journalists in June that Communists had not evolved into social democrats in Russia, as in Poland. On the contrary, their program reeked "not even of Khrushchev's era, but of long-ago Stalinist times, of the 1930s." He accused the KPRF of trying to hide its real face, which was that of its orthodox Communist members, such as Varennikov and Luk'ianov, who supported the GKChP conspiracy. And he blamed the Communists for polarizing Russian politics by creating the "image of the enemy."[35]

Increasingly as the final showdown between Yeltsin and Ziuganov approached, the president's team focused on negative aspects of the CPSU's whole seventy-year history rather than on Ziuganov's record or program. An important theme sounded repeatedly by Yeltsin and the democratic press was that if the KPRF came to power it would unleash bloodshed, turmoil, even civil war in an attempt to rearrange social and economic relations. Yeltsin held out to voters the simple, nonideological promise of "normal life."[36] But his KPRF opponents, according to him, were real revolutionaries. "I am sure," he asserted, "that they are preparing to act without any restraints, as happened after 1917. Let's not comfort ourselves with illusions: the opposition forces in Russia— these are not the 'leftists' of Eastern Europe or the Baltics. This is the party of revanche, whose ideology is based on the ideas of Marxism-Leninism." He warned that the Communists would settle accounts with all those who "had been able to reveal their talents, who began to live better, who saw the world."[37]

Yeltsin contrasted the Bolsheviks' traditional vengefulness toward their opponents with his leniency in August 1991. After all, he argued, his administration did not persecute ordinary members of the CPSU.[38] In other words, only Yeltsin could be counted on to guarantee the observation of legal rights. The choice again was framed in black-and-white terms: "Either back to revolution and upheaval or forward to stability and well-being," as Yeltsin announced after the conclusion of the first round of voting.[39] A new television commercial with a similar theme showed documentary footage of famine, civil war, and exile and asked voters to "save" Russia. Once again Yeltsin's ads did not use his name or defend his record; they simply created a stark choice between the past and the present.

Frequently the most virulent anticommunist propaganda, concentrating on the crimes of the Stalin era, came not from Yeltsin directly but from his media allies. Early in the race it became clear that Russian television and many other media had cast their lot with the president and were willing to use their resources to promote his victory.[40] National television channels, for instance, gave Yeltsin's campaign travels consistently detailed and flattering coverage in their nightly news programs, while they rarely mentioned his opponents' campaign activities. Although lack of coverage allowed Ziuganov, at least initially, to make farfetched claims with impunity, he indignantly and with good reason protested the evident media bias in its coverage of a single candidate.[41] Liberal journalists feared that efforts to blacken a candidate's reputation might create a backlash of sympathy for the underdog. Nevertheless, the main television channels risked flooding the airwaves with anticommunist programming in the form of documentary and fictional films on the eves of both rounds of the presidential elections. Any mention of the gulag, it seemed, had to work to Yeltsin's benefit.[42]

Yeltsin himself, despite the fact that he had been a major figure in the CPSU leadership during the last years of the Brezhnev regime, in no way associated himself with the politics of that era. In fact, in the context of the polarized politics they had promoted, Yeltsin and his team had to deal sensitively with the issue of the president's own Communist background. On the one hand, Yeltsin could not afford to alienate ordinary members or former members of the Party. On the other hand, he wanted his liberal supporters to remember him as a rebel who had challenged the Party hierarchy over issues of privileges and the pace of reforms.[43] Hence he claimed that he had been a sincere believer in Marxist teachings when he joined the CPSU, but that exposure to Party politics brought immediate disillusionment. With no explanation of why he remained in the CPSU if he had been frustrated by its practices from the first, Yeltsin skipped ahead to his perestroika-era martyrdom at the hands of Gorbachev and Party conservatives.[44] Having quit the Communist Party, Yeltsin washed his hands of any accountability that he might have borne as a former first secretary and Politburo member. He took responsibility only for the past five years—a narrow target compared with the seventy years that he ascribed to the KPRF—and even then he reminded voters that as president he had been seriously hampered by the CPSU's legacy of economic mismanagement.

On the eve of the second round of voting for the presidency, Yeltsin appealed to voters to put aside past dislikes and offenses and to vote for him as the guarantor of a better future for the next generation. He spoke gently to those who had trouble adjusting to new conditions and asked them to try to understand why change was necessary. Yeltsin expressed regret that he had not trusted the people to understand more, and hence had not explained from the start how difficult the country's economic situation really was. He also struck a final blow against nostalgia, reminding voters that in the past only Communist Party bosses had lived well. But at the same time he held out an olive branch, vowing that he was ready to cooperate with all who really had the best interests of the nation at heart. Returning to an earlier theme, he averred, "We all came out of the past and there's no reason to divide the country into Red and White."[45] Though Yeltsin hoped to gain the votes of citizens who had voted for third candidates in the first round, he clearly felt the need to reach out again to Ziuganov's presumed constituency of the economically depressed.[46] But having sharpened the tone of anticommunist rhetoric between the two rounds of voting, the president probably changed few minds by his last-minute call for reconciliation.

Running on the Past and from the Past

The Communist Party of the Russian Federation approached the 1996 elections with justifiable optimism. The party had united around a single candidate, Gennadii Ziuganov. It had taken advantage of its new strength in parliament to devote resources to reinvigorating its far-flung branches. Although local party organizations rarely contributed funds to the center, they provided both important networks for distributing literature and organizational resources for campaign rallies. Moreover, years of cultivating nationalist groups seemed to have paid off for Ziuganov when dozens of groups agreed to form a broad alliance—the Union of Popular Patriotic Forces—around his candidacy.[47] The backing of a relatively diverse coalition of organizations allowed Ziuganov to present himself as more than just the leader of the Communist Party.

Among the nationalists who rallied behind Ziuganov were such diverse figures as Yeltsin's former vice president, Aleksandr Rutskoi, and the anticommunist film director Stanislav Govorukhin, well known for his film *The Russia That We Lost*, which presented a sympathetic view of tsarist rule. Ziuganov's coalition seems less startling when one considers that, having acknowledged that "it is impossible to return to [the ideology] that led society for the last several decades," he had worked to forge a new "ideology of state patriotism" based on "traditional spiritual and cultural values" and composed of "the Russian idea, supplemented by the contemporary realities of life, and those social gains won by socialism during seventy years of Soviet power." At times Ziuganov frankly admitted that his goal was the "joining of the Red ideal of social justice . . . with the White ideal of a nationally interpreted statehood."[48] To this end, the KPRF had been working closely with a nationalist-religious-oriented think tank to reinforce the traditional link between Orthodoxy and a strong Russian state and to "Russify Marxism" by incorporating nationalist, spiritual, and statist elements strongly reminiscent of nineteenth-century concepts of Russian exceptionalism. In 1996 Ziuganov's interpretations of the national past were put to the test in his electoral battle.

The content of the "national Bolshevik" mix circa 1996 can be seen in articles in the pro-communist press, the candidate's speeches, and the Union of Popular Patriotic Forces' humble publicity efforts. Unlike Yeltsin, Ziuganov could not afford thousands of glossy posters and sophisticated television spots. The KPRF and its allies had to promote their candidate less expensively, with rallies and canvassing. The KPRF did have the support of the national newspapers *Sovetskaia Rossiia* and *Pravda*, both of which frequently published caricatures lampooning Yeltsin. Local activists pasted up the cartoons along with their own homemade posters, many of which depicted the blackened White House in 1993 or bemoaned Russia's economic and demographic losses since 1991.[49] Moreover, Ziuganov had free air time—each candidate got thirty minutes on three state-run channels in the month leading up to the first round of voting, and finalists received supplementary blocks of time before the second round—to present his mix of nationalist and socialist philosophy.

Ziuganov's campaign literature and speeches reveal that perhaps the strongest bond between post-1991 Communists and Russian nationalists consisted of their mutual distress at Russia's perceived loss of territory and decline in global status, military strength, and cultural influence. Ziuganov appealed to both Bolsheviks and monarchists with his concern for rebuilding a strong state with Russia at its center. At least one Orthodox clergyman justified his vote for Ziuganov on the grounds that Ziuganov intended to restore his "historic homeland" and to end the continued splintering of the nation and the church; a vote for Yeltsin, he argued, equaled "an involuntary admission that Russia's development over the course of a thousand years from separate principalities into a great nation was in error."[50]

To justify his calls for restoring old borders, however, Ziuganov abandoned Marxist-Leninist language about internationalism and adopted a traditional imperial vision of Russia as the center of Slavic and Orthodox civilization. Ziuganov characterized the Russian people as a nation that had always gathered together other peoples and that hence was a natural great power (narod sobiratelem, narod derzhavnikom).[51] Ziuganov did, however, incorporate Soviet leaders into his version of the Russian tradition of state-building. He praised Lenin not for overturning the old social, political, and economic order but for halting the territorial and economic disintegration under way when he returned to Russia in April 1917. In this interpretation, Lenin was a bearer of order rather than a revolutionary.[52] Ziuganov admired Stalin even more for his wartime leadership, especially his decision to imbue state doctrine with Russian nationalism. Stalin's display of respect for the Russian Orthodox Church and his interest in prerevolutionary military heroes were not temporary expedients, Ziuganov argued, but the start of a positive trend, which was interrupted by the leader's death. Now Ziuganov proposed to reunite Russians scattered by the collapse of the USSR.

A second point of convergence between Ziuganov's reform socialism and Russian nationalism was a shared belief in the exceptionalism of the Russian character, as evident in centuries of adherence to an ideal of collectivism. Ziuganov treated religious communitarianism (sobornost') as virtually the same as Communist collectivism. He praised the prerevolutionary peasant commune and alleged that Soviet village life was marked by the same spirit of selfless mutual aid. In contrast to the West, where "each pulls the blanket over himself," boasted one Ziuganov campaigner, "we were raised on the principle of all for one and one for all. . . . In our village we never respected the man who did everything for himself, who lived as a recluse—he was regarded with suspicion, no matter how well he managed for himself."[53] The natural Russian lifestyle, accordingly, was incompatible with liberal individualism and hence irreconcilable with Western capitalism. While the leaders of the KPRF denied that they would expropriate all private property, they asserted the superiority of collective forms of ownership, in part because they fitted with ancient Russian values.[54]

The third aspect of Ziuganov's patriotic blend of ideas relevant to the creation of a new historical narrative was his appropriation of traditional culture as a component of both Soviet and prerevolutionary Russian rule, but as lost at present in a sea of Western mass culture. As an example of Western cultural colonization, Ziuganov frequently cited the welter of English-language shop signs and advertisements surrounding Moscow's statue of the revered Russian poet Aleksandr Pushkin. From the perspective of Communists and of many other socially conservative Russians, Western culture united materialism, extreme individualism, violence, and sexual permissiveness—all qualities notably absent from Soviet works of art, literature, and film. Soviet censors, after all, followed both political and puritanical dictates. In this regard, Ziuganov claimed that while CPSU censorship often had been too harsh, it had been no worse for society than the current extreme of allowing pornography to flourish.

Willingly admitting that some members of the CPSU had denigrated all aspects of prerevolutionary Russian culture, including the classics of Russian literature and even the role of the Orthodox Church, Ziuganov argued that now "all people, regardless of their religious or materialist convictions, have recognized the positive role of churches, monasteries, and religious figures in the development of spiritual culture, the spread of literacy and enlightenment, in music and the fine arts." Just as empire-building and cultural achievements redeemed prerevolutionary Russia for Ziuganov, he urged noncommunist nationalists to admit that the emergence of writers such as Mikhail Sholokhov, Valentin Rasputin, Iurii Bondarev, and Aleksandr Tvardovskii during the Soviet period made it "a great epoch, worthy of study."[55]

In terms of cultural politics, Ziuganov sought common ground with Russian Orthodox believers and clergy who feared spiritual corruption from the West. Ziuganov played to a patriotic constituency by vowing to resist alien, Western ideas. "We won't allow Russia to be turned into a spiritual dumping ground, into a field of play for dark global forces, false prophets, and false teachers."[56] Though Ziuganov was less prone than some other ardent Russian nationalists to ascribe Russia's problems to the Jews, he also catered to anti-Semitism with veiled references, omissions, and pernicious stereotypes. His argument that it was "normal" for Russia to grant equal rights to "three classic religions—Orthodoxy, Islam, and Buddhism, religions that always placed spiritual-moral values higher than mercantile-consumer ones"—no doubt appealed to many religious Russian nationalists.[57]

Ziuganov's efforts to attract noncommunist nationalist voters did not prevent him from paying attention to the KPRF's main constituency, older people with a positive regard for the socialist legacy. Though Ziuganov did not campaign under the aegis of the Communist Party in 1996, he and his allies chose a name for their electoral alliance—the Union of Popular Patriotic Forces—that would resonate with Soviet patriots. The word "popular" had been used in the Soviet era as synonymous with the masses. Moreover, although the KPRF abandoned old doctrines of atheism, internationalism, and one-party rule, it preserved the symbols and slogans of the past. These familiar trappings may have reduced or even partially disguised the sting of internal party reforms.

Though Ziuganov rejected the architects of reform, he did endorse some of the consequences of perestroika. During the presidential campaign, he publicly disassociated himself from the views of extreme Marxists, noting with pride on national television that "our party has undergone an enormous evolution. It recognizes a mixed economy, and democratic methods of government."[58] Other results of perestroika—most notably the collapse of the USSR and the widening gap between rich and poor—he blamed squarely on Gorbachev, Yeltsin, and other reformers who seemed to have worked from within to bring down the old regime. The theory of the fifth column allowed Ziuganov to disown practices that now seemed reprehensible without having to apologize for them. Campaigning in regions with a strong Cossack tradition, for instance, he tried to convince those warriors that their persecution after the Civil War was the work of Leon Trotsky—that is, of a typically non-Russian "traitor" within the old CPSU. And in Novocherkassk he blamed the "liberal" Khrushchev for the 1962 massacre there of workers protesting against state-mandated price increases.[59]

When forced by their opponents to confront the tragedies or mistakes of the Soviet era, the Communists weighed them against both past accomplishments and current woes. In the 1995 parliamentary campaign they had answered accusations regarding the Bolsheviks' expropriation of property with reminders of the criminal privatization taking place in "democratic" Russia and countered allusions to the famine of the 1930s with references to current homelessness and undernourishment. Now they met Yeltsin's rhetoric about the Civil War, collectivization, and the purges with talk of interethnic conflict in the Caucasus, the unwilling "exile" of millions of Russians through the dissolution of the USSR, and Yeltsin's creation of a "concentration camp" in the center of Moscow when he sealed off the White House in October 1993.[60]

The fervor with which individuals who still identified themselves as Communists embraced such balancing acts can be seen in a letter to *Pravda* from a self-described "Communist since 1964." Responding to a local politician's appeal to voters to recall who had destroyed their places of worship, the letter writer urged fellow citizens to summon up a different set of memories:

Why not walk down memory lane before the presidential elections? Why shouldn't I, having worked on Sakhalin for 42 years, not remember 16 trips to sanatoria and rest homes from Yalta to Tbilisi? Why not recall that my daughter, having graduated from the Far East University, has been searching for a job for three years now? Why not remember the open theft of citizens' savings, the Belovezh accord [forming the CIS and ending the USSR], and the "new rich" who fatten themselves on the people's misery?[61]

The problem for the Union of Popular Patriotic Forces' candidate was to keep the public focused on the achievements of the old system and the shortcomings of the present government.

Ultimately during the 1996 campaign, Ziuganov had to defend not only the CPSU's record but also his own attempt to meld Russian nationalism and socialism. Yeltsin and his team frequently pointed out the disjuncture between Ziuganov's stance and the Soviet history of repressions against clergy and disapproval of nationalism of any sort. The Communist-nationalist bloc itself struggled to find an image that would capture the alleged natural convergence between the Russian Orthodox Church and the Soviet state. They frequently pointed to World War II as a time of cooperation, but this framework was complicated by the fact that while Stalin might be remembered as the leader of a heroic struggle against alien invaders, he had also been exposed as a ruthless executioner of his own people. Nevertheless, memories of wartime unity were frequently invoked. When asked why he himself did not attend church, Ziuganov explained, "One doesn't have to go to church to carry goodness and brotherhood in one's soul. Marshal Zhukov was not a churchgoer, but it's said that he carried the icon of the Kazan Mother of God, the protector of soldiers."[62]

The physical juxtaposition of nationalist and Communist symbols also struck a discordant note. At the final campaign rally for the Union of Popular Patriotic Forces, the Soviet red flag shared the stage with religious banners depicting Christ and the Virgin Mary, and various members of the audience toted portraits of Stalin and Dmitrii Donskoi, the grand duke of Moscow who successfully resisted Lithuania's attempts to invade Moscow in the fourteenth century. Soviet and Russian values might be equated in the abstract, but their symbolic embodiments looked odd side by side. The liberal newspaper *Izvestiia* highlighted this dissonance with a collage juxtaposing the persons listed by the rally's participants as inspirational heroes—Pushkin, Stalin, St. Sergei Radonezh, Dostoevsky, Lenin, and Dmitrii Donskoi—standing atop Lenin's tomb alongside Ziuganov and the radical Communist leader Viktor Anpilov. Politics do make strange bedfellows, the liberals implied.[63]

The People Vote

In the final days of the presidential race, supporters of both candidates urged citizens to remember their history, and presented their own heavily edited version of the important events of the past. The Yeltsin campaign dwelled on the chaos and destruction of the October Revolution and the famines and repressions of the 1930s before skipping ahead to remind people of the tedium and privations of the Brezhnev era. In his last address before the second round, Yeltsin declared, "Those who voted [in the first round] for the Communists voted after all not for a return to the past but against the hardships of the new life." But now, he urged, they should vote for the future, and not judge the very young Russian state too harshly.[64] Ziuganov, by contrast, cast a proud, loving eye over centuries of Russian history and singled out bright moments of military success, cultural achievement, and industrial progress. Despite

Ziuganov supporters at the final preelection rally of the Union of Popular Patriotic Forces, Moscow, June 12, 1996. (Photo by Kathleen E. Smith.)

his desire to avoid negative memories, Ziuganov felt compelled in his last appeal to voters to try once again to refute charges that he represented the party of civil war and the gulag.[65]

Yeltsin handily beat Ziuganov in the second round, receiving 54 percent of the vote to his opponent's 40 percent. Owing in part, no doubt, to having convinced Aleksandr Lebed to join the presidential team—an arrangement that lasted only a few months after the election—Yeltsin managed to widen significantly the 3-point lead he had held over Ziuganov in the first round of voting. It is impossible to measure the effect of the battle for control over the past on the ultimate outcome of the election, but Yeltsin's at first unwilling adoption of an anticommunist strategy undeniably contributed to his victory. The president's overwhelming personal unpopularity in the spring of 1996 certainly had diminished, but so too had fears of his opponent's revanchist tendencies increased. The division of voters into pro- and anticommunists had largely superseded the polarization between Yeltsin's opponents and supporters. Ziuganov had not been able to dispel or recast memories of the purges, repression of religion, and consumer shortages.

Whether anticommunist propaganda could continue to work to reformers' advantage in the long run remained to be seen. A few months after Yeltsin's reelection, the American political scientist Michael McFaul, for one, had already concluded that "the central organizing concept of the 1996 presidential election—communism versus anti-communism—has already disappeared."[66] He argued that the commitment of all the major players to abide by democratic procedures in the selection of officials had taken the force out of warnings that any particular vote meant a choice between two different systems. But Ziuganov and his allies had already been playing by democratic rules and espousing economic moderation for several years before 1996.

Yeltsin's anticommunist rhetoric worked not because of the KPRF's actual record but because the Communists had clung to their past identity even as they sought to give it a nationalist cast. Their use of familiar slogans, symbols, and names helped to hold the loyalty of people who identified with old institutions, yet left them vulnerable to criticism by those to whom the old system was anathema. Communists had worked diligently since 1992 to harness positive collective memories, but Russian/Soviet history remained in all its complexity as potential grist for their opponents as well. They could not avoid discussion of their own version of a usable past, and that version had a myriad of weaknesses, many of which were exploited by Yeltsin campaigners. Hence, as long as the Communist Party in some form remains a serious political force, reformers may again try to revive anticommunist formulas.

Yet in 1993 and 1995 few liberals ran campaigns that looked to the past. Promises of economic rationality and "normalization" certainly appealed to voters who were faring well after communism. For the majority of Russian citizens, who felt cast adrift in a sea of political and financial uncertainty, however, such campaigns could not provide a sense of belonging. Allusions to a shared history, even when that history is controversial, can stir up feelings of community. Having grasped the importance of campaigning on more than just the recent past, however, Yeltsin's team had few precedents for deploying Russian history to the liberals' advantage. Unlike the Communists, who had been finetuning new historical narratives since the demise of Soviet rule, liberals had little practice in conceptualizing a new patriotism. Hence Yeltsin's advisers, even though they would have preferred to set a more positive unifying tone, fell back on old antistalinist themes. Ultimately, dissatisfaction with crude, somewhat outdated divisions into Red and White may have finally convinced liberals of the merits of adopting a serious, constructive, and activist approach to framing collective memory.

Searching for a New Russian Idea

Just a few weeks after winning reelection, President Yeltsin announced that Russia needed a national idea. Unlike every other period of modern Russian history, he said, the new democratic era had no ideology. He called upon his supporters to "think about what national idea, what national ideology is the most important for Russia."[1] The administration quickly assembled a commission to head the search, and a major government newspaper immediately initiated a year-long contest for readers to identify or compose a set of principles capable of inspiring Russian citizens to unite as a nation. When Yeltsin stepped down as president three and a half years later, he had not found an idea for Russia. His concern for Russian patriotism, however, had become even stronger.

The notion that Russia was suffering from an identity crisis came as no surprise to the politically aware in 1996. The simultaneous collapse of Communist rule and the Soviet empire in late 1991 had given new life to centuries-old intellectual debates on the nature of Russia's national interest and the proper definition of the nation. But Yeltsin's admission that he and his allies had failed to unite citizens around democratic or other values raised the visibility of such philosophical debates and gave them new urgency. The "idea for Russia" contest served as a stimulus for democratic opinion makers to debate the appropriate content and form of Russian patriotism. It also spurred Yeltsin's advisers to take stock of the state of the nation's collective memories. Out of the discussion of what it meant to be Russian at the end of the twentieth century came a renewed interest on the part of the president's team in promoting some form of social reconciliation based on the depoliticization of national history.

Before we consider the hunt for a Russian idea itself, it is important to consider what motivated the members of the Yeltsin administration to take on such a mission at a juncture when they might have rested on their laurels. In part, the political establishment was motivated by the fear that the antistalinist and anticommunist rhetoric employed so frequently in Yeltsin's 1996 campaign would not suffice in the future to mobilize voters around economic reformers. As we have seen, liberal candidates in postsoviet elections had felt the lack of a positive patriotic core of symbols and myths. Although Yeltsin's advertising designers cleverly used individual life stories rather than national narratives to present reasons for voters to stick with the president in 1996, their output reflected democrats' inability to distill personal stories into simple symbols or historical analogies. Neither the Yeltsin administration nor liberal political parties had been able to discover or manufacture some potent, meaningful shorthand to communicate their principles to the public.[2] The failure to find the means to represent themselves graphically served as a reminder of the abnormality of the liberals' previous election campaigns.

The liberals' Communist opponents, by contrast, were seen as having at their disposal a symbolic repertoire replete with flags, songs, and myths of past military, scientific, and economic achievements.[3] Few elements of the Communists' patriotic armory appealed to the liberals per se, but some democrats now embraced the idea of having a set of positive memories to invoke as markers of a shared political identity. As Yeltsin's future adviser on the Russian idea put it on the eve of the presidential election, "When totalitarianism was being destroyed, the idea of ideology was being destroyed, too. The idea was formed that a national idea was a bad thing. But the baby was thrown out with the bath water. Our Kremlin polls show that people miss this."[4] In other words, whereas the Communists, in effect, had partially compensated for the unpopularity of Marxism-Leninism by rapidly embracing patriotism, democrats had mistakenly shunned patriotic rhetoric and rituals as somehow exclusive to totalitarian regimes.

By specifying that Russia needed its own idea, democrats now implicitly acknowledged that seeking "normality" patterned after the achievements of wealthy Western nations had not sufficed as a guiding principle for authority-building in Russia. Perhaps, as the American political scientist Michael Urban suggests, this decision was inspired by the fact that Western standards—economic and legal—clearly could not be met in Russia in the foreseeable future.[5] It may also have reflected the renewed popularity of centuries-old Slavophile theories, which insisted that Russia had a separate path to follow and that it should not betray its values and nature by blindly imitating the West. Ziuganov, after all, was by no means alone in his interest in such traditionally Russian values as state power (*derzhavnost'*) and community (*sobornost'*). But if they wanted to create a patriotic grounding for their authority, the liberals would have to find pieces of Russian history that somehow suited their own track record and goals.

The democrats' apparent "incapacity to create and cultivate new symbols"[6] should not be interpreted as entirely due to lack of effort. In 1993, Yeltsin, after failing to gain parliamentary support, acted by decree to make Mikhail Glinka's "Patriotic Song" the national anthem and the imperial two-headed eagle—complete with crowns, scepter, and orb—the state emblem. Moreover, his 1996 inauguration embodied an attempt to highlight prerevolutionary attributes and traditions and to add democratic accents. Against the background of the presidential banner—a tricolor bearing the two-headed eagle—Yeltsin was sworn in by the head of the Russian Constitutional Court in the ancient halls of the Kremlin, where generations of tsars had been crowned. Both the head of the Central Election Committee and the patriarch of the Russian Orthodox Church, who offered a blessing in the name of his church and all the "other traditional religions of Russia," spoke at the brief inauguration ceremony. At the reception that followed his swearing in, the seriously ill president essentially summed up the symbolic choices made by his administration when he toasted "the glorious, thousand-year-old and always young Russia."[7] For Yeltsin the state was both new and ancient but never middle-aged. His inauguration conspicuously omitted any Soviet symbols and rituals.

Many Russian politicians took offense at the practice of conflating ancient and modern Russia, and the Yeltsin government's adoption of tsarist heraldry sparked fierce controversy in parliament. KPRF deputies attacked the two-headed eagle with imperial trappings as both monarchical and colonialist, and hence as inappropriate for republican rule. Moreover, they hastened to note that there was nothing uniquely Russian about the two-headed eagle to justify its revival in the state heraldry. They preferred to keep the nation's first republican symbol—the hammer and sickle—in some form. The Communists and some nationalists similarly rejected the tricolor because it had been used during World War II by General Andrei Vlasov's Russian troops when they fought on the side of Germany against the USSR. For them this history outweighed the tricolor's 300 years of service as the flag of the Russian navy. Their complaints against Glinka's "Patriotic Song" were more trivial—that it had no words and was too complex to be hummed.[8]

Communist deputies recalled fondly the familiar, eminently singable, rousing Soviet anthem, which had lyrics that could be updated. Their claim that the familiar Soviet state attributes remained broadly popular did indeed carry some weight. In the Duma's 1997 vote on state symbols, the Soviet anthem garnered the support of 57 percent of the deputies, the old emblem 54 percent, and the red banner 53 percent.[9] These results, however, fell short of the two-thirds majority stipulated by the constitution for the establishment of the official Russian state attributes.

Given the nostalgia for Soviet symbols and the suspicion of imperial ones, Yeltsin's inauguration with its mix of tsarist and American elements and its omission of any homage to the Soviet experience was bound to be perceived as partisan. But resistance to the wholesale adoption of prerevolutionary state symbols came not only from Soviet patriots. From the very first days of the new Russian state, some liberals also questioned the suitability of reviving prerevolutionary symbolism. Though they generally considered such episodes as Vlasov's use of the Russian tricolor minor compared to the long bloody history of Communist rule under the red banner and hammer and sickle, they felt uneasy with the overtly imperial crowned eagle.[10] Liberal journalists therefore suggested that something national but not monarchical might be chosen to represent the new democracy. Indeed, polls showed that many Russians preferred the politically neutral bear to the two-headed eagle as a national symbol.[11] As in the dispute over changing the name of Leningrad back to St. Petersburg, prerevolutionary markers turned out to carry their own historical baggage.

Into this atmosphere of rancor and resentment Yeltsin and his advisers cast the idea of finding a unifying national idea. After the 1996 election, the Yeltsin administration organized a team of consultants under the supervision of Georgii Satarov, Yeltsin's long-time adviser. Philosophers, pollsters, and political scientists were all drafted to help in the search. The government newspaper, *Rossiiskaia gazeta*, took on the main task of opening a moderated public forum on the topic, with Satarov serving as a consultant. The editors solicited letters and comments from the public, and also sought out prominent politicians and intellectuals to provide their views on an idea for Russia. The newspaper encouraged participation by offering a cash prize for the best essay in the course of a year's debate on the topic.

Rossiiskaia gazeta accompanied its announcement of the "idea for Russia" contest with a reproduction of the nationalist painter Il'ia

Glazunov's well-known perestroika-era canvas *Eternal Russia*. The painting is a group portrait of a multitude of personages from Russian history. Famous individuals, including the patriarchs of the Russian Orthodox Church and members of the Politburo, surround a large figure of Christ on the cross. With this illustration the contest organizers seemed to be challenging their readers both to reexamine Russia's complex past and to mine it for heroes who might help in the nation's resurrection. The same page featured quotations from the prerevolutionary philosophers Vladimir Solov'ev and Ivan Il'in and from the Soviet-era dissidents Aleksandr Solzhenitsyn and Andrei Sakharov.[12] By implication, readers were directed to find some thread that connected these periods. Inspiration, it seemed, should stem from national history and homegrown thinkers; although, by using the construction "idea for Russia" (*ideia dlia Rossii*) rather than "Russian idea" (*Russkaia ideia*), the editors suggested that the unifying concept needed to be patriotic but not chauvinistic—an idea not just for ethnic Russians (*Russkie*) but for all citizens of the Russian Federation (*Rossiiane*).

Both the president's consultants and *Rossiiskaia gazeta*'s editors shied away from offering their own suggestions as to what might unite Russians. Instead, they cast the spotlight on society. After all, they argued, the goal was not to find an ideology for the state—the 1993 constitution prohibited a state ideology—but rather some "all-national progressive idea" capable of both binding together and energizing society. Yet organizers recognized that if the contest was to succeed, they would have to fight off the "pathological" fear of ideology generated by the Soviet experience. Hence they anticipated and dismissed complaints from liberal intellectuals that privileging any single idea would curb diversity and impose conformity. They pointed to the "American dream" and Israel's "promised land" as ideas that promoted rather than stifled national interests.[13]

Nevertheless, many liberal commentators attacked the very concept of a collective ideal as contradictory to the democratic principle of the sanctity of the individual. The outspoken former dissident Valeriia Novodvorskaia proclaimed: "A national idea—this is a gas mask that protects its 'wearer' from the external world, logic, common sense, and reality." Numerous others asked why the new constitution, with its defense of individual rights, was not sufficient to allow Russian citizens to flourish.[14] To have recognized in the three-year-old Russian constitution the embodiment of national ideals, however, would have defeated the contest's aims—to fill an allegedly sharply felt patriotic void. The constitution, moreover, as a long document open to amendment, did not fit the contest organizers' vision of a pithy, immutable, homespun formula.

By and large, those behind the search treated the Russian idea as something to be discovered rather than invented. They frequently implied that the idea already existed in nature and awaited articulation by someone who was perceptive and close to the people.[15] One critic likened this process to a restorer of churches "cleaning away the Soviet whitewash and finding under it an ancient fresco." This skeptical observer denied that there ever existed "some ideal Russia, completely genuine, totally true to itself."[16] But others remained convinced that Russia had distinct historical values that could be packaged to serve the present-day need for inspiration and harmony. Operating in this vein, the president's team of consultants made the first (and it seems ultimately the only) step in their work, a survey of writings in the press on the Russian idea.[17] If they could thus discover the right idea for Russia, they could avoid the accusations that they were trying to impose by decree an inherently partisan patriotism.

Having stipulated that an idea for Russia must come from outside the state apparatus, presidential advisers did not propose their own national formula. They did, however, try to steer the search in certain directions. First of all, they stressed that the idea must fit the whole Russian Federation and so must be civic, not "political, ethnic, or confessional." At the same time, however, it needed to be national and patriotic.[18] Second, although they expected intellectuals to help identify the idea for Russia, the president's consultants worried that such people might come up with something that suited only themselves, that did not provide ordinary people with a guide for living. Similarly, they worried that a search centered in Moscow would exclude the interests of the majority in the provinces.[19]

To a great extent, the editors of *Rossiiskaia gazeta* heeded the presidential team's guidelines in selecting commentaries to highlight. Consider, for instance, the essay by Gurii Sudakov that they chose to reward at the end of the first six months of the contest. Sudakov's piece, titled "Six Principles of Russianness," contrasted Western and Russian values. Its author, a historian, philologist, and local deputy from the Vologda region, in the north of Russia, praised his fellow countrymen for, among other characteristics, collective spirit, sociability, moral conscience, and striving to serve their country rather than to achieve individual wealth. Sudakov's definition of what it meant to be Russian applied to civic life, work, and morality, but it did not elevate any particular religion or social class. Sudakov also managed to distinguish between those who lived in Russia and those who lived in the West without stressing race.[20] Though lacking in brevity, Sudakov's essay adhered to many of the presidential advisers' stipulations.

Having singled out Sudakov midway through the contest, however, the editors of *Rossiiskaia gazeta* never followed up on their promise to declare a grand winner at the end of the first year of articles on the Russian idea theme. In the spring of 1997 the newspaper tapered off its publication of articles devoted to finding an idea for Russia and finally ceased to print them altogether without comment in July of that year. The president's advisers, too, apparently were frustrated by the quality of suggestions. Satarov belatedly argued in the summer of 1997 that the process, not the outcome, of the search was what really mattered. A few months later another of the president's consultants made the even more drastic suggestion that perhaps the nation needed a period of silent contemplation or a shift from words to practical deeds.[21]

Why did the search for an idea for Russia fizzle out? One problem was that the broad, abstract nature of the enterprise allowed for extreme diversity and encouraged high-minded rhetoric. Readers' ideas for the nation ranged from communication to repentance to empire.[22] Others tried to coin modern versions of the old imperial slogan "Orthodoxy, Autocracy, Nationality." One person suggested "Health, Unity (or Community [*sobornost'*]), Charity" as a new statement of priorities.[23] To a certain extent, the contest entries simply mirrored Russian society's diverse concerns about economic development, Russia's status in the world, federalism, the environment, and so forth. Yet, unlike the Communists' invocation of specific heroes and concrete collective memories, the liberals' discussion of cultural traditions did not excite any patriotic fervor. Lists of virtues or sets of priorities neither provided blueprints for action nor sparked strong emotion. It seemed that myths of national character could not substitute for narratives about statehood.

Despite the fact that the oceans of ink spent printing ruminations about Russia's special path produced no winning pithy formula or catchy slogan, the "idea for Russia" contest did offer several revelations about the potential grounds for "democratic patriotism" as of 1996–97. Not surprisingly, as a source of positive role models or moral lessons, the Soviet period was conspicuously absent from the pages of *Rossiiskaia gazeta*. The editors balanced rare opinion pieces from nationalistic Communists with harsh attacks on totalitarianism. Even a moderate left-wing essay arguing for democratic socialism had to share space with a story about a new book commemorating victims of communism.[24] In this context, publication in *Rossiiskaia gazeta* of Yeltsin's theses for a "Year of Reconciliation" to commence on November 7, 1996, created a problem for contest coordinators. Yeltsin's recasting of the anniversary of the Bolshevik Revolution as an occasion for forgiveness and mutual tolerance implied that they ought both to devote more space to the history of the Soviet period and to try to bring Communists and antistalinists closer together.

In the wake of Yeltsin's decree, contest organizers did publish several commentaries on the topic of reconciliation, but their chosen essays tended to add qualifications to the president's sweeping call for forgiveness. *Rossiiskaia gazeta*'s contributors posited that there could be no reconciliation without repentance, that one did not have to reconcile with criminals or the nouveau riche, and that the greatest contribution toward reconciliation would be a more civilized discourse free of accusations and name-calling.[25] But lacking any concrete ideas about how to promote peace between Reds and Whites without compromising their goal of formulating a liberal, civic patriotic ideal, the editors quickly dropped the topic of reconciliation in favor of a return to abstract discussions about tradition and culture.

A second interesting feature of the "idea for Russia" contest was its revelation of many liberal patriots' disdain for the dissident tradition. The opening announcement's quotations from Sakharov and Solzhenitsyn had suggested to contest participants that they might find the roots of a democratic Russian patriotism in the brave actions and intriguing philosophies of people who had dared to challenge Soviet rule. Yet few participants pointed to the dissidents as heroes, and several denigrated their role in the history of democratization. In a series of sharply written articles the political scientist Aleksei Kiva, a member of Yeltsin's Commission on Human Rights and a frequent contributor to *Rossiiskaia gazeta*, explained that the former dissidents had no place in modern Russian society. Having been accustomed to fighting authority and to mistrusting officials, according to Kiva, they had little to offer now that the time had come for constructive work. "For a long time, if not forever, they will feel closer to the person on the defendant's bench than to the person who guards him." These were not suitable candidates for government service.[26]

Indeed, just as Aleksandr Solzhenitsyn's return home in 1994 had provoked a fair amount of scorn for the would-be moral authority who came to Russia with harsh criticism for all politicians only after reform was well under way,[27] the whole dissident tradition came under fire from supporters of the Yeltsin regime for being overly judgmental. The dissidents' highly developed consciences had led them to hold all governments to strict standards. Such attitudes, Kiva believed, led former dissidents such as Sergei Kovalev to exacerbate Russian relations with the breakaway republic of Chechnia by siding with the underdogs rather than supporting the guardians of law and order. Kiva felt that too often human rights activists praised the West and scorned the idea of love for state and army. In short, he blamed the dissidents, along with radical democrats, for fostering Russians' inferiority complex.[28]

Similarly, for many participants in the "idea for Russia" contest, the key to uniting citizens of Russia lay in shaking off feelings of low national self-esteem. Echoing a favorite theme of postsoviet Communists, one liberal editorialist fiercely rejected any attempt to equate civilization with the West. If Russians were only true to themselves, he suggested, they could find the pride and self-confidence necessary to flourish as a nation.[29] In other words, what Russians needed was not a new way of life but rather satisfaction in their past and present efforts. After all, the point of defeating communism, according to the antistalinist philosopher Aleksandr Tsipko, was "to return to myself and my children historical memory, all the wealth of national culture, the right to be Orthodox"—not to open the way for American culture and worship of foreign lifestyles.[30] Human rights activists, with their appeals to international public opinion and their work with multinational institutions, seemed too oriented to the outside world.

In sum, from a variety of commentators in the late 1990s came the sentiment that previous liberal attitudes toward the national past had been too critical. Harsh antisoviet views no longer garnered praise. Though purveyors of a new patriotism certainly did not rush to embrace the Soviet period, they wanted all Russian citizens to be able to take satisfaction in their long shared history. Indeed, although Yeltsin did not directly contribute to the "idea for Russia" contest, he seemed to signal an important change of heart toward dealing with the past with his substantive statement on the merits of reconciliation on the anniversary of the Bolshevik Revolution in 1996. The president, who had fiercely opposed amnesty for his political opponents in 1994 and who had recently campaigned with harsh anticommunist rhetoric, now appeared ready to adopt a more forgiving attitude for the sake of harmony. By offering equality to all the victims of political disputes in the twentieth century, Yeltsin expressed willingness to suspend historical judgment to allow all Russians to mourn and honor their dead.

In practice, however, reconciliation promised to carry its own difficulties. Dueling rituals on November 7, for instance, suggested that for many Russians recognition of victims of the Civil War was a zero-sum game. To honor the White Army was by implication to dishonor the Red Army, and vice versa. Nevertheless, by the end of the 1990s, Yeltsin and his advisers seemed ready to try to make difficult conciliatory gestures for the sake of creating or reinforcing patriotic culture. After all, neither avoiding discussions of the national past nor condemning substantial sections of it had provided broad viable bases for civic self-esteem. Hence, in 1997–98, Yeltsin experimented with another course: he attempted to win public support for treating relics of the past with respect but not adulation.

The last Russian tsar, Nicholas II, who abdicated on the heels of the February Revolution in 1917, had been murdered together with his wife, four daughters, young son, and four loyal retainers in July 1918. The Bolsheviks concealed the story of their ruthless execution of the Romanovs for several years, and the fate of the bodies remained a well-kept secret, feeding rumors to this day that one or more of Nicholas's children escaped the slaughter. Boris Yeltsin himself even played a role in effacing the history of the murders when in 1977, as the new first secretary of the Communist Party in Sverdlovsk (now again Ekaterinburg), he carried out an order from the Central Committee of the CPSU to raze the house where the executions had taken place.

In the summer of 1991, however, with Yeltsin's permission and the help of two amateur historians who had located what they thought was the burial site of the tsar's family, local officials in Ekaterinburg arranged the exhumation of a grave in the woods outside the city. Two of the bodies—those of Tsarevich Aleksei and one of his sisters—were missing, believed to have been burned as part of the cover-up of the murders in 1918. Although subsequent multiple forensic investigations in Russia and the West confirmed the identity of the remaining Ekaterinburg bones, they were laid to rest only in 1998.[31]

The Russian government had begun planning an official ceremonial burial of the tsar's family in 1995, but numerous controversies—both technical and moral—had arisen to cause second thoughts. First, many people, including prominent Russian Orthodox clergymen, had doubts about the identity of the remains. Second, the church hierarchy hesitated to address the status of the last tsar. The Russian Orthodox Church Abroad, founded by émigrés who had fled Russia after the Revolution, had already canonized the family. But in Russia some worried that elevating Nicholas II to sainthood would encourage chauvinists and monarchists in their reverence for the often repressive autocratic regime. Arguably, the manner of their death qualified the members of the tsar's family as martyrs for their faith—so-called passion sufferers. Yet, though the tsar's relatives and supporters regarded him as a martyr for his country, he did not volunteer for death.[32] Others opposed Nicholas's canonization because of his poor leadership of the nation. Many people disapproved of his connection to the "mad monk" Grigorii Rasputin and his abdication. Even anticommunists could argue that Nicholas was not without blame for the coming of the Revolution, and hence bore some responsibility for the ills that followed.[33]

A ceremonial interment, however, had the merit of seemingly atoning for the Bolsheviks' harsh treatment of the royal family. It would also provide a proper grave where mourners might pay their respects. The idea that the souls of the dead cannot be at peace without fitting burials is widespread in Russia as elsewhere. In lobbying for the burial of Vladimir Lenin, for instance, the young liberal politician Boris Nemtsov, who headed Yeltsin's 1998 commission on disposing of the tsar's remains, admitted: "I have a mystical kind of feeling that as long as we don't bury Lenin, Russia is under an evil spell."[34] Moreover, many Russians could identify with the tsar and his family as fellow victims of communism. As the British historian Orlando Figes notes, "The slaughter of the children, in particular, has become a symbol of the moral degradation of a regime which went on to kill millions of other innocent people who do not have a grave that anybody knows."[35]

For Communists, of course, the notion of Nicholas II as an innocent victim rankled. Raised on the image of Nicholas as a bloody tyrant who danced the night away after thousands of common people had been injured and killed at the ceremonies in Khodynka field marking his coronation, they had little sympathy for Russia's last autocrat. For them to embrace Nicholas II as a martyr would be to renounce their belief in the Bolshevik Revolution as a progressive milestone. Indeed, some radical Communist fringe groups so opposed any tribute to the last tsar that, as mentioned earlier, they twice blew up Viacheslav Klykov's monument to him. And in July 1997, a previously unknown group calling itself the Fighting Partisans used explosives to damage a new memorial to the royal family in Moscow's Vagan'kov cemetery. The memorial had been inscribed "In memory of those tortured and murdered by the godless Bolsheviks"—a clear affront to Communist sensibilities.[36]

Moreover, Russian Communists worried that the interest in interring relics of the past would carry over to the body of Lenin. As early as 1989, liberal intellectuals had publicly called for burying Lenin as an act of Christian decency and common human kindness. Communists, however, justified Lenin's placement in an underground chamber in the mausoleum on Red Square as an appropriate form of burial and defended Lenin as the object of veneration of generations of Soviet people. Without referring to Lenin as the subject of a carefully cultivated cult, Communists admitted the importance of his mummified body, arguing that their opponents hoped to "erase the memory of the leader of October from popular consciousness" by obliterating his image.[37]

In the case of Lenin, as opposed to that of Nicholas II, burial would have lowered his status. Removal of his body from Red Square would have signaled that Lenin no longer belonged in the symbolic center of the state. Hence, though Yeltsin suggested that it could fit in his program of reconciliation, eviction of Lenin's remains from the mausoleum would have distressed many Russians. Indeed, threats to Lenin repeatedly mobilized picketers, and a poll taken at the time of the tsar's burial showed public opinion to be split on whether to bury Lenin.[38]

Hesitant to be drawn into a discussion of their predecessors' decision to execute the royal family, mainstream Communists said little about the planned burial. Ironically, nearly fatal protests came from a constituency that Yeltsin had hoped to please—the Russian Orthodox Church. After the Russian government's final decision to bury the remains together in St. Petersburg's Petropavlovsk Cathedral—the traditional resting place of the Romanov tsars—on the eightieth anniversary of the execution, the Russian Orthodox hierarchy announced that it would not accept DNA evidence as proof of the identity of the remains found in Ekaterinburg. A church synod wanted the bones buried in an anonymous memorial grave until such time as no doubt remained. Though the patriarch agreed to allow a member of the local clergy to perform the funeral service, he himself declined to attend. Moreover, in the week leading up to the burial, he underlined his lack of enthusiasm for the whole enterprise by declaring that the church would mark the anniversary of the murders (but not the event of the burial) with fasting and prayers for all those martyred by persecution.[39]

After the patriarch's announcements, Yeltsin also decided not to attend the St. Petersburg ceremony. He wanted reconciliation, not conflict. But his sudden withdrawal of support threatened to rob the whole ceremony of its gravity and status, especially when other prominent figures began to follow his lead. Shocked by Yeltsin's abrupt change of plans, prominent liberals, including the respected academician Dmitrii Likhachev, privately lobbied the president to lend his weight to the symbolic atonement for the cruelty shown Russia's last leader and his family. Ultimately, on the eve of the event, Yeltsin reversed himself and, citing the importance of publicizing the truth about what had happened so long ago, committed himself to attending the funeral.[40]

There, in the presence of some fifty members of the Romanov family, Yeltsin shunned the spotlight but contributed a short speech in which he described the current ceremony as an opportunity for Russians to ask forgiveness for "the sins of their forefathers." Bowing his head before the "victims of the Ekaterinburg tragedy," the president did not limit the need for repentance to a small circle of actual executioners, but counted himself among those who had erred by hiding the truth. Moreover, he extolled the liberating and revitalizing effects of facing up to the past. Yeltsin argued that, regardless of their political views or ethnic and religious differences, Russians—and he as president in particular—had a duty to the next generation to "end this century, which for Russia had become a century of blood and lawlessness, with repentance and reconciliation." In this spirit, Yeltsin called upon his listeners to recall all of the "innocent victims of hatred and violence."[41]

Without praising the tsar's life, Yeltsin lamented his cruel death. Treating the tsar as just one of many Russians who had suffered from violence over the centuries, Yeltsin appealed to his countrymen to take the opportunity offered by the burial of Nicholas II to learn from the past that "any efforts to change life through force are doomed."[42] With remarkable grace, Yeltsin neither gilded the past nor ducked his share of responsibility. The history of Nicholas II's reign did not provide Yeltsin with material for mythologizing the prerevolutionary past, but the occasion of burying the last emperor allowed him to set a personal example of how to treat national history with respect. Most significant, rather than use the burial as a pretext for delivering an anticommunist tirade, Yeltsin sought to make it a source of nonpartisan, conciliatory lessons.

Thousands of people turned out in Ekaterinburg and St. Petersburg to pay their respects to the family of the last tsar. This rare civic gesture by ordinary citizens clearly demonstrated that Yeltsin's humane gesture had touched an emotional chord. Less evident was whether his conciliatory message had been taken to heart. By downplaying Nicholas II's record, Yeltsin had avoided showing favor to any one interpretation of the end of the Russian empire. Yet, while depoliticization reduced the ceremony's potential to cause offense, it simultaneously robbed the event of any heroic cast. In other words, in the absence of a reevaluation of national history, rectification of the Bolsheviks' mistreatment of the Romanovs and their remains provided little grounds for mythmaking. Sympathy for the tsar and his family for the manner of their deaths may have touched many hearts, it but did not necessarily translate into positive sentiments about the Russian past. Moreover, the burial was a one-time act of respect, not the basis of a new tradition. Ultimately, Yeltsin's gesture of reconciliation was controversial and fleeting.[43]

As Yeltsin entered the final years of his tenure as the president of a new Russian state, he yearned to solve his nation's identity crisis. Having finally come to the conclusion that normal states, not just communist regimes, encouraged patriotism, Yeltsin and his administration looked hard for some unifying ideas or traditions. Their "idea for Russia" contest produced many ideal types of Russian citizens and numerous lists of aspirations for the Russian state, but the moral principles that the contest identified as potentially supporting an inclusive civic conception of Russia provoked little popular reaction. Abstract ideas had little hold on the public imagination. Lists of virtues similarly seemed to have little to do with the demands of real life—physical and economic survival and finding new ways of living.

The Communists also portrayed themselves as the guardians of certain values, but they placed these qualities in the context of the historical record. For instance, Communist politicians and commentators proudly cited a tradition of self-sacrifice for the national good as epitomized by CPSU leadership during World War II. By contrast, Sudakov's claim in his prize-winning essay that Russians put national interest over individual wealth certainly did not seem to fit with the brief record of the new Russian state. Would-be democratic patriots had trouble identifying collective memories that might be mobilized to serve their cause.

Yeltsin's own imperfect record and the absence of prerevolutionary exemplars of democratic virtue put liberals in a bind. The invocation of imperial symbols and traditions made many democrats uncomfortable. The use of tsarist sites and emblems in Yeltsin's inauguration, for instance, lent authority to the ritual but left the unpleasant impression that a new monarch had just been crowned. Those who wished to support the current government seemingly could not even invoke the inspiring legacy of Soviet dissidents who fought for basic freedoms. Human rights activists were now taking Yeltsin to task for his government's violations of basic norms, especially regarding the war in Chechnia; to cite them as heroes would have boosted the status of the regime's critics.

When condemnation of Soviet history became increasingly unappealing as a strategy for winning public favor, Yeltsin was left trying to popularize the idea of reconciliation. Yeltsin cast his actions as a means of clearing the way for new generations to escape acrimony stemming from the past. In effect, he endorsed forgiving with a dose of forgetting. During perestroika liberals strove to fill in blank spots in national history. Now Yeltsin would have Russians shift to an ideal of putting past controversies to rest rather than investigating them. Yet he did not advocate total amnesia about the Revolution or tsarism. Rather, he urged everyone to share the responsibility for past misdeeds and to move on with life.

Manipulation of the past to promote a basic level of social consensus is not an uncommon phenomenon. The renowned scholar of American historical memory Michael Kammen identifies just such an impulse in the decades after the American civil war. To reknit the fabric of the nation then, he notes, "amnesia emerged as a bonding agent far preferable to memory."[44] Yeltsin's plan for reconciliation based on depoliticization of the past, however, had clear flaws. Unilateral efforts to defuse controversies carry little guarantee of success. Under the new conditions of pluralism, Yeltsin's opponents could openly contest the government's plans to make November 7 a holiday that did not celebrate the anniversary of the Russian Revolution, for instance. Moreover, acts of atonement provided little material for building traditional patriotism. Pride in nation and state typically rests on narratives of achievement, not on expressions of remorse and apology.

Patriotic Divisions

In November 1998 a prominent Duma deputy urged that the monument to Feliks Dzerzhinskii be restored to its former place of pride in front of the security services headquarters in central Moscow. The very presence of "Iron Feliks" would deter crime and disorder, averred Nikolai Kharitonov, the leader of the legislature's Communist-allied Agrarian faction. By returning the statue of the USSR's first secret police chief, the Russian parliament would send the message that it was taking a strong stand against lawlessness. Kharitonov also invoked the Soviet-era myth of Dzerzhinskii as a man of "fiery heart, cool head, and clean hands" to support his suggestion that Dzerzhinskii would be an ideal role model for today's police. Communist and nationalist deputies, ignoring a chorus of liberal indignation, responded by voting overwhelmingly to resurrect Dzerzhinskii. One legislator even put the proposal on a moral par with the restoration of old churches.[1]

Liberals associated Dzerzhinskii with a different set of values. They recalled the Soviet secret police's early history of using violent measures against Civil War opponents and "class enemies." Duma deputy Iulii Rybakov, a long-time human rights activist and a member of Russia's Democratic Choice, characterized Dzerzhinskii as "one of the most horrible butchers in history, with a multitude of innocent victims on his conscience."[2] For liberals, Dzerzhinskii—like Lenin—also bore responsibility for the excesses later carried out by the institutions he created. Dzerzhinskii was the hero of the organization that had carried out the purges and masterminded the persecution of dissidents. Yet the outcry by democratic politicians and intellectuals was accompanied by the protests of only a few dozen elderly gulag survivors, who gathered in front of the Lubianka to warn against what they saw as an omen of a return to old Stalinist ways.[3] Then head of the KGB's successor, the FSB, Vladimir Putin had no comment.

Meanwhile, Communists countered criticism of Dzerzhinskii with their now familiar postsoviet themes. Dzerzhinskii, they claimed, had been not just a revolutionary but a state-builder (*gosudarstvennik*), who contributed to the restoration of a powerful nation in the aftermath of World War I and the Civil War. He had brought order to a chaotic situation, in particular by organizing children's homes to shelter war orphans and reduce delinquency. Communists also remembered Dzerzhinskii as a paragon of honesty and dedication to his work—in contrast to today's corrupt and irresponsible "democratic" bureaucrats.[4] In presenting him as a morally upright figure, they tapped an old myth that the KGB was a bastion of incorruptibility and efficiency. Under Brezhnev, careerists might have penetrated other institutions, but the KGB allegedly had been staffed by loyal servants of the state.

The significance of the monument to Dzerzhinskii, however, no longer lay just in its subject matter. The statue's return would clearly signify a reversal of the events of August 1991. The monument's removal would be understood as vandalism rather than as popular justice, Communists would demonstrate their dominance over democrats in the legislature, and the old regime's humiliation would be erased. Since the erection of monuments in Moscow falls under the jurisdiction of the city government, however, the Duma's endorsement of Dzerzhinskii's transfer from relative obscurity in the statue park outside the Central House of Artists entailed no practical consequences.[5] After all, Luzhkov had no desire to honor such a politicized figure. Nevertheless, Communist and nationalist deputies' strong support for the proposal delivered a harsh reminder that antistalinism had fallen out of favor, and that the status of August 1991 as a triumphal founding moment in the history of the new Russian state had been severely undermined.

Even though Dzerzhinskii did not take up his old guard post by the state security headquarters, Aleksandr Iakovlev, the so-called architect of perestroika, greeted the Duma's show of respect for him with despair. Seemingly weary of fighting against Communist myths nearly a decade after the start of liberal reform, Iakovlev interpreted the open efforts to restore Dzerzhinskii as evidence of a creeping Communist revanche. He warned that nostalgia was a threat to democracy, and he laid much of the blame for the allure of the past at the democrats' feet—not for their policies of painful economic reform but for their neglect of propaganda. "Since 1991," he observed, "no one has tackled debolshevization—the Communist Party was not banned, Lenin was not removed from the mausoleum. Everything was done impulsively and hence

Monument to Feliks Dzerzhinskii back on its pedestal in the "statue graveyard" at the Central House of Artists, Moscow, 1996. (Photo by Kathleen E. Smith.)

many opportunities were simply wasted. Today," he concluded, "we must begin again from the beginning."[6]

Indeed, upon coming to power in 1991, the democrats both neglected to expose the misdeeds of the old regime systematically and let slip opportunities to consolidate collective memories of the struggle for democracy that might have bolstered their own legitimacy. The fact that the trial of the CPSU came about only when the Communists took Yeltsin to court shows how little concerned the democrats were in 1991–92 with setting out a strong negative interpretation of Communist rule. Having spent the years of perestroika publicizing the horrors of collectivization and the gulag, many liberals believed in 1991 that an antistalinist, if not antileninist, consensus had been firmly established. Popular resistance to the conservative Communist coup seemed then to have underscored society's disillusionment with the old system and its values. Liberals did not anticipate a revival of the Communist Party or a renewal of respect for Soviet idols like Dzerzhinskii.

Ruling democrats' disinterest in 1991 in further attacks on Soviet icons can be attributed largely to their confidence that communism as an ideology and as a political movement had been discredited. Their laissez faire attitude over the next few years toward commemorating the founding of a new regime and their general wariness of patriotic rituals, however, were rooted in the Soviet experience. Regarding holiday celebrations in independent Ukraine, Catherine Wanner observes that "the long history of Soviet manipulation of historiography, compounded by state domination of the public sphere, leaves nationalist leaders in post-Soviet society in a delicate bind. How can a revised historical narrative be accepted as authentic if it is presented in a public space that has been discredited as a forum of lies?"[7] Russian democrats shared a suspicion of ritual displays as "Soviet." Having formed an aversion to the practices of the old regime, democrats also forswore both invoking the past for self-serving purposes and building up new national heroes and myths. In addition, having been at the center of an empire rather than at the periphery, they were suspicious of nationalism as an illiberal phenomenon.

The use of history for political ends, however, is hardly a prerogative of communist regimes. Democratic politicians in the West also play a role as historians, not necessarily by writing about the past within the confines of the historical discipline or even by overseeing the creation of new educational programs, but more often by refining and wielding collective memories to justify present-day institutions and policies.[8]

The very conception of the nation in the public imagination is often shaped by state-sponsored public art that commemorates some aspect of the shared past. Politicians, moreover, routinely weave threads of a common past into their electoral campaigns to give themselves an aura of historical legitimacy.

In the crucial 1996 elections, Yeltsin and his allies did show themselves capable of mobilizing collective memories. Motivated in part by the need to distract voters from their own unpopular market ideology, the ruling democrats worked to connect their rivals with a Bolshevik tradition of violence and intolerance. The initial hesitation of Yeltsin's campaign managers to summon up bad memories of the Soviet period stemmed not from a belief that "normal" countries did not dwell on the past but from fear that the public was sick of bleak depictions of their history. Faced with the Communists' sophisticated and aggressive recasting of Soviet and prerevolutionary history to bolster their own candidate, democrats had little choice but to address interpretations of the national past. But by 1996, patriotism had made a comeback.

Whereas once only conservative Communists had warned against nihilism as the likely result of too many attacks on Soviet history, now intellectuals across the political spectrum discussed the need to promote positive bases of patriotism. Liberals and Communists alike had come to deplore Russians' low national self-esteem, and no one wished to be seen as contributing to the problem of lack of respect for the nation. Stirring up unhappy memories of suffering and failure or neglecting national history, therefore, seemed unlikely to serve democrats' long-term aim of fostering attachment to a new democratic Russia. But, insofar as liberals were concerned, attractive pieces of national history proved a scarce resource in postsoviet Russia.

The short history of the Yeltsin regime provided few unabashedly popular moments. The defense of the Russian White House in August 1991 had been a noticeable exception. But, as we have seen, liberals watched with dismay as a combination of historical contingency and clever Communist propaganda swept away the memory of August 1991 as a populist, democratic victory. The October events and the opposition's relentless depictions of August as a tragic farce overshadowed the work of liberal journalists and civic activists to preserve the images of Yeltsin heroically climbing atop a tank and of demonstrators bravely manning the barricades.[9] The ruling democrats' choice of a different founding event—the adoption of state sovereignty on June 12, 1990— failed to make a positive impression on the public. Instead of contributing to the legitimizing genealogy of a new Russia, Independence Day was a source of confusion for the public and an object of ridicule for the opposition.

When it seemed as if the revived Communist Party might also monopolize positive memories of victory in World War II, both in the trophy art debate with their passionate defense of Soviet sacrifices and in the ceremonial realm with their organized Victory Day parades, democrats finally entered the fray. In 1995 they invested state resources in imposing public commemorations of the fiftieth anniversary of victory, and propagated their own myth of victory as having come in spite of, not because of, Communist Party leadership. Other than battling to reclaim the legacy of valor and loss in World War II, however, the Yeltsin regime did not try to adapt Soviet history to its advantage. For Yeltsin, the Soviet era remained the antithesis of what he sought to create.

Unfortunately for Yeltsin, prerevolutionary Russian history also provided little patriotic fodder for most liberals. Certainly Russia had no experience with democracy that could be tapped for inspiration. Not surprisingly, then, when Yeltsin imposed the two-headed eagle emblem on the Russian state over the Duma's objections, he did so without drawing any connections between the imperial government and the postsoviet system. Though his critics saw the autocratic symbol as a good fit for Yeltsin, the president did not embrace any specific tsarist heritage. The emblem had value simply because it was Russian. Similarly, Mayor Luzhkov honored Peter the Great with a huge statue and rebuilt churches that had marked the Russian Empire's military feats without putting his grand gestures in context. Luzhkov did not incorporate Peter into a narrative of reform from above, and when he took over the reconstruction of Christ the Saviour Cathedral from ultranationalists, he dropped their militarist and often chauvinist myths of the church's significance. Luzhkov decorated the capital city with Russian motifs but did not work at harnessing collective memories of military success or Orthodoxy to a civic identity for a democratic Russian state.

By the end of 1998, the task of finding an inclusive unifying ideal for Russia had also defeated Yelstin's advisers. Their "idea for Russia" contest had begun with quotations from prerevolutionary philosophers and modern dissidents, but neither Slavophile theories nor a commitment to critical thinking satisfied the liberal establishment's quest for a pithy formula that would bind citizens to Russia's new institutions. The contest had tapped new and old conceptions of national character. Lists of virtues, however, lacked the resonance of collective memories, especially those polished into dramatic narratives by years of Soviet propaganda. Liberal patriotic myths remained appealing but elusive.

Unsuccessful in his attempts to mobilize inspiring memories, Yeltsin strove to gain popularity toward the end of his second term with a new approach to the past. Yeltsin wanted to promote stability and reconciliation, but without encouraging historical amnesia. After the liberals' struggle in the 1980s to expose the distortions and omissions of Soviet historiography, he and his advisers could not easily advocate forgetting the many unpleasant aspects of the national past. They could, however, urge a nonpartisan reckoning with painful divisive episodes. In the 1992 trial of the Communist Party, reformers had already displayed their willingness both to accept a share of accountability for ills of the old regime and to atone for them. Yeltsin himself had apologized in 1991 for failing to save the lives of the three youths who died defending the White House. In 1998 he again personally atoned for his past at the funeral of Nicholas II. Though Yeltsin never expressed remorse for many of his government's failings, including the use of force in October 1993 and the war in Chechnia, he did sometimes try to make individual humility part of national loyalty. He also demonstrated a willingness to tolerate depoliticized approaches to Russian history if they would promote civic unity.

Yeltsin waited in vain, however, for the opposition to reciprocate his call for greater harmony in respect to the past. Communist loyalists, for instance, maintained their practice of scapegoating. As they had done in their first efforts to salvage their party's reputation in 1992, Communist leaders continued to cast all the blame for Russia's past and present woes on others. Gorbachev, Iakovlev, and Yeltsin were behind the collapse of Communist Party rule. They, not the members of the GKChP, had betrayed the Party from within. Similarly, Communist propagandists attributed Soviet-era events that were now regretted—such as persecution of the Russian Orthodox Church and the purges of the 1930s— to members of a fifth column. By splitting the Party in two in retrospect, Ziuganov's reform Communists justified their unwillingness to apologize for past misdeeds. They also spared Party members the need to search their consciences regarding past behavior or loyalties.

The leaders of the KPRF facilitated the natural urge to avoid feelings of guilt or responsibility for problems in other ways as well. Along with blaming the Communist Party's failings on a small minority, they promoted the self-serving notion that most Party loyalists were victims. The keystone of the CPSU's defense before the Constitutional Court in

1992 was the notion that Communists had been deprived of their rights by the Yeltsin regime. The leaders of the reconstituted Communist Party of the Russian Federation extended the status of victim to include all Soviet citizens who suffered under economic reforms. Russians, they argued, were victims of Western powers and their lackeys in the Yeltsin government. Drawing on Soviet myths of reconstruction after the Revolution and World War II, however, KPRF representatives promised that self-sacrifice and collective action under familiar leadership could redeem Russians. At a time when Russia's economy and military both seemed to be collapsing, Communists stressed their past history of state-building. Hence, as in the case of Dzerzhinskii, revolutionaries were no longer remembered as such. Creating institutions, not destroying them, was cast as heroic action.

Like the democrats, the leaders of the Communist opposition appreciated the value of positive collective memories for uniting a weary and disillusioned public. Indeed, they acted ahead of liberals to stake a claim to the most important moment in the history of several living generations—Russia's ultimate victory in World War II. As was evident in the debate over trophy art, Communists' sensitivity to the ease with which criticism of Stalin's wartime leadership could be perceived as a slur against the sacrifices of a nation served them well. By framing the return of artworks as evidence that the Yeltsin regime did not respect Soviet veterans and that it was kowtowing to the West, the Communists captured the mantle of patriots. Stalin's wartime rapprochement with the Orthodox Church also appealed to the KPRF, whose leaders wanted to highlight positive continuities with prerevolutionary Russian culture.

In short, the leaders of the revived Communist Party had little incentive to embrace Yeltsin's call for depoliticized interpretations of history. In their new role as political opposition, the KPRF benefited by undermining democrats' efforts to unite citizens around the current political system. Moreover, the Communist opposition, unlike the ruling democrats, had worked steadily and often successfully in multiple arenas to summon up collective memories to support partisan and patriotic goals. They mined the drama of Russia's ultimate victory in World War II for mythmaking material, and promoted their national Bolshevik synthesis in holiday demonstrations and electoral campaigns. Their heavily edited and often repeated presentation of Soviet history drew on a living generation's memories of achievements. The version of the past salvaged by reform Communists served as a good substitute for less popular ideology.

During the 1996 election campaign, liberals successfully targeted the weak points in the Communists' account of Russian history. Yet, despite the resources at its disposal, the Yeltsin administration never invested heavily in propagating countermemories of the Soviet period or in institutionalizing its own heroes or myths. Yeltsin left office without having built a consensus behind the symbols of the new state and without having created commemorative traditions to preserve positive memories of Russia's founding moment or its adoption of a new constitution. But accountability and reconciliation remained concerns for Yeltsin even as he stepped down from his post and endorsed a successor. Upon his unexpected resignation on December 31, 1999, he again asked for forgiveness. Announcing his intent to make way for a new generation on the eve of a new century, Yeltsin apologized for his inability to spare Russians the hardships of reform.[10]

Yeltsin's chosen heir, Vladimir Putin, easily won the early presidential elections in March 2000. Hardly bothering to campaign, Putin ran largely on the basis of his character, and he presented himself as an unabashed patriot, committed to strengthening the state. As one Western observer wryly noted, "He speaks of the state almost as a sacred object, with a reverence that previous leaders, such as Gaidar and Chubais, had reserved for the concept of 'reform.' "[11] Indeed, Putin had already made clear that he thought young people in Russia needed a better patriotic upbringing. A self-proclaimed successful product of Soviet patriotic education, Putin averred that materialism and liberal values alone were insufficient to inspire love for the nation. "Sausage and freedom" would not do as an idea for Russia, Putin had warned university students in one of his first speeches as prime minister.[12]

During his first year in office, President Putin revealed more about his idea of patriotism. In December 2000 he took up the issue of Russia's state symbols, the national anthem in particular. As we have seen, many people had expressed dissatisfaction with the complex, wordless music by Glinka that Yeltsin had endorsed. A contest to find suitable lyrics had produced nothing satisfactory, and after entertaining the notion of trying again to solicit words to Glinka's "Patriotic Song," Putin opted to support the revival of the popular music of the Soviet anthem with unspecified new verses to replace old lines about Communist ideals. He proposed to the legislature that it ratify Yeltsin's choice of the two-headed eagle emblem and tricolor while adopting the music of the Soviet anthem and restoring the red flag as the banner of the armed forces.[13] Communist deputies hailed the surprising concession on the national anthem as a victory, but liberals refused to accept the compromise deal.

Liberal politicians and intellectuals accused Putin of pandering to public opinion and of honoring a repressive regime with the restoration of the Soviet anthem. Even Yeltsin criticized his heir: "The president of a country should not blindly follow the mood of the people. On the contrary, it is up to him to actively influence it."[14] But Putin defended the compromise that finally brought Russia a full set of state symbols. He told the nation, "If we agree that the symbols of the preceding epochs, including the Soviet epoch, must not be used at all, we will have to admit then that our mothers' and fathers' lives were useless and meaningless, that their lives were in vain. Neither in my head nor in my heart can I agree with this." Putin, in terms reminiscent of Ziuganov's campaign speeches, reminded opponents of the anthem that the Soviet period had consisted of more than "Stalin's prisons and repression." He cited Soviet achievements in space and culture, while noting that the tsarist regime "had repressed peoples and dissidents of its own."[15] Centrist and Communist parliamentarians happily agreed with the president to split the difference, and the compromise laws on state symbols quickly passed in both houses of the legislature.

Yeltsin had been willing to appease veterans by producing the red banner on Victory Day, but it was one thing to recognize a historic relic as such and another thing to adopt an old symbol as relevant and fitting in the present. Liberals never endorsed forgetting that Russians had fought, sometimes died, and finally triumphed in World War II under the Communist flag. But they had come to power on the strength of a promise to replace the Soviet regime with a democratic one, and even though that promise had not been fully realized, they could not look at the old system as anything other than a foil to what they wanted to create. Yeltsin had tried to mend the breach between those who looked back with nostalgia and those who scorned the past by urging the depoliticization of history. By burying the Romanovs, he removed one locus of acrimony, but Yeltsin and his allies could not really reconcile with the Soviet era.

Putin, by contrast, seemed free of the liberal habit of soul-searching. He expressed no regrets or qualms about his career in the KGB, apparently seeing no contradictions between his past work and his more recent service in ostensibly democratic administrations—first under Sobchak in St. Petersburg and then under Yeltsin. His choice of an amalgam of Soviet and Russian symbols for the state was in accord with his personal history, and clearly showed that he did not share earlier democratic leaders' self-consciousness about borrowing from the Soviet political repertoire or their discomfort with patriotic pomp.

Yet Putin's disdain for invoking inverse legitimacy—that is, for holding up the old regime as a negative example—should not be ascribed solely to a more tolerant attitude toward communism. It also reflects the priority that the new president has given to strengthening state power. Whereas Yeltsin was motivated by the tasks of transition to underscore breaks with the past, Putin acts in accordance with the idea that consolidation can be promoted by avoiding divisive memories whenever possible.[16] In theory, both transition and consolidation could involve extracting positive lessons from the past, but Russian liberals never identified some golden age from which to draw guidance or inspiration. Some intellectuals were happy to live without historic myths, preferring a critical approach to the past to patriotic simplification, but humility regarding the nation's common history created the impression of weakness and even shame, sentiments unappealing to state-builders.

In the debate over state symbols Putin showed himself to be ready to invoke positive collective memories and downplay negative ones. His attempt to have the best of both worlds with the national anthem— keeping the form while changing the content—is unlikely, however, to have the desired effect of resolving the controversy over state symbols. The multiplicity of Russia's anthems—from "God Save the Tsar" to the "Internationale" to Stalin's anthem to Glinka's "Patriotic Song"— faithfully reflects the nation's turbulent history. Twice Russia has had music without words: first after Khrushchev's denunciation of Stalin, when lyrics praising the late leader proved an embarrassment, and again in 1991, when a new melody was chosen but suitable words could not be found. Given the fundamental divisions in Russia today, the writer Vladimir Voinovich considers that the recent absence of words in the national song was appropriate. The words of the anthem should express national identity, he notes, but "what image can we have if we ourselves don't know who we are? We know what the Soviet Union was, and tsarist Russia also. But what is Russia today? Some pray to Jesus Christ, while others bow down before the chief atheist in the mausoleum."[17] Putin's pragmatic approach to overcoming the deadlock on state symbols by granting concessions to the Soviet partisans could not end the battle over what to take from the past. It simply reaffirmed the deep divisions among the Russian people.

The emotions unleashed by the reinstatement of Stalin's anthem, complete with new lyrics by one of the co-authors of the original version, serve as a reminder that historical amnesia has not prevailed in Russia.[18] On the contrary, memory remains a potent weapon in the battle for political influence. Political actors' efforts to subordinate memory to partisan purposes, however, have not always succeeded. When Communists, liberals, and statists have attempted to strip symbols of their context, all have encountered resistance. Images of the past are not infinitely malleable. The Russian experience shows that politicians can neither escape the past nor mold it completely to their will. Collective memories are shaped gradually and hence the struggle over interpretations of the nation's common history will persist as Russians continue to forge new identities.

Notes

Chapter 1. Memory and Postcommunist Politics

1. On the flood of historical revelations during perestroika, see, for instance, R. W. Davies, *Soviet History in the Gorbachev Revolution* (Bloomington: Indiana University Press, 1989); Rosalind Marsh, *History and Literature in Contemporary Russia* (New York: New York University Press, 1995).

2. Significantly, the liberal candidates for president of the RSFSR and for mayor of Leningrad won by much higher margins than the name St. Petersburg.

3. Cited in Viktor Khamraev, "Gennadii Ziuganov: KPRF prevedet k vlasti upravlentsev-professionalov," *Segodnia*, Aug. 29, 1995, p. 2.

4. As the Hungarian philosopher G. M. Tamás observes, "If you would like to coin the most successful slogan in Eastern Europe [including the former USSR], surely it would be, 'No slogans!' ": Tamás, "Victory Defeated," *Journal of Democracy* 10, no. 1 (January 1999): 67.

5. Cynthia M. Koch, "Teaching Patriotism: Private Virtue for the Public Good in the Early Republic," in *The Bonds of Affection: Americans Define Their Patriotism*, ed. John Bodnar (Princeton: Princeton University Press, 1996), p. 22.

6. Katherine Verdery, *The Political Lives of Dead Bodies: Reburial and Postsocialist Change* (New York: Columbia University Press, 1999), p. 35.

7. In Eastern Europe and the Baltic states, by contrast, pre–World War II political parties and associations have sometimes been revived.

8. Michael Schudson, *Watergate in American History: How We Remember, Forget, and Reconstruct the Past* (New York: Basic Books, 1992), p. xiii.

9. Mary Catherine Bateson, *Peripheral Visions: Learning along the Way* (New York: HarperCollins, 1994), p. 11.

10. John R. Gillis, "Memory and Identity: The History of a Relationship," in *Commemorations: The Politics of National Identity*, ed. Gillis (Princeton: Princeton University Press, 1994), p. 4.

11. See, for instance, Steven L. Solnick, *Stealing the State: Control and Collapse in Soviet Institutions* (Cambridge: Harvard University Press, 1998).

12. I am not interested in "political culture" as it has generally been used by political scientists to characterize values at an arbitrary point in time

and then to project them into analyses of all successive periods. Such approaches tend to be overly deterministic, even when they postulate competing strands of political culture. See, for instance, Nicolai N. Petro, *The Rebirth of Russian Democracy* (Cambridge: Harvard University Press, 1995). For other appeals to broaden the study of politics to include attention to symbolism, the construction of identities, and legitimacy myths, see Verdery, *Political Lives of Dead Bodies*, pp. 22–27, 34–35; and David I. Kertzer, *Politics and Symbols: The Italian Communist Party and the Fall of Communism* (New Haven: Yale University Press, 1996), pp. 3–5.

13. Maurice Halbwachs, *The Collective Memory*, trans. Francis J. Ditter Jr. and Vida Yazdi Ditter (New York: Harper & Row, 1990), p. 50.

14. Alon Confino, "Collective Memory and Cultural History: Problems of Method," *American Historical Review* 102, no. 5 (December 1997): 1386. For the term *lieux de mémoire*, see Pierre Nora, "Between Memory and History," *Representations* 26 (Spring 1989): 7–25.

15. David Lowenthal, "Fabricating Heritage," *History & Memory* 10, no. 1 (Spring 1998): 8.

16. Yael Zerubavel, *Recovered Roots: Collective Memory and the Making of Israeli National Tradition* (Chicago: University of Chicago Press, 1995), p. 5.

17. David Lowenthal, *Possessed by the Past: The Heritage Crusade and the Spoils of History* (New York: Free Press, 1996), p. xi; see also Alon Confino, *The Nation as a Local Metaphor: Württemberg, Imperial Germany, and National Memory, 1871–1918* (Chapel Hill: University of North Carolina Press, 1997), p. 12.

18. Eric Hobsbawm and Terence Ranger, eds., *The Invention of Tradition* (Cambridge: Cambridge University Press, 1983).

19. Confino, *Nation as a Local Metaphor*, p. 11.

20. Confino, "Collective Memory and Cultural History," p. 1394.

21. Even monumental art can be exploited for popular ends; consider, for instance, the Krasnoiarsk workers who protested the wage arrears crisis by erecting in their factory courtyard a tombstone to the memory of their wages. See Aleksei Tarasov, "Zarplata, my tebia pomnim!" *Izvestiia*, Oct. 17, 1996, p. 1.

22. Confino, "Collective Memory and Cultural History," pp. 1393–1395.

23. Ibid., p. 1389.

24. Nina Tumarkin, *The Living and the Dead: The Rise and Fall of the Cult of World War II in Russia* (New York: Basic Books, 1994); Victoria E. Bonnell, *Iconography of Power: Soviet Political Posters under Lenin and Stalin* (Berkeley: University of California Press, 1997).

25. I borrow the characterization of attitudes toward mythmaking as "laissez faire" from Lyn Spillman, *Nation and Commemoration: Creating National Identities in the United States and Australia* (Cambridge: Cambridge University Press, 1997).

Chapter 2. Rewriting Communist Party History in the Constitutional Court

1. "O deiatel'nosti KPSS i KP RSFSR," *Rossiiskaia gazeta*, Nov. 9, 1991, p. 2.

2. The Russian Supreme Soviet passed a law creating the Constitutional Court in July 1991, but elected the court's justices only in October of the same year.

3. For early statements of the GKChP, see Victoria Bonnell, Ann Cooper, and Gregory Freidin, eds., *Russia at the Barricades* (Armonk, N.Y.: M. E. Sharpe, 1994), pp. 33–41; quotation, p. 34.

4. In June 1990, the Russian Republic had followed the lead of several other republics that made up the Union of Soviet Socialist Republics by declaring sovereignty. A year later, Russians elected Boris Yeltsin as their first president.

5. Victoria E. Bonnell and Gregory Freidin, "Televorot: The Role of Television Coverage in Russia's August 1991 Coup," in *Soviet Hieroglyphics: Visual Culture in Late Twentieth-Century Russia*, ed. Nancy Condee, (Bloomington: Indiana University Press, 1995) pp. 27–33.

6. "Vstrecha s M. S. Gorbachevym," *Rossiiskaia gazeta*, Aug. 24, 1991, p. 1.

7. "Vystuplenie Prezidenta RSFSR B. N. El'tsina po 'Radio Rossii' 29 Avgusta 1991 goda," *Rossiiskaia gazeta*, Aug. 31, 1991, p. 1.

8. "Ob otstranenii ot ispolneniia obiazannostei predsedatelei ispolkomov oblastnykh Sovetov narodnykh deputatov" and "O nekotorykh voprosakh deiatel'nosti organov ispolnitel'noi vlasti v RSFSR," *Rossiiskaia gazeta*, Aug. 27, 1991, p. 3.

9. The Russian branch of the CPSU was formed only in 1990. Controlled by conservatives, it had expelled Aleksandr Rutskoi and other reformers at its summer 1991 plenum. See Robert Orttung, *From Leningrad to St. Petersburg* (New York: St. Martin's Press, 1995), pp. 163–185; Valerii Vyzhutovich, "Zalozhniki printsipov," *Izvestiia*, Aug. 8, 1991, p. 1; "O priostanovlenii deiatel'nosti Kommunisticheskoi partii RSFSR," *Rossiiskaia gazeta*, Aug. 27, 1991, p. 3.

10. "O partiinykh arkhivakh" and "Ob arkhivakh Komiteta gosudarstvennoi bezopasnosti SSSR," *Rossiiskaia gazeta*, Aug. 27, 1991, p. 3; "Ob imushchestve KPSS i Kommunisticheskoi partii RSFSR," ibid., Aug. 30, 1991, p. 2.

11. "Vystuplenie Prezidenta RSFSR." On Yeltsin's 1987 ordeal, when he was summoned from his hospital bed on Gorbachev's orders to face a round of abuse from the Moscow Party Committee before being dismissed from his post as Moscow first secretary, see Boris El'tsin, *Ispoved' na zadannuiu temu* (Moscow: PIK, 1990), pp. 134–140.

12. Gorbachev quoted in "In the Case of the Verification of the Constitutionality of Edicts of the President of the Russian Federation No. 79 of 23 August 1991, 'On the Property of the CPSU and the Communist Party of the RSFSR,' and No. 169 of 6 November 1991, 'On the Activity of the CPSU and the CP RSFSR,' as well as of the Verification of the Constitutionality of the CPSU and the CP RSFSR," *Statutes and Decisions: The Laws of the*

USSR and Its Successor States 30, no. 4 (July–August 1994): 36. See also Jonathan Steele, *Eternal Russia* (Cambridge: Harvard University Press, 1994), pp. 138–140.

13. "O deiatel'nosti KPSS i KP RSFSR."

14. Iurii Slobodkin, "Prezident Rossii perestupil konstitutsiiu, no reshitsia li konstitutsionnyi sud reabilitirovat' kompartiiu?" *Pravda*, May 16, 1992, pp. 1–2; E. Sorokin and A. Shinkin, "Partiia zapreshchena: Opasnyi pretsedent," ibid., Nov. 13, 1991, p. 2; "Opasnyi pretsedent: Zaiavlenie gruppy uchenykh-pravovedov po povodu Ukaza Prezidenta RSFSR ot 6 noiabria 1991 goda 'O deiatel'nosti KPSS i KP RSFSR,' " *Sovetskaia Rossiia*, Nov. 22, 1991, p. 2.

15. On the spectrum of new parties, see Joan Barth Urban and Valerii D. Solovei, *Russia's Communists at the Crossroads* (Boulder, Colo.: Westview Press, 1997), pp. 20–33.

16. Liudmila Aleksandrova, untitled commentary accompanying "O deiatel'nosti KPSS i KP RSFSR," *Rossiiskaia gazeta*, Nov. 9, 1991, p. 2; see also Elizabeth Teague and Vera Tolz, "CPSU R.I.P.," *Report on the USSR*, Nov. 22, 1991, pp. 1–8, and Boris Pugachev, "Tragicheskii opyt vlastvovaniia KPSS mozhet ostat'sia plokho usvoennym urokom," *Rossiiskaia gazeta*, July 7, 1992, p. 2.

17. Anatolii Sobchak, *Zhila-byla kommunisticheskaia partiia* (St. Petersburg: Lenizdat, 1995), p. 130.

18. Disinterest in holding the CPSU accountable was not universal among the public; see letters to the editor from N. Zuev and S. Aleksandrov in *Ogonek*, Sept. 21–28, 1991, p. 6, and Sept. 28–Oct. 5, 1991, p. 4, respectively.

19. Mikhail Karpov, "Konstitutsionnyi sud ob''edinil dva khodaistva v odno delo," *Nezavisimaia gazeta*, May 27, 1992, p. 2.

20. In keeping with the practice of the trial's participants, and as confirmed in the court's decision, I generally treat the CP RSFSR as a constituent and subordinate part of the CPSU. After all, as of August 1991, the CP RSFSR had no separate membership cards, charter, or program.

21. Note that the two teams partially overlapped, and both included representatives of both moderate and nationalist strands of the neocommunist movement. For details, see F. M. Rudinskii, *"Delo KPSS" v konstitutsionnom sude: Zapiski uchastnika protsessa* (Moscow: Bylina, 1999), pp. 43–46. For a typology of different tendencies, see Barth Urban and Solovei, *Russia's Communists*, pp. 11–60.

22. Sergei Shakhrai served as a deputy in the Russian legislature before becoming one of Yeltsin's legal advisers. Mikhail Fedotov worked for the Copyright Protection Agency. The lawyer Andrei Makarov was best known for his defense of Brezhnev's son-in-law in his trial for corruption in 1988.

23. David Remnick, "The Trial of the Old Regime," *New Yorker*, Nov. 30, 1992, pp. 112–114.

24. Iu. Slobodkin, D. Stepanov, and V. Sevast'ianov in *Materialy dela o*

*proverke konstitutsionnosti Ukazov Prezidenta RF, kasaiushchikhsia
deiatel'nosti KPSS i KP RSFSR, a takzhe o proverke konstitutsionnosti
KPSS i KP RSFSR*, 4 vols. (Moscow: Spark, 1996–1997), 1: 7–9, 29, 54–55.

25. V. Zorkal'tsev, ibid., p. 9.

26. V. Kuptsov, ibid., p. 229. See also I. Osadchii, ibid., 2: 386.

27. G. Ziuganov, ibid., 1: 276–277; Kuptsov, ibid., 3: 464; interrogation of
A. Iakovlev, ibid., 4: 315–355; Inna Mura'veva, "Partiia nevinna: Kak inkviz-
itsiia . . . ," *Rossiiskaia gazeta*, Nov. 5, 1992, pp. 1–2; Viktor Kozhemiako,
"Gde zhe logika, Mikhail Sergeevich?" *Pravda*, Oct. 14, 1992, p. 1.

28. F. Rudinskii in *Materialy*, 4: 549; see also Osadchii, ibid., 2: 424.

29. "Valentin Kuptsov: Nadeemsia, chto vostorzhesvuiut pravo,
spravedlivost'," *Pravda*, Nov. 14, 1992, p. 2.

30. Kuptsov in *Materialy*, 1: 229; N. Ryzhkov, ibid., 3: 542; E. Ligachev,
ibid., 4: 16.

31. Stepanov, ibid., 1: 28.

32. Valentina Nikiforova and Viktor Trushkov, "V konstitutsionnom
sude RF: Nachalas' duel' storon," *Pravda*, July 9, 1992, p. 2.

33. V. Falin in *Materialy*, 4: 233.

34. A. Denisov and Osadchii, ibid., 2: 195, 430; "Vladimir Kalashnikov:
Pravo—iskusstvo dobra i spravedlivosti," *Pravda*, Nov. 18, 1992, p. 2.

35. Ryzhkov in *Materialy*, 3: 549. See also Zorkal'tsev and Stepanov,
ibid., 1: 9, 29.

36. G. Veretennikov, ibid., 2: 80; A. Vol'skii, ibid., 3: 482, 489.

37. Rudinskii, ibid., 1: 269.

38. "Kuptsov: Nadeemsia"; see also V. Zorkal'tsev, quoted in Murav'eva,
"Partiia nevinna."

39. Kuptsov in *Materialy*, 1: 229; Iu. Belov and Osadchii, ibid., 2: 276,
412, 424, 428; Viktor Trushkov, "I Minina s Pozharskim v sud?" *Pravda*,
June 25, 1992, p. 1.

40. G. Skliar, L. Oleinik, and A. Mal'tsev in *Materialy*, 1: 348–376,
396–414; V. Tiurin and Mal'tsev, ibid., pp. 370, 401.

41. David Remnick quotes Vladimir Ivashko as remarking during a break in
the trial, "This is a coup? No, I am sorry. This was a drama, designed to crush
the Communist Party and create bourgeois power in Russia": "Trial of the Old
Regime," p. 110; see also V. Bokov and Kuptsov in *Materialy*, 1: 44, 227.

42. Ziuganov in *Materialy*, 1: 273. See also the exchange between V.
Guliev and B. Kurashvili, ibid., 2: 340; O. Latsis, ibid., 1: 555; Veretennikov
and Osadchii, ibid., 2: 80, 423; Ryzhkov, ibid., 3: 567; Ligachev and
Iakovlev, ibid., 4: 103, 355.

43. V. Vishniakov, B. Kurashvili, V. Martem'ianov, S. Bogoliubov, V.
Khangel'dyev, and V. Iliukhin, "Slovo dlia zashchity," *Pravda*, July 4,
1992, p. 1.

44. "Vladimir Kalashnikov: Pravo . . ."; V. Dolgikh in *Materialy*, 4: 6–7.

45. Slobodkin and Martem'ianov in *Materialy*, 1: 35–36, 53.

46. On Russians' affinity for the status of victim, see Nancy Ries, *Russian Talk: Culture & Conversation during Perestroika* (Ithaca: Cornell University Press, 1997), esp. pp. 105–110, in which she describes tendencies toward "competitive litanizing," a process in which speakers "assert themselves or their groups as the supreme victims."

47. S. Kovalev, V. Bukovskii, and G. Iakunin in *Materialy*, 2: 85–103, 233–250, 261–273; V. Solodin, V. Belov, and V. Ivanenko, ibid., 1: 578–593 and 2: 16–37; E. Albats, ibid., 2: 44–60; Evgeniia Albats, "Partiia—sud, pressa, armiia, gosbezopasnost' nashei epokhi," *Moskovskie novosti*, June 12, 1992, pp. 6–7.

48. Makarov in *Materialy*, 1: 134, 191.

49. V. Bakatin, ibid., 4: 372. See also the exchange between Justice Morshchakova and Ivan Rybkin on this subject, ibid., 1: 59.

50. See, for instance, Makarov, ibid., 1: 206, 210.

51. Oleg Rumiantsev, "Podtverdit' ochevidnoe," *Rossiiskaia gazeta*, July 7, 1992, p. 2; Sergei Shakhrai and Andrei Makarov in *Materialy*, 1: 108, 125.

52. Latsis in *Materialy*, 4: 554–555. See also Iurii Feofanov, "Zhertvy—kaialis', palachei—zashchishali," *Izvestiia*, Aug. 24, 1992, p. 2; Makarov in *Materialy*, 1: 213.

53. Shakhrai in *Materialy*, 1: 72; Feofanov, "Zhertvy—kaialis'."

54. Mikhail Fedotov, Andrei Makarov, and Sergei Shakhrai, " 'Delo KPSS,' ili Kakuiu organizatsiiu my poteriali," *Izvestiia*, July 2, 1992, p. 3; Inna Murav'eva, "Nakanune godovshchiny Velikogo Oktiabria," *Rossiiskaia gazeta*, Nov. 7, 1992, p. 2. Even Chief Justice Valerii Zorkin sharply rebuked the Communist side for referring to "repressions" against them—a charge that he said was refuted by their very presence in the courtroom. *Materialy*, 3: 498.

55. D. Zlatopol'skii in *Materialy*, 3: 62; see also Sergei Pogrel'skii, "Oleg Rumiantsev protiv KPSS," *Pravda*, June 30, 1992, p. 2; Trushkov, "I Minina."

56. Interviews with Ernest Ametistov and Valerii Zorkin cited in Lynne M. Tracy, "Prospects for an Independent Judiciary: The Russian Constitutional Court and the CPSU Trial," *Akron Law Review* 26, no. 3–4 (Winter/Spring 1993): 596.

57. "In the Case of the Verification," pp. 36–38.

58. Ibid., pp. 29–34.

59. Ibid., pp. 26–29.

60. "Zhiva Kompartiia Rossii!" *Pravda*, Dec. 3, 1992, pp. 1–2; Barth Urban and Solovei, *Russia's Communists*, pp. 49–55; Ametistov cited in Valerii Vyzhutovich, "Doigryvanie otlozhennoi partii," *Izvestiia*, Feb. 13, 1993, p. 5.

61. Trials of old regimes normally serve both as "the constitutive acts of the new order" and as reminders of past injustices that need to be remedied: Paul Connerton, *How Societies Remember* (Cambridge: Cambridge University Press, 1989), p. 7.

62. Inna Murav'eva, "Kommunisty snimaiut s sebia otvetstvennost' i za proshloe, i za nastoiashchee," *Rossiiskaia gazeta*, July 14, 1992, p. 1; Iurii

Feofanov, "XX S''ezd KPSS v zale konstitutsionnogo suda," *Izvestiia*, July 8, 1992, p. 3.

Chapter 3. Remembering August 1991: Founding Moment or Farce?

1. Moscow Central Television, Aug. 24, 1991, in *Federal Broadcast Information Service Daily Report (FBIS-SOV)*, Aug. 26, 1991, pp. 20–21, 74–75; quotation, p. 74.

2. Victoria E. Bonnell and Gregory Freidin, "Televorot: The Role of Television Coverage in Russia's August 1991 Coup," in *Soviet Hieroglyphics: Visual Culture in Twentieth-Century Russia*, ed. Nancy Condee (Bloomington: Indiana University Press, 1995), p. 43.

3. Viktor Masliukov and Konstantin Truevtsev, comps., *V Avguste 91-go: Rossiia glazami ochevidtsev* (Moscow and St. Petersburg: Limbus-press, 1993), p. 217.

4. Interview with Konstantin Truevtsev, president of Living Ring, June 3, 1996.

5. Russian Television Network, Aug. 21, 1992, in *FBIS-SOV*, Aug. 24, 1992, p. 15; "Obrashchenie prezidenta k sograzhdanam," *Izvestiia*, Aug. 20, 1992, pp. 1–2.

6. Alla Latynina, " 'No voriugi mne milei, chem krovopiitsy . . . ,' " *Moskovskie novosti*, Aug. 23, 1992, p. 22. On how the dramatized version of the storming of the Winter Palace replaced the duller one even in participants' memoirs, see James von Geldern, *Bolshevik Festivals, 1917–1920* (Berkeley: University of California Press, 1993), pp. 199–207.

7. See, for instance, Donald J. Raleigh, "A View from Saratov," in *Russia at the Barricades*, ed. Victoria E. Bonnell, Ann Cooper, and Gregory Freidin (Armonk, N.Y.: M. E. Sharpe, 1994), pp. 131–146.

8. Vitalii Tret'iakov, "19 Avgusta k nam prishla svoboda," *Nezavisimaia gazeta*, Aug. 19, 1992, p. 1.

9. Radio Mayak, Aug. 17, 1992, in *FBIS-SOV*, Aug. 18, 1992, pp. 21–22; *Moskovskie novosti*, Aug. 23, 1992, ibid., Aug. 24, 1992, pp. 30–32.

10. Pavel Zakharov, "Tel'man Gdlian: Zhdu vtoroi volny," *Kuranty*, Aug. 18, 1992, p. 4; Galina Starovoitova, untitled commentary, *Literaturnaia gazeta*, Aug. 19, 1992, p. 11.

11. "Otchego krasneiut tseny (Moskva)," and Igor' Saltykov, "Oranzhevaia palatka na fone 'Belogo doma,' " *Pravda*, Aug. 18, 1992, p. 1; Viacheslav Gerasimov, Natal'ia Ivanova, and Elena Gutova, ". . . A Gorbachev s Burbulisom 'preobreli negativ,' " ibid., Aug. 22, 1992, p. 1.

12. Russian Television Network, Aug. 21, 1992, in *FBIS-SOV*, Aug. 24, 1992, p. 23.

13. V. S., "Nash den'!" *Kuranty*, Aug. 20, 1992, p. 1; "Panikhida na Vagan'kovskom," ibid., Aug. 22, 1992, p. 1; Vladimir Strakhov, "Svecha gorela na zemle, svecha gorela . . . ," ibid., p. 2; P. Bykov, "U K. Borovogo svoi prazdnik," ibid., Aug. 18, 1992, p. 5.

14. Yeltsin cited in Petr Zhuravlev, "Gusenitsy istorii," *Itogi*, June 18, 1996, pp. 17–18.

15. "Soobshchenie Tsentralnoi komissii vserossiiskogo referenduma," *Rossiiskaia gazeta*, May 6, 1993, p. 1.

16. Russian Television Network, Aug. 19, 1993, in *FBIS-SOV*, Aug. 19, 1993, pp. 13–15.

17. "Vspominaia avgust-91," *Pravda*, Aug. 17, 1993, pp. 1–2. On Ziuganov's absence from Moscow in August 1991, see David Remnick, "Hammer, Sickle, and Book," *New York Review of Books*, May 23, 1996, p. 46.

18. See, for instance, Iuliia Kokhanova and Inna Semenova, "Lebedinyi tanets dva goda spustia," *Pravda*, Aug. 20, 1993, p. 2.

19. VTsIOM poll of 1,300 Muscovites in *Moskovskie novosti*, Aug. 22, 1993, p. 8.

20. Grigorii Kakovin, "Smysl Avgusta: Neiubileinaia stat'ia," *Nezavisimaia gazeta*, Aug. 20, 1993, p. 2; Vitalii Tret'iakov, "Dva goda nazad v etot den' v Moskvu voshli tanki: Segodnia my po prezhnomu ne znaet konkretnykh, opredelennykh sudom vinovnikov . . . ," ibid., Aug. 19, 1993, p. 1.

21. Cited in Nikolai Andreev, "Dva goda posle putcha," *Kuranty*, Aug. 19, 1993, p. 4.

22. "Vo vremia demonstratsii nash korrespondent podvergsia napadeniiu," *Pravda*, Aug. 20, 1993.

23. Russian Television Network, Aug. 19, 1993, in *FBIS-SOV*, Aug. 19, 1993, p. 19; Interfax, Aug. 20, 1993, ibid., Aug. 19, 1993, p. 23; Ivan Rodin and Ol'ga Odintsova, "Prezident pishet pis'mo deputatam, parlament plodotvorno truditsia, a narod guliaet na mitingakh . . . ," *Nezavisimaia gazeta*, Aug. 21, 1993, p. 1.

24. Andrei Kolesnikov, "Vkhod tol'ko dlia belykh," *Nezavisimaia gazeta*, Aug. 29, 1993, p. 2.

25. Gleb Pavlovskii, ed., *93 Oktriabr' Moskva: Khronika tekushchikh sobytii* (Moscow: Vek XX i Mir, 1993), pp. 4–10.

26. Rutskoi's appeal of Sept. 23, 1993, is in *Listovki Belogo doma: Moskovskie letuchie izdaniia 22 Sentiabria–4 Oktiabria 1993*, comp. Boris Belenkin and Elena Strukova (Moscow: 1993), p. 45; see also pp. 28–33.

27. See, for instance, Iurii Feofanov, "Ne gosudarstvennyi perevorot, a vykhod iz konstitutsionnogo tupika," *Izvestiia*, Oct. 1, 1993, p. 4.

28. *Listovki Belogo doma*, p. 113.

29. Alexander Buzgalin and Andrei Kolganov, *Bloody October in Moscow: Political Repression in the Name of Reform*, trans. Renfrey Clarke (New York: Monthly Review Press, 1994), pp. 80–95.

30. Jamey Gambrell, "Moscow: Storm over the Press," *New York Review of Books*, Dec. 16, 1993, p. 69.

31. "Chislo postradavshikh vo vremia sobytii 3–4 oktiabria v Moskve ustanovleno," *Izvestiia*, Dec. 25, 1993, p. 1.

32. Aleksandr Kasatov, "Nasha vina, nasha beda," and Boris Zhukov, "Eto prazdnik so sliunoiu na gubakh . . . ," *Stolitsa*, no. 41, 1993, pp. 5–7;

Liudmila Telen', "Reformy perenosiatsia v XXI vek," *Moskovskie novosti,* Oct. 17–24, 1993, p. 11.

33. Viktor Loshak, "Russian Procurator-General: 'There Will Be No Mass Arrests,'" *Moscow News,* Sept. 1–8, 1991, p. 11; Wendy Slater, "The Trial of the Leaders of Russia's August 1991 Coup," *RFE/RL Research Report* 2, no. 48 (Dec. 3, 1993): 25–27; Valerii Rudnev, "Delo KPSS: Nas ozhidaiet ne politicheskii protsess, a ugolovny," *Izvestiia,* Jan. 21, 1992, pp. 1–2.

34. Aleksandr Golovenko, "Gennadii Ianaev: 'U nas ne bylo drugogo vykhoda . . . ,'" *Pravda,* Sept. 26, 1992, p. 3; Valerii Rudnev, "Delo GKChP: Podsudimye nedovol'nyi khodom sudebnogo protsessa," *Izvestiia,* Apr. 28, 1993, p. 2.

35. Anatolii Golovenko, "Valentin Pavlov: Sudu gotovat rol' 'troiki,'" *Pravda,* Mar. 23, 1993, p. 4; Golovenko, "Gennadii Ianaev"; Golovenko, "Anatolii Luk'ianov: 'Osuzhdaiu stremlenie k samovlast'iu,'" *Pravda,* July 21, 1992, pp. 1–2.

36. See *Gosudarstvennaia Duma: Stenogramma zasedanii,* 5 vols. (Moscow: Respublika, 1995) (hereafter *GD*).

37. Iu. P. Ivanov and V. G. Vishniakov in *GD,* 2: 414–415, 491–495.

38. Indeed, when first put to a vote in the Duma on Feb. 17, LDPR's draft on political and economic amnesty failed. *GD,* 2: 707.

39. "Memorandum o soglasii," *Rossiiskaia gazeta,* Feb. 26, 1994, p. 4. A number of factions protested that there was no need to drop the investigation of the October events. Shakhrai, however, contended that a long, partisan examination of the conflict would only stir up the very enmity that the amnesty was meant to defuse. *GD,* 3: 33–35.

40. S. M. Shakhrai and V. S. Medvedev, *GD,* 3: 33–35, 38–40.

41. V. V. Zhirinovskii, ibid., pp. 29–33.

42. M. K. Dobrovol'skaia, ibid., pp. 3–4.

43. *GD,* 3: 818.

44. A. E. Shabad, *GD,* 2: 501.

45. "Strategicheskaia tsel'—sozdat' prosvetaiushchuiu stranu" and "Ob ukreplenii Rossiiskogo gosudarstva," *Rossiiskaia gazeta,* Feb. 25, 1994, pp. 1–7; Sergei Parkhomenko, "Sorok bochek arestantov," *Segodnia,* Feb. 25, 1994, p. 1.

46. Yeltsin's adviser Iurii Baturin cited in "Amnistiia: Reshenie priniato, posledstviia—v tumane," *Trud,* Feb. 25, 1994, p. 2. See also "Priniav postanovlenie ob amnistii, Duma vstupila v konfrontatsiiu s Prezidentom i pravitel'stvom," *Rossiiskaia gazeta,* Feb. 24, 1994, p. 2. Nevertheless, Prosecutor General Aleksei Kazannik released the prisoners before the president could challenge the Duma's decision. He resigned immediately thereafter. Dmitrii Pushkar', "Priznaniia General'nogo prokurora," *Moskovskie novosti,* Feb. 27–Mar. 6, 1994, pp. 1, 8; Tamara Zamiatina, "Vopreki politicheskoi vole Prezidenta," *Rossiiskaia gazeta,* Mar. 1, 1994, p. 1.

47. Varennikov accompanied Boldin, Oleg Shenin, Secretary of the CPSU

Central Committee, and Oleg Baklanov, First Deputy Chairman of the National Defense Council, to Foros on Aug. 18, 1991, to try to secure Gorbachev's acquiescence in the state of emergency or his resignation. V. Varennikov, "General Varennikov otkazyvaetsia ot amnistii," *Pravda*, May 5, 1994, p. 1; " 'Ia schital svoim dolgom . . . ,' " *Moskovskii zhurnal*, May 1995, pp. 7–8; Valerii Rudnev, "Delo GKChP: Obdumannyi khod generala Varennikova," *Izvestiia*, June 7, 1994, p. 5.

48. Valentina Nikforova, "General prodolzhaet boi," *Pravda*, June 23, 1994, p. 1; " 'Ia schital svoim dolgom . . . ,' " p. 9; Leonid Nikitinskii, "Iavlenie Gorbacheva," *Izvestiia*, June 16, 1994, p. 4.

49. Sander Thoenes, "Coup Trial: Prosecutor Said No Case from Start," *Moscow Times*, Aug. 11, 1994, and "Acquittal Ends Trial, but Verbal War Goes On," ibid., Aug. 12, 1994.

50. Otto Latsis, "Chto spasali putchisty v avguste-91," *Izvestiia*, Aug. 19, 1994, p. 4; see also Mikhail Leont'ev, "Den' samoubiistva SSSR," *Segodnia*, Aug. 19, 1994, p. 1; Iurii Shchekochikin, "My oderzhali porazhenie?" *Literaturnaia gazeta*, Aug. 24, 1994, pp. 1–2.

51. ITAR-TASS, Aug. 20, 1994, in *FBIS-SOV*, Aug. 22, 1994, p. 20.

52. *Nauchno-prakticheskaia konferentsiia "Uroki avgusta 1991 goda"* (Moscow: Iuridicheskaia literatura, 1994). One liberal critic called the event "a formal, top-down, unrepresentative, pseudo-democratic, ersatz conference": Arkadii Udal'tsov, "19–21 Avgusta s. g. po vine rukovodstva strany pobedili riazhenye," *Literaturnaia gazeta*, Aug. 24, 1994, p. 1.

53. Viktor Kozhemiako, "Chto mozhno vlozhit' v usta i v golovu prezidentu El'tsinu?" *Pravda*, Aug. 26, 1995, p. 2.

54. *Komsomolskaia pravda*, Aug. 19, 1995, in *FBIS-SOV*, Aug. 21, 1995, pp. 22–26; quotation, p. 24.

55. *Kuranty*, Aug. 23, 1994, p. 1.

56. Vitalii Tret'iakov, "19.08.91: To, chto proizoshlo, Rossiia osoznala poslednei," *Nezavisimaia gazeta*, August 19, 1996, p. 1; "Komanda 'Pobeditelei' Avgusta 1991-go," ibid., Aug. 18, 1994, p. 5; Iurii Solomonov, "Sladkii son o gosudarstve i revoliutsii," *Literaturnaia gazeta*, Aug. 23, 1995, pp. 1–2.

57. Tat'iana Malkina, "V kustakh igrushechnye volki glazami strashnymi gliadiat," *Itogi*, Aug. 20, 1996, p. 32.

58. Aleksandr Sargin, "GKChP: Chetyre goda spustia," *Argumenty i fakty*, no. 34, 1995, p. 1; Dmitrii Gutenev, "Dmitrii Iazov: 'My obnadezhili narod. On poveril, chto my zashchitim SSSR ot razvala,' " *Pravda*, Aug. 19, 1994, pp. 1–2; Varennikov cited in Carlotta Gall, "Hundreds Gather to Relive Intense Days of Coup," *Moscow Times*, Aug. 23, 1994.

59. Dmitrii Okskii, "Viktor Anpilov prizval oppozitsii izbrat' edinogo vozhdia," *Segodnia*, Aug. 23, 1994, p. 2.

60. Evgenii Krasnikov, "Rossiia skromno otmetila godovschinu krakha GKChP," *Nezavisimaia gazeta*, Aug. 23, 1994, p. 1; "Blagotvoritel'nost' Vasiliia Blazhenogo," *Segodnia*, Aug. 24, 1994, p. 2; Leonid Bershidsky, "Years Blur Sharp Lines of '91," *Moscow Times*, Aug. 22, 1995; Marina An-

drusenko, "Prazdnik 'Vivat, Rossiia!' sostoitsia," *Nezavisimaia gazeta*, Aug. 17, 1996, p. 2.

61. Aleksei Vorob'ev, "Panikhida na meste tragedii," *Nezavisimaia gazeta*, Oct. 4, 1994, p. 2; "Mitingi oppozitsii v Moskve ne sobrali bol'shikh tolp," *Izvestiia*, Sept. 21, 1995, p. 1; author's observations, Oct. 4, 1996.

62. Typical accounts include Viktor Kharlamov, "Ostavalas' tol'ko noch'," *Pravda*, Oct. 4, 1994, pp. 2, 4; and Vladimir Maslennikov, "Pered rasstrelom," *Sovetskaia Rossiia*, Oct. 3, 1996, p. 3.

63. Aleksandr Zinov'ev, "Zavershenie russkoi kontrrevoliutsii," *Pravda*, Oct. 1, 1994, pp. 1–2.

64. Boris Yeltsin, *The Struggle for Russia*, trans. Catherine A. Fitzpatrick (New York: Random House, 1994), pp. 258, 272, 267, 280.

65. "My zhivem uzhe v drugoi Rossii," *Rossiiskaia gazeta*, Oct. 5, 1994, p. 1.

66. Vladimir Kuz'mishchev, "Posleslovie k oktiabriu," *Rossiiskaia gazeta*, Oct. 4, 1994, p. 1.

67. Sergei Parkhomenko, "God s tekh por, kak menia ne povesili," *Segodnia*, Oct. 4, 1994, p. 1; Viktoria Shokhina, "V rossii ne vyveshivaiut traurnykh flagov: Oktiabr'skaia godovshchina na teleekrane," *Nezavisimaia gazeta*, Oct. 8, 1994, p. 5; Grigorii Voskoboinikov and Dmitrii Khitarov, "Litsa bezlikoi istorii," *Itogi*, Oct. 1, 1996, pp. 12–13; "V oktiabre 93-go nas khoteli vernut' v oktiabr' 17-go," *Literaturnaia gazeta*, Oct. 5, 1994, p. 3.

68. "Narod i soldaty na barrikadakh, intelligentsiia v razdum'iakh," *Nezavisimaia gazeta*, Oct. 4, 1994, pp. 1, 4; "V oktiabre 93-go nas khoteli"; "Ten' ot Belogo doma," *Nezavisimaia gazeta*, Oct. 4, 1996, p. 5; Aleksandr Golovkov, "Drama Oktiabria," *Izvestiia*, Oct. 3, 1995, p. 5.

69. "Lish' kazhdyi desiatyi rossiianin schitaet podavlenie putcha GKChP pobedoi demokratii," *Izvestiia*, Aug. 19, 1999, p. 1.

70. "Zabyt'? Prostit'? Nachat' s nachala? Proshlo tri goda. No eto ne povod putat' greshnoe s pravednym," *Moskovskii Komsomolets*, Oct. 3, 1996, p. 2; *Argumenty i fakty* poll in *Current Digest of the Post-Soviet Press* 45, no. 42 (Nov. 17, 1993): 16.

71. Pavel Gutionov, "The Investigation Is Not Over. Will We Forget?" *Chas pik*, Mar. 2, 1994, in *Current Digest of the Post-Soviet Press* 46, no. 9 (Mar. 30, 1994).

72. "Prezident dali srok. Uslovno," *Kuranty*, Aug. 23, 1994, p. 1.

73. Solomonov, "Sladkii son."

Chapter 4. Disposing of the Spoils of World War II

1. For a thorough account of German art acquisitions during the war, see Lynn H. Nicholas, *The Rape of Europa* (New York: Knopf, 1994). Jonathan Petropolous, *Art as Politics in the Third Reich* (Chapel Hill: University of North Carolina Press, 1996), describes Nazi collecting in the East and analyzes art collecting as a reflection of Nazi leaders' worldviews.

2. Konstantin Akinsha and Grigorii Kozlov, with Sylvia Hochfield,

Beautiful Loot: The Soviet Plunder of Europe's Art Treasures (New York: Random House, 1995), pp. 12–15.

3. Suzanne Massie, *Pavlovsk: The Life of a Russian Palace* (Boston: Little, Brown, 1990), pp. 265–273.

4. Nicholas, *Rape of Europa*, pp. 369–370, 383–400; General Clay cited, p. 385.

5. Kozlov and Akinsha, *Beautiful Loot*, pp. 19–22, 32–40, 44–45.

6. Ibid., pp. 99–105, 159–166; Hector Feliciano, *The Lost Museum* (New York: Basic Books, 1997), pp. 206–208; Caroline Moorehead, *The Lost Treasures of Troy* (London: Phoenix Giants, 1995), pp. 288–290.

7. Konstantin Akinsha and Grigorii Kozlov, "Restitutsiia: Mezhdu mifami i katalogami," *Itogi*, May 14, 1996, pp. 63–65. Suzanne Massie (*Pavlovsk*, pp. 293–308) chronicles how the curator of Pavlovsk, Anatolii Kuchumov, worked alone to find and retrieve items taken from the Leningrad palaces.

8. Akinsha and Kozlov, *Beautiful Loot*, pp. 181–185.

9. Ibid., pp. 195–196.

10. Ibid., pp. 203–216, 222–223.

11. Evgenii Kuz'min, "Taina tserkvi v Uzkom," *Literaturnaia gazeta*, Sept. 18, 1990, p. 10; Savelii Iamshchikov, "Vozvrashchat' ili ne vozvrashchat'?" *Nezavisimaia gazeta*, Apr. 21, 1994, pp. 1, 3; Akinsha and Kozlov, *Beautiful Loot*, pp. 243–246.

12. Article 16 of the Treaty Between the Federal Republic of Germany and the Union of Soviet Socialist Republics on Good Neighborliness, Partnership, and Cooperation is reprinted in *The Spoils of War: World War II and Its Aftermath: The Loss, Reappearance, and Recovery of Cultural Property*, ed. Elizabeth Simpson (New York: Harry N. Abrams, 1997), pp. 304–306; quotation, p. 305. Yeltsin is cited in Akinsha and Kozlov, *Beautiful Loot*, p. 244.

13. Aleksei Rastorguev, "Trofei 2-i mirovoi voiny v Sovetskom Soiuze," *Russkaia mysl'* (Paris), Jan. 18, 1991; Konstantin Akinsha and Grigorii Kozlov, "Spoils of War: The Soviet Union's Hidden Art Treasures," *Artnews*, April 1991, pp. 130–141.

14. Viktor Remizov, "Shedevry s grifom 'sekretno,'" *Izvestiia*, Apr. 8, 1991, p. 3; Konstantin Akinsha, "A Soviet-German Exchange of War Treasures?" *Artnews*, May 1991, pp. 137–139.

15. Aleksei Rastorguev, "Voennoplennoe iskusstvo," *Literaturnaia gazeta*, June 26, 1991, p. 8.

16. Antonova cited in Akinsha and Kozlov, *Beautiful Loot*, p. 235; S. Maslov, "Molchanie—zoloto: K tomu zhe Troianskoe," *Komsomol'skaia pravda*, Oct. 30, 1991, p. 4.

17. Akinsha and Kozlov, *Beautiful Loot*, p. 237; Alexey Rastorguev, "A Little Glasnost, but No Action," *Daily Telegraph* (London), Oct. 28, 1991, p. 14.

18. Gubenko cited in Eleanor Randolph, "The Soviet Stonewall on Nazi Art," *Washington Post*, Oct. 26, 1991, p. D1. See also Helen Womack, "Moscow Silent on Fate of Art Treasures," *Independent* (London), Oct. 26, 1991, p. 8.

19. Akinsha cited in Pavel Kriuchkov, "Proizvedeniia iskusstva: Granitsy i dolgi," *Nezavisimaia gazeta*, Feb. 19, 1992, p. 6.

20. Kuz'min, "Taina tserkvi v Uzkom."

21. Rastorguev, "Voennoplennoe iskusstvo."

22. E. Maksimova, "Arkhivy frantsuzkoi razvedki skryvali na Leningradskom shosse," *Izvestiia*, Oct. 8, 1991, p. 8.

23. M. Murzina, "Schet pred'iavliut iskusstvovedy," *Izvestiia*, Nov. 7, 1991, p. 4. See also the opinions of Dmitrii Likhachev and B. Ugarov, president of the USSR Academy of Arts, in the commentary to G. Vzdornov, "Skol'ko stoit bestsennoe?" *Izvestiia*, May 14, 1991, p. 8.

24. Savelii Iamshchikov, "Khranit' vechno . . . chtoby pogubit'," *Izvestiia*, Apr. 11, 1991, p. 3.

25. Kuz'min, "Taina tserkvi v Uzkom."

26. Cited in Jamie Gambrell, "Displaced Art," *Art in America*, September 1995, p. 94.

27. Mikhail Shvidkoi, "Boi s ten'iu," *Nezavisimaia gazeta*, May 6, 1994, p. 5; Sergei Martynov, "Trofeinye knigi: Zapozdaloe vozvrashchenie dolgov," ibid., Nov. 17, 1992, p. 6; Savelii Iamshchikov, "Problemu khudozhestvennykh trofeev ne mogut reshat' politiki," ibid., July 1, 1994, p. 2.

28. Vitalii Kolbasiuk, "Rossiia otdaet Germanii Gotskuiu biblioteku," *Nezavisimaia gazeta*, Mar. 24, 1994, pp. 1, 3. Ironically, Hungary faces political divisions over what to do with art left for safekeeping in national museums by Jews who fled German occupation. See Judith H. Dobrzynski, "Claims for Art Collection Pose a Challenge to Hungary," *New York Times*, July 7, 1998, pp. E1, 7.

29. Andrei Kovalev, "Sekretnoe oruzhie Stalina," *Nezavisimaia gazeta*, July 28, 1992, p. 7; for another protest against "commercial" exchanges, see G. Vzdornov in Anton Zverev, "Kuda izchezaiut trofeinye shedevry?" *Izvestiia*, Jan. 9, 1992, p. 7.

30. Iamschikov, "Vozvrashchat' ili ne vozvrashchat'?"

31. The treaty is reproduced in Simpson, *Spoils of War*, p. 307.

32. Vitalii Kolbasiuk, "Troianskii kon' ministra kultury," *Nezavisimaia gazeta*, June 24, 1993, p. 2; Aleksandr Polotskii, "Storony 'ochen' udovletvoreny,' " ibid., Feb. 13, 1993, p. 1; Dmitrii Gornostaev, "Shedevry nakhodiat svoikh khozaev," ibid., May 26, 1993, p. 2.

33. Iamshchikov, "Problemu khudozhestvennykh trofeev"; Aleksei Rastorguev, "Zoloto Shlimana naideno," *Nezavisimaia gazeta*, Aug. 4, 1993, pp. 1, 7; Iurii Kovalenko and Ella Maksimova, "Skandal, ne dostoinyi Rossii," *Izvestiia*, Sept. 8, 1994, p. 5; Viktor Litovkin, "Trofeinoe iskusstvo vernetsia v Bremen," *Izvestiia*, Feb. 24, 1993, p. 7. See also Patricia

Kennedy Grimsted, " 'Trophy' Archives and Non-Restitution: Russia's Cultural 'Cold War' with the European Community," *Problems of Post-Communism* 45, no. 3 (May/June 1998): 8.

34. Stephen White, "Electoral Statistics, 1993–1996," in *Party Politics in Post-Communist Russia*, ed. John Lowenhardt (London: Frank Cass, 1998), p. 265; Petr Zhuravlev, "Usluzhlivost' Minkul'tury nastorozhila senatorov," *Segodnia*, June 2, 1994, p. 2; Konstantin Akinsha and Grigorii Kozlov, "To Return or Not to Return," *Artnews*, October 1994, pp. 154–159.

35. Debate of May 20 reproduced in *Gosudarstvennaia Duma: Stenogramma zasedanii* (hereafter *GD*), 11 vols. (Moscow: Respublika, 1995), 5: 455–472; speeches by E. I. Sidorov and E. S. Krasnitskii (KPRF), pp. 469–472.

36. The 1994 draft is reprinted in V. M. Teteriatnikov, *Problema kul'turnykh tsennostei, peremeshchennykh v rezul'tate vtoroi mirovoi voiny* (Moscow: Obozrevatel', 1996), pp. 86–95; May 1996, July 1996, and March 1997 drafts are in the author's archive.

37. The alternative draft is reproduced in Teteriatnikov, *Problema*, pp. 96–105.

38. Ibid. See also "O prave sobstvennosti na kul'turnye tsennosti, peremeshchennye na territoriiu Rossiskoi Federatsii v rezul'tate vtoroi mirovoi voiny: O Vyvoze i vvoze kul'turnykh tsennostei," *Dumskii vestnik*, no. 7, 1995, pp. 43–53.

39. Petr Zhuravlev, "Problemu peremeshchennykh tsennostei Duma poka reshit' ne smogla," *Segodnia*, June 8, 1995, p. 2; Emina Kuzmina, "Politikanstvo i patriotizm," *Nezavisimaia gazeta*, Nov. 12, 1996, p. 5; Liudmila Lunina, "Sovetskie vlasti ne planirovali tselenapravlennogo grabezha," *Segodnia*, July 12, 1995, p. 10.

40. "Popravki k proektu federal'nogo zakona 'O kul'turnykh tsennostiakh peremeshchennykh v soiuz SSR v rezul'tate Vtoroi mirovoi voiny i nakhodiashchikhsia na territorii Rossiiskoi Federatsii,' " author's archive.

41. Aleksandr Sevast'ianov, "Tret'e ograblenie Rossii," *Nezavisimaia gazeta*, May 6, 1994, p. 5; Irina Antonova, commentary on Valerii Kulishov, "Dyshlo vmesto zakona," ibid., Apr. 4, 1997, p. 7; Mark Boguslavskii, "Legal Aspects of the Russian Position in Regard to the Return of Cultural Property in Russia," in Simpson, *Spoils of War*, pp. 186–190; Lunina, "Sovetskie vlasti."

42. Nikolai Nikandrov, "The Transfer of the Contents of German Repositories into the Custody of the USSR," in Simpson, *Spoils of War*, p. 120.

43. Vladimir Vishniakov, "Krov' i zoloto," *Pravda*, May 16, 1995, pp. 1, 4.

44. V. N. Maksimov in *GD*, biulleten' no. 74 (Feb. 5, 1997), p. 19; M. V. Seslavinskii and V. G. Vishniakov, ibid., biulleten' no. 27 (May 17, 1996), pp. 35–36.

45. Rosalind Gray, "Pushkin Exhibit Counters German Claims," *Moscow Times*, May 11, 1995; Irina Antonova, "My nikomu nichego ne

dolzhny," *Nezavisimaia gazeta*, May 6, 1994, p. 4; Andrei Chegodaev, "Pravda o trofeinykh tsennostiakh," *Kul'tura*, Nov. 30, 1991, p. 14.

46. Piotrovskii quoted in Jean MacKenzie, " 'Trophy Art' Debut Delayed," *Moscow Times*, Mar. 31, 1995, and in "Hermitage Trophies to Set Art World Afire," ibid., Oct. 19, 1994; Mikhail Piotrovsky, "Preface," in Albert Kostenevich, *Hidden Treasures Revealed: Impressionist Masterpieces and Other Important French Paintings Preserved by the State Hermitage Museum, St. Petersburg*, trans. Elena Kolesnikova and Catherine A. Fitzpatrick (New York: Harry N. Abrams, 1995), p. 7.

47. Kostenevich, *Hidden Treasures*, p. 12.

48. Aleksandr Sevast'ianov, "Moral' buivola," *Nezavismaia gazeta* (book review supplement), Feb. 20, 1997, p. 3; Gubenko et al. cited in Konstantin Akinsha, "The Turmoil over Soviet War Treasures," *Artnews*, December 1991, pp. 110–115. See also Vladimir Teteriatnikov, "Kto komu dolzhen?" *Zavtra*, May 17, 1996, p. 8.

49. E. A. Stroev and G. V. Kulik in *GD*, biulleten' no. 108 (June 7, 1995), pp. 37–38, 40–42; Stroev in *Sovet Federatsii Federal'nogo sobraniia*, biulleten' no. 3 (Mar. 23, 1995), p. 278; Grigorii Zaslavskii, "Ne 'krasnyi,' a spravedlivyi," *Nezavisimaia gazeta*, Feb. 26, 1997, p. 1; Valery Koulichkov, "The History of the Soviet Repositories and Their Contents," in Simpson, *Spoils of War*, p. 173. For a claim that Germans never returned any cultural objects, see Vladimir Vishniakov, " 'Logika mira' sulit dividendy?" *Pravda*, May 15, 1996, p. 4. Regarding items returned to the Soviet Union, see Grimsted, " 'Trophy' Archives," p. 13.

50. Sevast'ianov, "Tret'e ograblenie."

51. Vladimir Teteriatnikov, "Pochemu lukavit deputat," *Pravda*, June 23, 1995, p. 2, and "Proshchanie s shedevrami," *Pravda*, June 11, 1994, p. 1.

52. Stroev in *Sovet Federatsii Federal'nogo sobraniia*, biulleten' no. 3 (Mar. 23, 1995), p. 279.

53. Aleksandr Sevast'ianov, "Bol'she, chem trofei," *Nezavisimaia gazeta*, Sept. 14, 1996, p. 6; Gubenko in *GD*, biulleten' no. 89 (Apr. 4, 1997), p. 16, quotation p. 18.

54. Mark Boguslavskii, "S tochki zreniia prava," *Itogi*, May 14, 1996, p. 67; Vasilii Fartyshev, "Taina 'Gotskoi biblioteki,' " *Pravda*, May 11, 1994, pp. 1, 3.

55. Kostenevich, *Hidden Treasures Revealed*, pp. 10–11; MacKenzie, " 'Trophy Art' Debut."

56. Teteriatnikov, *Problema*, pp. 82–83. Conservative Communists also accused other former Soviet republics that returned trophies of selling out their principles. See, for instance, Mark Nikiforov, "Nashe vam s knizhechkoi . . . ," *Pravda-5*, Nov. 2, 1996, p. 3.

57. *GD*, biulleten' no. 27 (May 17, 1996), p. 32.

58. Savelii Iamshchikov, "My vse gliadim v napoleony," *Nezavisimaia gazeta*, May 6, 1994, p. 5.

59. "Arkhivisti protiv politikov" (interview with Mikhail Shvidkoi), *Itogi*, May 14, 1996, pp. 68–69; Evgenii Sidorov, "Bol'shoe iskusstvo kak bol'shaia politika," *Izvestiia*, May 7, 1994, p. 5.

60. Mikhail Shvidkoi, "V nachale byla voina: A potom uzhe voznikla problema restitutsii," *Nezavisimaia gazeta*, May 8, 1996, p. 2; Shvidkoi, "Russian Cultural Losses during World War II," in Simpson, *Spoils of War*, p. 67.

61. Shvidkoi, "V nachale byla voina."

62. "Arkhivisti protiv politikov."

63. Akinsha and Kozlov, "Restitutsiia."

64. Dmitry Zaks, "Court Rules against Yeltsin on Trophy Art," *Moscow Times*, Apr. 7, 1998; Konsantin Akinsha and Grigorii Kozlov, "Russian Deposits: No Return?" *Artnews*, June 1998, p. 62; Konstantin Katanian, "Spor mezhdu vetviami vlasti razreshit sud," *Nezavisimaia gazeta*, Jan. 24, 1998, p. 3; Oksana Yablokova, "Court Finds 'Trophy Art' Nuances," *Moscow Times*, July 21, 1999, pp. 1–2.

65. Dina Goder, "Milyi chelovek v bol'shom kabinete," *Itogi*, Aug. 18, 1998, p. 70.

66. Kulishov, "Dyshlo vmesto zakona."

67. Carol Duncan, *Civilizing Rituals: Inside Public Art Museums* (London: Routledge, 1995), pp. 22–27.

Chapter 5. Recasting the Commemorative Calendar

1. See, for instance, letter from E. Grishina, *Ogonek*, no. 48, 1991, p. 7.

2. "Zhizn' vechnyi prazdnik," *Itogi*, Oct. 6, 1998, p. 5. Christel Lane defines commemorative rites as those that "present the past to the present and justify and strengthen the one by reference to the other": *The Rites of Rulers: Ritual in Industrial Society—The Soviet Case* (Cambridge: Cambridge University Press, 1981), p. 153.

3. David Cressy, *Bonfires and Bells: National Memory and the Protestant Calendar in Elizabethan and Stuart England* (Berkeley: University of California Press, 1989), p. xi.

4. Susan G. Davis, *Parades and Power: Street Theatre in Nineteenth-Century Philadelphia* (Philadelphia: Temple University Press, 1986), p. 9.

5. Christopher A. P. Binns, "The Changing Face of Power: Revolution and Accommodation in the Development of the Soviet Ceremonial System," pt. 1, *Man*, no. 14, 1979, p. 588.

6. On holidays and memory, see Catherine Wanner, *Burden of Dreams: History and Identity in Post-Soviet Ukraine* (University Park: Pennsylvania State University Press, 1998), p. 142.

7. Aleksei Portanskii, " 'Po sluchaiu natsional'nogo prazdnika . . . ': S chem nas budut pozdravliat' 7 noiabria?" *Izvestiia*, Sept. 19, 1991, p. 1.

8. James von Geldern, *Bolshevik Festivals, 1917–1920* (Berkeley: University of California Press, 1993), p. 43. See also Richard Stites, "The Origins of Soviet Ritual Style: Symbol and Festival in the Russian Revolution,"

in *Symbols of Power*, ed. Claes Arvidsson and Lars Erik Blomqvist, (Stockholm: Almqvist & Wiksell, 1987), pp. 23–42.

9. Von Geldern, *Bolshevik Festivals*, p. 209.

10. Lane, *Rites of Rulers*, pp. 25–26, 188. On the role of rituals, see also Robert A. Schneider, *The Ceremonial City: Toulouse Observed, 1738–1780* (Princeton: Princeton University Press, 1995), p. 10.

11. "Ot Oktiabr'skoi do Kremlia," *Pravda*, Nov. 9, 1991, p. 1; Iulii Lebedev, "Kommunisty v oppozitsii: Pervaia massovaia demonstratsiia v Moskve," *Nezavisimaia gazeta*, Nov. 9, 1991, p. 2.

12. Nikolai Ul'ianov and Ivan Rodin, "Demokraty proveli traurnuiu tseremoniiu," *Nezavisimaia gazeta*, Nov. 9, 1991, p. 1; "Kakie budni, takie i prazdniki," *Izvestiia*, Nov. 9, 1991, p. 1; Andrei Zhdankin, "Trudnoe proshchanie s oktiabrem," *Rossiiskaia gazeta*, Nov. 9, 1991, p. 1; Boris Khodorovskii, " 'Vivat, Sankt-Peterburg!' Pod etim devizom prazdnoval gorod na Neve," *Nezavisimaia gazeta*, Nov. 9, 1991, p. 2.

13. Evgenii Krasnikov, "Kommunisticheskii prazdnik v moskve proshel spokoino," *Nezavisimaia gazeta*, Nov. 11, 1992, p. 1.

14. "Liudei teper' ne stroiat v prazdnichnye kolonny: No Oktiabr' s narodom," *Pravda*, Nov. 11, 1992, p. 1; Aleksandr Cherniak, "Revoliutsiia sovershilas'!" ibid., Nov. 7, 1992, pp. 1–2.

15. Viktor Trushkov, "Sotsializm vyderzhal ekzamen istorii," *Pravda*, Nov. 6, 1992, pp. 1–2.

16. In 1993, despite a ban on public gatherings in Moscow in the wake of the October events, some 3,000 Communists gathered just outside the city limits to mark their holiday.

17. Iulii Lebedev, "Demokraty opiat' kritikovali Lenina," *Nezavisimaia gazeta*, Nov. 7, 1994, p. 1; Viktor Khamraev, "Oppozitsiia predlagaet novuiu revoliutsiiu v kratchaishie sroki," *Segodnia*, Nov. 9, 1994, p. 2; Jean MacKenzie, "10,000 Rally to Mark 1917 Revolution," *Moscow Times*, Nov. 9, 1995; Iurii Belkin, "Deviz prazdnichnykh kolonn: Trud, narodovlastie, sotsializm!" *Pravda Rossii*, Nov. 9, 1995, p. 1; Patrick Henry, "Reds Rally for a Lost Holiday," *Moscow Times*, November 10, 1996; Valeria Korchagina, "Apathy Marks Revolution's 80th Anniversary," *Moscow Times*, Nov. 11, 1997, p. 5.

18. Viktor Trushkov, "Nasledie na veka: Razmyshleniia o budniakh nakanune prazdnika," *Pravda Rossii*, Nov. 6, 1996, pp. 1–2; Boris Slavin, "Oshibka istorii ili proryv v budushchee," *Pravda*, Nov. 12, 1996, pp. 1–2.

19. Vitalii Marsov, "Krasno-beloe koleso Rossiiskoi istorii: 7 noiabria—obychnyi prazdnichnyi den' otechestvennogo kalendaria," *Nezavisimaia gazeta*, Nov. 5, 1995, p. 1.

20. "O dne soglasiia i primireniia," *Rossiiskaia gazeta*, Nov. 10, 1996, p. 2.

21. Sergei Ptichkin, "Togda vystoiali: Vydiuzhim i seichas," *Rossiiskaia gazeta*, suppl., Nov. 2–10, 1996, p. III.

22. Titus Sovetolog 16-i [Vitalii Tret'iakov], "O protsesse soglasiia," *Nezavisimaia gazeta*, Nov. 11, 1996, p. 1.

23. Ziuganov cited in Lee Hockstader, "Yeltsin Finds New Use for Old

Holiday," *Washington Post*, Nov. 8, 1996, p. A21; "Den' 7 noiabria, kak i Den' Pobedy, po pravu stal gosudarstvennym prazdnikom nashei velikoi Rodiny," *Pravda*, Nov. 6, 1996, p. 1.

24. On the cult of World War II in the USSR, see Nina Tumarkin, *The Living and the Dead: The Rise and Fall of the Cult of World War II in Russia* (New York: Basic Books, 1994).

25. *Pravda*, May 9, 1991, in *Federal Broadcast Information Service Daily Report* (hereafter *FBIS-SOV*), May 9, 1991, p. 19.

26. Vitalii Tret'iakov, "Den' Pobedy: Den' radosti, skorbi i voprosov, na kotorye net otveta," *Nezavisimaia gazeta*, May 7, 1991, p. 1 (emphasis added); Pavel Gutionov, "Sol' i rany," *Izvestiia*, May 8, 1991, p. 1.

27. *Pravda*, May 7, 1991, in *FBIS-SOV*, May 8, 1991, pp. 27–28.

28. Aleksei Tarasov, "Dve zhizni Gennadiia Demenchuka," *Izvestiia*, May 9, 1992, p. 6. For stories challenging old myths, see Nikolai Burbyga and Valerii Rudnev, "Iapontsy v SSSR ne vtorgalis', no v Russkom plenu byli," ibid., May 7, 1992, p. 8; Boris Slavinskii, "Sovetskii desant na Khokkaido i Iuzhnye Kurily: Mify i deistvitel'nost'," ibid., May 12, 1992, p. 6; Anatolii Chernev, "Lichnye dela trekh Marshalov," ibid., May 8, 1992, p. 3.

29. ITAR-TASS and Interfax, May 9, 1992, in *FBIS-SOV*, May 8, 1992, p. 24.

30. Nikolai Krivomazov, "Ne zabyvai, malysh, pobedili, vse-taki my!" *Pravda*, May 13, 1992, p. 1; Viktor Baranets, Aleksei Golovenko, and Viktor Kharlamov, "Front i tyl srazhalis' za stranu, kotoroi bol'she net . . . ," ibid., pp. 1–2; "My slyshim vas, frontoviki," ibid., May 9, 1992, p. 1.

31. Viktor Kozhemiako, "Eto ona, nasha Zoia!" *Pravda*, May 7, 1992, p. 4; Kharlamov, "Front i tyl"; "My slyshem vas, frontoviki."

32. Nikolai Ul'ianov, "Prazdnik," *Nezavisimaia gazeta*, May 12, 1993, p. 1; ITAR-TASS, May 9, 1993, in *FBIS-SOV*, May 10, 1993, p. 20; Irina Kretova et al., "Mai: Den' Pobedy," *Rossiiskaia gazeta*, May 12, 1993, p. 1.

33. Inna Komarova, "Oppozitsiia opiat' vyhodit iz okopov," *Kuranty*, May 11, 1994, p. 2; Russian Television, *Vesti*, May 9, 1993, in *FBIS-SOV*, May 10, 1993, pp. 19–20; Ekaterina Deinego, Elena Chepkasova, Dmitrii Donskoi, and Vladimir Svartsevich, "Den' Pobedy kazhdyi otmetil po-svoemu," *Nezavisimaia gazeta*, May 11, 1994, p. 1.

34. Viola Egikova, "Skorb' i radost' ne stroiat v sherengi," *Moskovskaia pravda*, May 8, 1993, p. 1.

35. "Pobediteli i provokatory—po raznye storony barrikad," *Kuranty*, May 8, 1993, p. 5.

36. Quoted in Lee Hockstader, "Politics in the Aftermyth of War," *Washington Post*, May 10, 1996, p. A32.

37. Vasilii Kononenko, "V svoikh vystuplenniiakh v dni prazdnovaniia 50-letiia pobedy B. El'tsin nameren izbezhat' mentorstva i sensatsii," *Izvestiia*, May 6, 1995, p. 2; Moscow Russian Television, May 8, 1995, in *FBIS-SOV*, May 9, 1995, pp. 1–4; Evgenii Aleksandrov, "Nastoiashchii prazdnik ne otmenit nikto: 9 maia—Den' Pobedy," *Nezavisimaia gazeta*,

May 7, 1994, p. 1; Otto Latsis, "My ne zabudem, kto bral Berlin, dazhe esli komu-to ne khochetsia ob etom vspominat'," *Izvestiia*, May 7, 1994, p. 1.

38. Evgenii Krasnikov, "Oppozitsiia," *Nezavisimaia gazeta*, May 11, 1995, p. 1.

39. Boris Slavin and Valentina Nikiforova, "Pobeda rvet gromadu let, shagaia cherez golovy pravitel'stv," *Pravda*, May 11, 1995, p. 1; *Ekho Moskvy*, May 9, 1995, and ITAR- TASS, in *FBIS-SOV*, May 9, 1995, pp. 21–22; Gennadii Ziuganov, "Vash podvig bessmerten," *Sovetskaia Rossiia*, May 8, 1997, p. 1.

40. "Skol'ko let svobodnoi Rossii?" *Rossiiskaia gazeta*, June 10, 1995, p. 4.

41. "Komu den' svetlyi, komu—chernyi," *Rossiiskaia gazeta*, June 12, 1992, p. 1; "Spasut svobodnuiu Rossiiu" (interview with Boris Yeltsin), *Izvestiia*, June 11, 1992, pp. 1, 3.

42. Robert Minasov, "Prazdnik, kotoryi budet s nami," *Rossiiskaia gazeta*, June 11, 1992, p. 1; Viktor Trushkov, "Tak vyrastaiut . . . anekdoty," *Pravda*, June 15, 1993, p. 2.

43. "1990–1992-i: Sobytiia v fotodokumentakh," *Rossiiskaia gazeta*, June 12, 1992, pp. 1–5; Inna Murav'eva, "Tiazhelo narodu—tiazhelo Prezidentu," ibid., pp. 1–2.

44. Liudmila Dianova and Evgeniia Pishchikova, "Kazhdyi vybiraet svobodu: Po sebe," *Rossiiskaia gazeta*, June 11, 1993, pp. 1, 2, 4; "Shest' let: Svobody ne vidat'," *Moskovskii komsomolets*, June 11, 1997, p. 1.

45. Vitalii Tret'iakov, "Zavtra—den' nezavisimosti Rossii: Nepravil'nyi prazdnik s nepravil'nym nazvaniem," *Nezavisimaia gazeta*, June 11, 1994, p. 1. For the continuation of this theme, see Sergei Mulin, "Semiletka Rossiiskoi vol'nitsy," ibid., June 14, 1997, p. 2.

46. Boris Pugachev, "Ot deklaratsii o suverenitete do voiny konstitutsii," *Rossiiskaia gazeta*, June 11, 1993, pp. 1–2; "Iubilei nezavisimosti vlasti ot naroda," *Pravda*, June 11, 1994, p. 1; Shod Muladzhanov, "Ten' nezavisimosti," *Moskovskaia pravda*, June 11, 1997, p. 1; "Pervaia Rossiiskaia piatiletiia: Postroili tol'ko pervyi etazh, a krysha uzhe poekhala," *Moskovskii komsomolets*, June 10, 1995, p. 3.

47. Quoted in Ivan Boltovskii, "Prazdnik chuzhoi ulitsy," *Pravda*, June 15, 1994, p. 1.

48. Ruslan Armeev, "Glavnyi prazdnik—12 iiunia? . . ." *Izvestiia*, June 11, 1994, p. 2; Aleksei Portanskii, "Inostrannym diplomatam razreshili ne rabotat' v ponedelnik," ibid.

49. Mulin, "Semiletka Rossiiskoi vol'nitsy"; Iurii Aidinov, "Nash put' ne khudshii: Proiti by," *Vecherniaia Moskva*, June 12, 1997, p. 1; S. R., "V Moskve opiat' vyveshivaiut flagi, no ne vse znaiut zachem," *Moskovskii komsomolets*, June 11, 1995, p. 1.

50. "Spasut svobodnuiu Rossiiu"; "Idem svoim putem" (interview with Sergei Filatov), *Rossiiskaia gazeta*, June 8, 1995, pp. 1–2.

51. An exception was Mikhail Pozdniaev, who urged people to take consolation in the fact that whereas old holidays "marked what was, the new

[mark] what perhaps someday will be": "Den' nezavisimosti ot kogo?" *Obshchaia gazeta,* June 11–18, 1997, p. 1.

52. "Rossiia obiazatel'no vozroditsia! Obrashchenie Prezidenta k Rossiianam," *Rossiiskaia gazeta,* June 14, 1997, p. 1.

53. Jean MacKenzie, "Festivities Set for Independence Day," *Moscow Times,* June 11, 1994; Sophia Coudenhove, "Independence Day: Muted Celebration," ibid., June 14, 1995; Sergei Karkhanin, "Vivat-nezavisimost'!" *Rossiiskaia gazeta,* June 7, 1996, p. 2; "Rossiia—nash dom," *Rossiiskaia gazeta,* suppl., June 14, 1997, p. I.

54. Sergei Chugaev, "V Rossii mozhet byt' vozrozhdena traditsiia provedenniia voennykh paradov," *Izvestiia,* Mar. 31, 1998, p. 2; *Rossiiskaia gazeta,* June 10, 1995, p. 1.

55. Ol'ga Churakova, "Den' nezavisimosti otmechali shiroko," *Nezavisimaia gazeta,* June 14, 1996, p. 2.

56. Viktor Bondarev, "Rossiiskii prezident, kotorogo my ne znali," *Kuranty,* June 11, 1994, p. 3; *Kuranty,* June 11, 1993, p. 1.

57. Vladimir Kuz'mintsev, "U naroda otniali prazdnik," *Rossiiskaia gazeta,* Dec. 10, 1994, p. 1.

58. For a variety of opinions, mostly regarding the constitution's lack of influence at present, see "Primaia rech'," *Kommersant-Daily,* Dec. 11, 1997; "U nas est' pravo na zashchitu svoikh prav," *Trud,* Dec. 11, 1997, p. 6; "Opros AiF," *Argumenty i fakty,* no. 50, 1997, p. 1.

59. "Tsivilizovannye ramki svobody" (interview with Boris Yeltsin), *Izvestiia,* Dec. 10, 1994, pp. 1–2; "God pod znakom konstitutsii," *Rossiiskaia gazeta,* Dec. 10, 1994, pp. 1, 5.

60. Viktoriia Molodtsova, "Svoboda—sladkoe slovo: I nosha," *Rossiiskaia gazeta,* Dec. 9, 1995, p. 1; Boris Oleinik in "Opros AiF"; "Boris El'tsin: Sledovat' bukve i dukhu Konstitutsii," *Rossiiskaia gazeta,* Dec. 15, 1998, p. 1.

61. On identity crises, see Wanner, *Burden of Dreams,* p. xxvi.

62. For more details on the Day of Remembrance of Victims of Political Repressions, see Kathleen E. Smith, *Remembering Stalin's Victims: Popular Memory and the End of the USSR* (Ithaca: Cornell University Press, 1996), pp. 160–163.

63. Holidays are often co-opted by new authorities. As the anthropologist Margaret Paxson shows in a fascinating study of Troitsa in a Russian village, Soviet holidays competed with Russian Orthodox ones, but both sometimes lost out to pagan traditions: "The Festival of the Holy Trinity (Troitsa) in Rural Russia: A Case Study in the Symbolic Topography of Memory," *Anthropology of Eastern Europe Review,* November 1998, pp. 53–58.

64. Aleksandr Rudakov, "Paskha stanovitsia obshchenatsional'nym prazdnikom," *Nezavisimaia gazeta,* suppl., Apr. 15, 1998, p. 1.

Chapter 6. Remaking the Capital's Landscape

1. Brian Ladd, *The Ghosts of Berlin: Confronting German History in the Urban Landscape* (Chicago: University of Chicago Press, 1997), pp. 1, 2.

2. Francis X. Clines, "Communist Street Signs in Moscow Go the Way of a Spurned Ideology," *New York Times*, Nov. 6, 1990, p. 4.

3. Between 1990 and 1993 more than 150 Moscow streets changed names, but outside the boulevard ring many Soviet-period names remain. Moscow still has streets named for the Comintern, the Communist Party, and the secret police officials V. R. Menzhinskii and V. S. Abakumov. On the technical difficulties resulting from altering toponyms, see "O vozvrashchenii istoricheskikh naimenovanii, prisvoenii novykh naimeno-vanii i pereimenovaniiakh moskovskikh ulits," *Vestnik merii Moskvy*, no. 24 (December 1994), pp. 14–19.

4. Avner Ben-Amos, "Monuments and Memory in French National-ism," *History & Memory* 5, no. 2 (1993): 53.

5. On the Bolshevik precedent, see John E. Bowlt, "Russian Sculpture and Lenin's Plan of Monumental Propaganda," in *Art and Architecture in the Service of Politics*, ed. Henry F. Millon and Linda Nuchlin, (Cambridge: MIT Press, 1978), pp. 185–188.

6. Iurii Luzhkov, *My deti tvoi, Moskva* (Moscow: Vagrius, 1996), pp. 275–276.

7. Mikhail Yampolsky, "In the Shadow of Monuments: Notes on Icono-clasm and Time," in *Soviet Hieroglyphics: Visual Culture in Late Twenti-eth-Century Russia*, ed. Nancy Condee (Bloomington: Indiana University Press, 1995), pp. 106–107.

8. Jamey Gambrell, "Moscow's Monuments Come Tumbling Down," *Art in America*, October 1991, p. 7.

9. Sergei Panarin, "Delo svobody prazdnik naroda," *Nezavisimaia gazeta*, Sept. 11, 1991, p. 2.

10. Andrei Baiduzhii and Ivan Rodin, "Perestavliaia Lenina," *Nezavisi-maia gazeta*, Nov. 6, 1991, p. 6, and "Vozhd snova pereezhaet v Gorki," *Segodnia*, Aug. 17, 1995, p. 12.

11. Vitaly Komar and Alexander Melamid, "What Is to Be Done with Monumental Propaganda?" in *Monumental Propaganda*, ed. Dore Ashton (New York: Independent Curators, 1994), p. 9.

12. Nina Tumarkin, "Story of a War Memorial," in *World War II and the Soviet People*, ed. John Garrard and Carol Garrard (New York: St. Martin's Press, 1993), p. 126.

13. Sergei Kavtaradze, "Pamiatnik pobedy: Dostoinyi li my ego us-tanovit'?" *Arkhitektura i stroitel'stvo Moskvy*, no. 3, 1989, p. 9; see also Tu-markin, "Story of a War Memorial," pp. 129–132, and Iu. Iziumov, "Vremia pyshnykh monumentov proshlo," *Literaturnaia gazeta*, June 1, 1988, p. 2.

14. Tumarkin, "Story of a War Memorial," pp. 132–141; Mikhail Utkin, "Nakanun vybora?" *Arkhitektura i stroitel'stvo Moskvy*, no. 9, 1989, pp. 10–12. Klykov is cited in Nina Tumarkin, *The Living and the Dead: The Rise and Fall of the Cult of World War II in Russia* (New York: Basic Books, 1994), p. 218.

15. Ella Maksimova, "Na poklonnoi gore otlivaiut v zolote stalinskii mif

o voine," *Izvestiia*, Mar. 25, 1992, p. 3; Stepan Il'in, "Tak chto zhe postroeno na Poklonnoi gore?" *Literaturnaia gazeta*, Aug. 10, 1994, p. 15.

16. "O stroitel'stve v 1993 g. ob'ektov pamiatnika pobedy v velikoi otechestvennoi voine 1941–1945 gg.," *Vestnik merii Moskvy*, no. 7 (April 1993), pp. 8–9; Igor' Nekrasov, "Poslednii pamiatnik sovetskoi monumental'noi propagandy," *Nezavisimaia gazeta*, Apr. 15, 1995, p. 1.

17. "Zmeia nastrugali, kak kolbasu," *Argumenty i fakty*, no. 37, 1995, p. 9; see also Ivan Tarasov, "Uroki Poklonnoi gory," *Nezavisimaia gazeta*, Sept. 12, 1996. The quotation is from E. M. Kukina and R. F. Kozhevnikov, *Rukotvornaia pamiat' Moskvy* (Moscow: Moskovskii rabochii, 1997), p. 170.

18. Robin Wagner-Pacifici and Barry Schwartz, "The Vietnam Veterans Memorial: Commemorating a Difficult Past," *American Journal of Sociology* 97, no. 2 (September 1991): 382.

19. Aleksandr Burtin, "Smena simvolov," *Moskovskie novosti*, June 11–18, 1995, p. 19.

20. Letter from A. Smirnov in "O tom, kakuiu voinu dolzhen uvekovechit' memorial na pokolonnoi gore," *Izvestiia*, May 13, 1992, p. 3.

21. Maksimova, "Na poklonnoi gore"; Il'in, "Tak chto zhe"; Burtin, "Smena simvolov."

22. James Mayo, quoted in Wagner-Pacifici and Schwartz, "Vietnam Veterans Memorial," p. 380.

23. Burtin, "Smena simvolov"; Nikolai Aksenov, "Eshche raz o simvolike memoriala pobedy," *Nezavisimaia gazeta*, May 18, 1996, p. 6.

24. Roza Sergazieva, "Nam nuzhen eshche odin pamiatnik," *Argumenty i fakty*, Moscow section, no. 3, 1998, p. 1.

25. Mariia Chegodaeva, "Ne ugnetaite nas tragizmom," *Moskovskie novosti*, May 26–June 2, 1996, p. 36.

26. See, for instance, "Park uzhasov na poklonnoi gore," *Nezavisimaia gazeta*, Apr. 2, 1996, p. 1; Elena Egorova, " 'Tragediia narodov' perevratilas' v tragediiu Moskvy," *Moskovskii komsomolets*, Aug. 23, 1996, p. 1.

27. Vladimir Budaev, "Pyl' i solntse nad poklonnoi gore," *Nezavisimaia gazeta*, Apr. 27, 1996, p. 2.

28. One report claims that Moscow paid half the costs for the mosque; see Svetlana Sukhova, "Ptitsa schast'ia zavtrashnego dnia," *Segodnia*, July 22, 1997, p. 2; Il'ia Riazantsev, "Memorial'naia mechet' na Poklonnoi gore otkryta," *Nezavisimaia gazeta*, suppl., Sept. 25, 1997, p. 4; Sergei Cherniak-Brodskii, "On prishel dat' nam Toru: Mer Moskvy prevel v vostorge tsvet mirovogo evreistva," *Itogi*, Sept. 8, 1998, pp. 46–47.

29. Grigorii Rezvin, "Novaia moskovskaia arkhitektura," *Kommersant-Daily*, Sept. 9, 1997, p. 5.

30. Iakov Krotov, "Deti podzemel'ia krasiat nebo," *Moskovskie novsosti*, Aug. 13–20, 1995, p. 5; Vladimir Bushin, "Glumlenie na Poklonnoi gore," *Pravda-Piat'*, Oct. 11–18, 1996, p. 2; Cherniak-Brodskii, "On prishel dat' nam Toru."

31. Zurab Tsereteli, "Novomu obshchestvu nuzhny novye obrazy," *Nezavisimaia gazeta*, Aug. 28, 1996, p. 2.

32. See, for instance, Dmitrii Shimanskii, "Tretii rim epokhi raspada," *Nezavisimaia gazeta*, Jan. 24, 1996.

33. Lev Kolodnyi, "Vivat, Petr!" *Moskovskaia pravda*, Oct. 22, 1996, p. 7.

34. Lev Kolodnyi, "Liliputy i gullivery," *Moskovskaia pravda*, June 7, 1997, p. 3. See also Valeria Korchagina, "Protests Slam City Funding for 'Ugly' Tsereteli Creations," *Moscow Times*, Jan. 16, 1997, and "City Commission Rules Peter the Great Can Stay," *Moscow Times*, June 3, 1997, p. 3.

35. Sergei Antonov, "Petra I sobiralis' vzorvat' vo slavu Lenina," *Segodnia*, July 7, 1997, p. 1; "Petr Pervy v vode ne tonet i v ogne ne sgorit," *Kommersant-Daily*, July 8, 1997, p. 1.

36. Ia. E. Brodskii, *Moskva ot A do Ia* (Moscow: Moskovskii rabochii 1994), pp. 92–93, 112.

37. Ella Maksimova, "Kamennoe nashestvie tsarei na Moskvu," *Izvestiia*, Apr. 17, 1996, p. 6; José Alaniz, "Monument to Nicholas II Unveiled," *Moscow Tribune*, May 28, 1996, pp. 1–2; Valeria Korchagina, "Mystery Explosion Dethrones Nicholas," *Moscow Times*, Apr. 2, 1997, pp. 1–2; Julia Solovyova, "Another Statue of Tsar Blown to Bits," *Moscow Times*, Nov. 3, 1998.

38. For evidence from St. Petersburg, see Kira Dolinina, "Tsar i Chizhik—novye figury v peterburgskom panteone," *Kommersant-Daily*, July 6, 1996, p. 16.

39. Aleksei Komech quoted in Maksimova, "Kamennoe nashestvie." See also Oleg Antonov, "Dar ot pravitel'stva," *Nezavisimaia gazeta*, Apr. 25, 1997, p. 7.

40. Chris Bird, "Mask of Sorrow Unveiled in East," *Moscow Tribune*, June 13, 1996, p. 5; Irina Shcherbakova, "Stolitsa Kolymskogo kraia," *Itogi*, June 30, 1996, p. 36.

41. Aleksei Butorov, *Khram Khrista Spasitelia: Istorii stroitel'stvo i razrushenie* (Moscow: Iunyi khudozhnik, 1992), pp. 4–11, 21–26; Franklin Sciacca, "The Iconography of Moscow's Cathedral of Christ the Saviour," paper presented at AATSEEL conference, Toronto, December 1993, p. 8.

42. Butorov, *Khram Khrista Spasitelia*, pp. 13, 34; Irina Ilovaiskaya-Alberti, "Introduction," in *The Destruction of the Church of Christ the Saviour (Samizdat Photographs)* (London: Overseas Publications, 1988), pp. 8–10.

43. E. I. Kirichenko, *Khram Khrista Spasitelia v Moskve* (Moscow: Planeta, 1992), pp. 220, 250; Selim Khan-Magomedov, "K istorii vybora mesta dlia Dvortsa Sovetov," *Arkhitektura i stroitel'stvo Moskvy*, no. 1, 1988, pp. 21–22.

44. For detailed accounts of the creation and destruction of the cathedral, see Kathleen E. Smith, "An Old Cathedral for a New Russia: The Symbolic Politics of the Reconstructed Church of Christ the Saviour," *Religion, State and Society* 25, no. 2 (1997): 164–166; and Andrew Gentes, "The Life,

Death, and Resurrection of the Cathedral of Christ the Saviour," *History Workshop Journal*, no. 46 (1998), pp. 63–85.

45. Yitzhak M. Brudny, *Reinventing Russia: Russian Nationalism and the Soviet State, 1953–1991* (Cambridge: Harvard University Press, 1998), pp. 45, 67–70, 138–142; Vladimir Soloukhin, *A Time to Gather Stones*, trans. Valerie Z. Nollan (Evanston: Northwestern University Press, 1993), p. 230.

46. Georgii Kokun'ko, " 'Beloe piatno' na Krasnoi ploshchadi," *Arkhitektura i stroitel'stvo Moskvy*, no. 5, 1989, p. 15.

47. V. P. Mokrousov, "Blagoe delo spasitel'no," and Vladimir Potapov, "Narodnaia sviatynia," both in *Khram Khrista Spasitelia: Sozdanie-Razrushenie-Vozrozhdenie* (a special edition of *Pravda*), April 1992, pp. 1, 2.

48. Elena Alekseeva, "Spasitelia simvol nashei very" (interview with V. Mokrousov), *Rus' Derzhavnaia*, no. 5–7, 1996, p. 5; Alla Bossart, "Teatr vremen Luzhkova i Sinoda," *Stolitsa*, no. 2 (Jan. 8, 1995), p. 12.

49. Vladimir Sidorov, "Pamiatnik pobedy-khram," *Literaturnaia Rossiia*, no. 14, 1989, p. 7; "Pod kliuch? Net, pod krest!" (interview with Appolos F. Ivanov), *Literaturnaia Rossiia*, no. 38 (Sept. 28, 1989), pp. 10–11; Vladimir Soloukhin, "Eshche raz o vozrozhdenii Khrama Khrista Spasitelia," *Literaturnaia Rossiia*, no. 5 (Feb. 2, 1990), pp. 8–9.

50. Vladimir Zamanskii, "Eto Khram nashego pokoianie," *Rus' Derzhavnaia*, no. 5–7, 1996, p. 4. "Pod kliuch? Net, pod krest!"; letter from S. Iu. Rybas in *Khram Khrista Spasitelia*, (Moscow: Stolitsa, 1996) p. 240; Alekseeva, "Spasitelia simvol nashei very."

51. Iu. Borisov, "Khramu byt'!" in *Khram Khrista Spasitelia* (Moscow: Stolitsa, 1996), pp. 221–224.

52. For an invaluable and elegant account of conflicts over preservation in one Russian city, see Blair Ruble, *Money Sings: The Changing Politics of Urban Space in Post-Soviet Yaroslavl* (Cambridge: Cambridge University Press, 1995), pp. 76–103.

53. "Khram Khrista Spasitelia budet vosstanovlen uzhe v 1997 godu," *Segodnia*, Apr. 2, 1994, p. 6; "Ob obrazovanii obshchestvennogo nabliudatel'nogo sovete po kontroliu za vossozdaniem Khrama Khrista Spasitelia," *Vestnik Merii Moskvy*, no. 18 (September 1994), pp. 4–6.

54. "O vossozdanii Khrama Khrista Spasitelia v g. Moskve po ul. Volkhonke," *Vestnik Merii Moskvy*, no. 14 (July 1994), pp. 37–39; Chrystia Freeman, "Moscow Puts Its Faith in a Capital Project," *Financial Times*, Aug. 24, 1995, p. 2.

55. Vladimir Gromov, "Pokaianie za schet biudzheta?" *Rossiiskaia gazeta*, Jan. 6, 1995, p. 8; Richard Lein, "Cathedral Reconstruction to Begin in Weekend Ceremony," *Moscow Tribune*, Jan. 6, 1995, p. 17; Natal'ia Olenich, "Aleksandr Livshits: Put' biudzhetnykh ssud slishkom neiasen," *Segodnia*, June 7, 1995, p. 1; Sergei Varshavchik, "Chto khram griadushchii nam gotovit," *Ogonek*, no. 45 (November 1995), pp. 28–29.

56. Quoted in Nikolai Ziat'kov, "Kto stroit nash dom?" *Argumenty i fakty*, no. 34, 1995, p. 3.

57. Luzhkov quoted in "Vo chto by to ni stalo," *Segodnia*, Nov. 18, 1994, p. 6; "Obrashchenie prezidenta Rossiiskoi federatsii k chlenam obshchestvennogo nabliudatel'nogo soveta po vossozdaniiu Khrama Khrista Spasitelia," in *Khram Khrista Spasitelia* (Moscow: Stolitsa, 1996), p. 214.

58. Kavtaradze, "Pamiatnik pobedy."

59. Liudmila Lunina, "Tsentr Novoi Utopii? Snova eshche raz pro vosstanovlenie khrama Khrista Spasitelia," *Segodnia*, Feb. 18, 1995, p. 10; Otto Latsis, "Poddel'naia Rossiia: Ne pomozhet dukhovnomu vozrozhdeniiu obshchestva," *Izvestiia*, Nov. 24, 1994, p. 5; B. Salmanov, "Gosudarstvo ne dolzhno stroit' khramy—eto zabota veruiushchikh," *Izvestiia*, Sept. 24, 1994, p. 4; Viktor Litovkin, "V Khrame Khrista Spasitelia . . . ," *Izvestiia*, July 12, 1995, p. 2.

60. Elena Gureva, "Novaia staraia Moskva: Aleksei Komech: 'My ponimaem gorod fasadno,' " *Itogi*, Oct. 8, 1996, pp. 58–59; Bossart, "Teatr vremen Luzhkova," p. 11; "Stolichnaia duma razbiraetsia s khramom," *Segodnia*, June 28, 1995, p. 12.

61. Aleksandra Tolstikhina and Mikhail Tolpegin, "Khram Khrista Spasitelia nachal razrushat'sia," *Segodnia*, Dec. 10, 1998, p. 1; Diakon Andrei Kuraev, *Razmyshleniia pravoslavnogo pragmatika o tom, nado li stroit' Khram Khrista Spasitelia* (Moscow: Otdel religioznogo obrazovaniia i katekhizatsii Moskovskogo Patriarkhata, 1995), p. 4.

62. Grigorii Rezvin, "Post-modernizm kak 'kultura dva,' " *Nezavisimaia gazeta*, Jan. 25, 1997, p. 7. See also Natalya Shulyakovskaya, "Defining the Moscow Style," *Moscow Times*, May 21, 1998.

63. Valeria Korchagina, "Sculptor Plans Historical Decor for Manezh," *Moscow Times*, Nov. 23, 1996; Svetlana Sukhova, "Kopaite, Shura, kopaite: Vam zachetsia," *Segodnia*, June 20, 1997; Sukhova, "Popast' iz XVII veka v XIX mozhno na lifte," *Segodnia*, Sept. 10, 1997.

64. For instance, the centerpiece of festivities for Moscow's 850th anniversary in 1997—for which Luzhkov turned the whole city into a stage—was a folk opera on Red Square.

65. Rustam Rakhmatullin, "Vid monumental'noi peremeny," *Nezavisimaia gazeta*, Sept. 4, 1997, p. 7.

66. David Lowenthal, *Possessed by the Past: The Heritage Crusade and the Spoils of History* (New York: Free Press, 1996), pp. x, 128.

67. Appeal from Archimandrate Petr (Poliakov), president of the Fund for Financial Support of the Re-creation of the Cathedral of Christ the Saviour, in *Khram Khrista Spasitelia*, (Moscow: Stolitsa, 1996), p. 252.

68. Dmitrii Shvidkovskii, "Samoe pravdivoe iz iskusstv," *Itogi*, June 18, 1996, p. 75.

69. Andrei Kolesnikov, "Moskovskii upravdom," *Novoe vremia*, nos. 18–19, 1996, p. 17.

70. Nikolai Troitskii, "Nizenkii, v kepke, no ne Lenin," *Itogi*, June 11, 1996, p. 34.

Chapter 7. Campaigning on the Past

1. David I. Kertzer, *Politics and Symbols: The Italian Communist Party and the Fall of Communism* (New Haven: Yale University Press, 1996), pp. 3–4.

2. I do not aspire to offer a methodologically sophisticated analysis of the effectiveness of campaign rhetoric on voter behavior. Instead, I tackle the less rigorous but so far neglected work of identifying and interpreting symbolic and historical representations. For similar attempts to learn from the use of historical and cultural referents in campaign propaganda in a newly democratized nation, see Daina Stukuls, "Imagining the Nation: Campaign Posters of the First Postcommunist Elections in Latvia," *East European Politics and Societies* 11, no. 1 (Winter 1997): 131–154; and Eve Bertelsen, "Selling Change: Advertisements for the 1994 South African Election," *African Affairs*, no. 95 (1996), pp. 225–252.

3. Earlier parliamentary elections were rich in illustrations of the use of collective memories, but the overwhelming importance of the presidential race and the small number of serious candidates involved in it allows for treatment of the main tendencies—nationalist communism and liberal reformism—in greater depth. Moreover, the timing of the presidential election—nearly five years after the collapse of Communist rule—also offers a good vantage point for examining the evolution of political strategies toward the national past.

4. An analysis of the campaigns for single-mandate seats would require numerous in-depth case studies to have been conducted at the time of the elections.

5. M. Steven Fish, *Democracy from Scratch: Regime and Opposition in the New Russian Revolution* (Princeton: Princeton University Press, 1995).

6. The ban on the KPRF was lifted Oct. 18, 1993, and *Pravda* was allowed to resume publication Nov. 2. See Joan Barth Urban and Valerii D. Solovei, *Russia's Communists at the Crossroads* (Boulder, Colo.: Westview Press, 1997), p. 106.

7. For instance, My Fatherland featured the singer Iosif Kobzon, the academician Stanislav Shatalin, and the former general Boris Gromov, while the Congress of Russian Societies promoted the former general Aleksandr Lebed, the economist Sergei Glaz'ev, and the politician Iurii Skokov.

8. Christian Democrats in 1995 also used a fish for their logo. They chose a simple line drawing of a fish that is widely recognized as a Christian symbol, whereas Rybkin used a cartoonlike sketch of a cheerful fish in some literature and a realistic-looking silhouette of a fish as his ballot symbol.

9. Strangely enough, Iabloko often used a stylized red circle and green wedge to represent an apple, geometric forms echoing a famous Bolshevik poster that featured a red wedge in a white circle and the slogan "Reds drive a wedge into the Whites."

10. In 1993 the Russia's Choice party had used a stylized representation of the famous Bronze Horseman statue of Peter the Great, though without any elaboration on Peter's Westernizing reforms. Two years later the broader Russia's Democratic Choice coalition had dropped the Bronze Horseman symbol and, although some literature featured a soaring seagull logo, the movement did not supply an official symbol for inclusion on the ballot.

11. Egor Gaidar, *Besedy s izbirateliami* (Moscow: Evraziia, 1995), p. 43.

12. I am grateful to Boris Belenkin of the Interregional Memorial Society, Moscow, and to Elena Strukova of the Historical Library in Moscow for granting me access to their collections of political posters and other campaign ephemera.

13. *OMRI Special Report*, no. 9 (Nov. 28, 1995), by electronic mail.

14. Ironically, only Zhirinovsky attempted to use the image of Andrei Sakharov in a national ad, but his spot claiming the support of Sakharov and other historical figures was banned by the Central Election Committee on the grounds that it was not true. *OMRI Daily Digest*, no. 224 (Nov. 16, 1995) by electronic mail.

15. *Vpered, Rossiia!* (party newspaper), Oct. 25, 1995.

16. *Za nashu Sovetskuiu Rodinu! Predvybornaia platforma Kommunisticheskoi partii Rossiiskoi Federatsii* (Moscow: Informpechat', 1995).

17. Ibid., pp. 3–4, 17.

18. "Imia iz spiska," *Pravda Rossii*, Nov. 2, 1995, p. 1, and Nov. 16, 1995, p. 1.

19. "Za nashu sovetskuiu Rodinu!" *Pravda Rossii*, Nov. 23, 1995, p. 2.

20. The more radical Communist parties did not discuss prerevolutionary history. Having stated that "our flag is red, our symbol is the star with the hammer and sickle," Communists–Working Russia–For the Soviet Union really felt no need for long explanations of who they were or what period they took as their ideal.

21. *Za nashu Sovetskuiu Rodinu!* pp. 8, 17–18.

22. Alena Solntseva, "Kandidat v assortimente: Politicheskii plakat kak indikator politicheskoi zrelosti," *Itogi*, June 11, 1996, p. 70; Yekaterina Yegorova, "Selling Gray Candidates," *Moscow Times*, Dec. 15, 1995.

23. Sergei Parkhomenko, "Fol poslednei nadezhdy," *Segodnia*, Dec. 16, 1995, p. 1. Yeltsin cited in ibid.

24. Stephen White, "Electoral Statistics, 1993–1996," in *Party Politics in Post-Communist Russia*, ed. John Lowenhardt (London: Frank Cass, 1998), pp. 98–127, 265–266.

25. For a succinct and fascinating account of the organization of the Yeltsin campaign, see Michael McFaul, *Russia's 1996 Presidential Election:*

The End of Polarized Politics (Stanford: Hoover Institution Press, 1997), pp. 15–27.

26. Sergei Mulin, "Podrobnosti," *Nezavisimaia gazeta,* Apr. 9, 1996, p. 3; Viacheslav Nikonov quoted in Iurii Aidinov, "El'tsinu ne za chto opravdyvat'sia," *Vecherniaia Moskva,* May 12, 1996, p. 3.

27. Speech of Apr. 9, 1996, in *Obshcherossiiskoe dvizhenie obshchestvennoi poderzhki B. N. El'tsina na vyborakh Prezidenta Rossiiskoi Federatsii* (Mocow: Pressa, 1996), p. 6.

28. On the creation of these ads, see Natal'ia Arkhangel'skaia, "Reklama prezidenta bez prezidenta," *Kommersant-Daily,* May 29, 1996, p. 3.

29. Quoted in Jonas Bernstein, "From Subtle to Strange, Ads Blitz TV," *Moscow Times,* June 14, 1996, p. 2.

30. "Milyi, dorogoi, liubimyi, edinstvennyi," *Izvestiia,* May 23, 1996, p. 2.

31. "Telefon doveriia prezidentu rabotaet," *Izvestiia,* May 31, 1996, p. 2.

32. Grigorii Zaslavskii, "Intelligentnyi reklamnyi biznes," *Nezavisimaia gazeta,* June 8, 1996, p. 6; Elena Dikun, "Letiat pevtsy vo vse kontsy," *Obshchaia gazeta,* May 30–June 5, 1996, p. 8; Irina Petrovskaia, "Golosui ili Khruishei stanesh'!" *Izvestiia,* June 1, 1996, p. 5.

33. "Viktor Astaf'ev: U kommunistov lozungi vsegda byli krasivymi, a dela—chernymi," *Izvestiia,* May 17, 1996, p. 2.

34. I saw this poster and a similar one warning of "red chaos" displayed prominently in shop windows in Moscow and Saratov. In Moscow, at least, city authorities handed them out to shopkeepers, who felt obliged to display them. See Elizabeth Owen, "Shops Get Hard Sell for Yeltsin," *Moscow Times,* June 29, 1996, p. 4.

35. Interview with Filatov in *Vercherniaia Moskva,* June 9, 1996, reproduced in *Ot El'tsina k El'tsinu: Prezidentskaia gonka-96* (Moscow: Terra, 1997), p. 428.

36. Tat'iana Malkina, "Boris El'tsin obeshchaet 'prosto normal'nuiu zhizn','" *Segodnia,* June 1, 1996, p. 1.

37. "Ia uveren v svoei pobede" (interview with Boris Yeltsin), *Delovye liudi,* May 1996, p. 8.

38. *Piat' desiat sem' voprosov izbiratelei prezidentu Rossii* (Moscow, 1996), p. 74.

39. B. El'tsin, "Vmeste—my pobedim!" *Rossiiskaia gazeta,* June 18, 1996, reproduced in *Ot El'tsina, k El'tsinu,* p. 489.

40. The president of NTV, Igor' Malashenko, actually joined the Yeltsin campaign as an adviser. He described the liberal Russian media as being caught in a dilemma: "If we work strictly according to objective, professional, unbiased, nonpartisan rules and tomorrow Ziuganov wins, we'll know we've dug our own graves. If to avoid this we stand on Yeltsin's side and begin to play up to him, then the mass media have been transformed into a propaganda tool": quoted in Irina Petrovskaia, "Predvybornaia lovushka dlia TV," *Izvestiia,* Apr. 19, 1996, p. 6.

41. Alessandra Stanley, "Russia's Press Edits Out a Communist," *New York Times,* Mar. 31, 1996, pp. 1, 4.

42. Sergei Kudriavtsev, "Ne goriui, chto skoro budet konets sveta," *Kommersant-Daily,* June 8, 1996, p. 15.

43. Iurii Luzhkov touted Yeltsin as the sole rebel in the Politburo: *Obshcherossiiskoe dvizhenie,* p. 44.

44. *Piat'desiat sem' voprosov,* pp. 72–73.

45. Leonid Lokotov, "Nagornaia propoved' s Kremlevskogo kholma," *Kommersant-Daily,* June 28, 1996, p. 1.

46. In particular, Yeltsin counted on picking up some of the 15% of voters who had supported Aleksandr Lebed, whom he had just made head of the Security Council.

47. Ziuganov claimed 200 organizations had signed on to the bloc, but closer examination revealed that of the 171 signatures affixed to the coalition charter, 69 belonged to individuals and only 31 were from groups that had registered officially with the Ministry of Justice. See Viktor Khamraev, "Koalitsiiu Ziuganova ulichaiut v pripiskakh," *Segodnia,* May 16, 1996, p. 2.

48. G. A. Ziuganov, "Dlia menia glavnoi partiei iavliaetsia Rossiia," *Pravda Rossii,* Sept. 6, 1995, reprinted in *G. A. Ziuganov i o G. A. Ziuganov,* ed. V. A. Mal'tsev (Perm, 1995), p. 199; and Ziuganov quoted in James P. Scanlan, "The Russian Idea from Dostoevskii to Ziuganov," *Problems of Post-Communism* 43, no. 4 (July/August 1996): 41.

49. My observations supplemented by the Historical Library's collection of election ephemera. Regarding local KPRF activism, see Andrei Aderekhin, "Labinsk protsvetaet, no toskuet o proshlom," *Izvestiia,* June 1, 1996, p. 2; Ekaterina Deeva et al., "Sekret bol'shoi kampanii," *Moskovskii komsomolets,* Apr. 27, 1996, pp. 1, 5.

50. Konstantin Bufeev, "Devat' dovodov k voprosu, pochemu pravoslavomu khristianinu sleduet golosovat' za kommunista Ziuganova," *Pravda-5,* June 7–14, 1996, p. 6.

51. Ziuganov, "Dlia menia glavnoi partiei iavliaetsia Rossiia," p. 200.

52. G. A. Ziuganov, *Ia Russkii po krovi i dukhu* (Moscow: Izbiratel'nyi fond kandidata na dolzhnost' Prezidenta RF G. A. Ziuganova, 1996), pp. 16, 44.

53. "Liudmila Zaitseva: 'Nashe znamia u nas ne otniat', " *Pravda,* June 29, 1996, p. 4.

54. "Dlia menia glavnoi partiei iavliaetsia Rossiia," p. 198; on the links between nationalist and new communist economic theories of a Russian "third way," see Veljko Vujacic, "Gennadiy Zyuganov and the 'Third Road'," *Post-Soviet Affairs* 12, no. 2 (1996): 118–154.

55. G. Ziuganov, "S nami sovest' nashei zemli," *Sovetskaia Rossiia,* May 25, 1996, p. 2.

56. G. A. Ziuganov, "K pravoslavnym liudiam," *Sovetskaia Rossiia,* June 11, 1996, p. 3. On the Orthodox Church's fears of competition from West-

ern religious groups see, for instance, "Net vlasti ne ot boga," ibid., June 20, 1996, p. 5; "Beseda pered vyborami 17 Dekabria 1995 goda," *Antikhrist v Moskve,* no. 2 (Moscow: Obshchestvennyi komitet "Za nravstvennoe vozrozhdenie otechestva," 1996), pp. 61–63.

57. Ziuganov, "Dlia menia glavnoi partiei iavliaetsia Rossiia," p. 200.

58. Excerpts from an interview by Evgenii Kiselev on "Geroi dnia," reprinted as "Ia boius' za Rossiiu," *Sovetskaia Rossiia,* June 13, 1996, p. 3.

59. G. A. Ziuganov, "Rodina vnov' zovet vas zashchishchat' i oberegat' ee," *Sovetskaia Rossiia,* May 30, 1996, p. 3; Oleg Cherkovets, "Chto na serdtse u Novocherkasska?" ibid., June 20, 1996, p. 3; *Itogi,* NTV, June 9, 1996.

60. "Za nashu sovetskuiu rodinu," *Pravda Rossii,* Nov. 23, 1995, p. 1; Gennadii Ziuganov, "My vmeste vozrodim Rossiiu," *Pravda,* July 1, 1996, p. 1; "Ne ver'te," *Sovetskaia Rossiia,* June 14, 1996, p. 8.

61. Ivan Savenko, "Vspomnim vse," *Pravda Rossiia,* May 16, 1996, p. 1.

62. Quoted in Vasilii Ustiuzhanin, "O zvezdakh, o liubvi i prochem," in *G. A. Ziuganov i o G. A. Ziuganove,* p. 274.

63. Rustam Arifdzhanov, "Vstanet li s Gennadiem Ziuganovym Sergii Radonezhskii?" *Izvestiia,* June 13, 1996, p. 1.

64. Interview with Yeltsin in *Rossiiskie vesti,* July 1, 1996, reproduced in *Ot El'tsina k El'tsinu,* p. 543.

65. "Vse vmeste vozrodim rossiiu," *Sovetskaia Rossiia,* July 1, 1996, p. 1.

66. McFaul, *Russia's 1996 Presidential Election,* p. 92.

Chapter 8. Searching for a New Russian Idea

1. "El'tsin o 'nasional'noi idee,' " *Nezavisimaia gazeta,* July 13, 1996, p. 1.

2. Regarding awareness of the need to translate ideas into "a language of images, metaphors," see Aleksandr Rubtsov, "V ozhidanii idei," *Nezavisimaia gazeta,* Nov. 4, 1997, p. 5; see also Michael Urban's discussion of " 'technologies of discourse' which shape the social world by establishing the ensemble of words, expressions and symbols that can be meaningfully communicated about it": "Remythologising the Russian State," *Europe-Asia Studies* 50, no. 6 (1998): 969.

3. Awareness that the KPRF had seized the initiative regarding patriotism was not new in 1996. After the 1995 parliamentary elections, the leaders of Russia's Democratic Choice held a press conference to denounce the KPRF's effort to portray itself as the party of patriots. They themselves, however, still insisted that Russia needed to follow a "normal path, common for all humanity and not some special path": Aleksei Uliukhaev quoted in Aleksandr Zhelenin, "Demokraticheskii patriotizm," *Nezavisimaia gazeta,* Dec. 15, 1995, p. 2.

4. Georgii Satarov quoted in David Remnick, "Hammer, Sickle, and Book," *New York Review of Books,* May 23, 1996, p. 46. See also Viacheslav Kostikov, "Vremia vlastvovat' postupkami," *Moskovskie novosti,* Sept. 22–29, 1996, p. 28.

5. Urban, "Remythologising the Russian State," p. 975.

6. L. A. Stepnova, "Sotsial'naia simvolika Rossiia," *Sotsis*, no. 7, 1998, p. 95.

7. Ivan Rodin and Vitalii Marsov, "Boris El'tsin snova vstupil v dolzhnost'," *Nezavisimaia gazeta*, Aug. 10, 1996, pp. 1–2.

8. Debate of Dec. 8–9, 1994, especially report by Deputy O. Shenkarev (KPRF), in *Gosudarstvennaia Duma: Stenogramma zasedanii* (hereafter *GD*) (Moscow: Respublika, 1995), 11: 210–215; see also *GD*, biulleten' no. 88 (Apr. 2, 1997), pp. 28–31, 37.

9. *GD*, biulleten no. 88 (Apr. 2, 1997), p. 39.

10. In defense of the tricolor, see G. Vilinbakhov in *GD*, 11: 218. On discomfort with imperial symbols, see, for instance, Denis Babchenko, " 'Bozhe, tsaria khrani!' Ne konstitutsionnye u nas ne tol'ko pasporta, no i dengi," *Segodnia*, Aug. 8, 1998, p. 2.

11. Kim Smirnov, "Imperskii orel ne k litsu demokraticheskoi Rossii," *Izvestiia*, May 12, 1992, p. 7; Stepnova, "Sotsial'naia simvolika Rossiia."

12. "Kto my? Kuda my idem? Konkurs 'Ideia dlia Rossii,' " *Rossiiskaia gazeta*, July 30, 1996, p. 1.

13. "Ne putaite gosudarstvennuiu ideiu s lichnoi" (interview with G. Satarov), *Rossiiskaia gazeta*, Nov. 14, 1996, p. 3; Anatolii Karpychev and Sergei Trunov, "Soedinennye odnoi sud'boi na odnoi zemle," ibid., Oct. 9, 1996, pp. 1, 3; Anatolii Iurkov, "O chem zvoniat kolokola," ibid., July 30, 1996, pp. 1–2.

14. Valeriia Novodvorskaia, "Po liubi etu vechnost' bolot," *Novoe vremia*, no. 41, October 1996, p. 9. See also Andrei Zagorodnikov, "Sviato mesto pusto ne byvaet," *Nezavisimaia gazeta*, July 30, 1996, p. 2; Sergei Koliadin, "Lichnaia tsel' vyshe dvuglavnogo orla," *Rossiiskaia gazeta*, Oct. 17, 1996, p. 4; and in *Rossiiskaia gazeta*, Sept. 17, 1996, Nikolai Ovsiannikov, "Likha beda nachalo," p. 5, and Georgii Nikolaev, "Kto shagaet ne v nogu?" p. 4.

15. One well-known democratic intellectual examined Russian folklore and aphorisms at length for common values: Igor' Chubais, *Rossiia v poiskakh sebia* (Moscow: NOK "Muzei bumagi," 1998).

16. Grigorii Pomerants, "Maastrikt ili Saraevo?" *Novoe vremia*, no. 41, October 1996, p. 6.

17. Aleksandr Rubtsov, comp., *Rossiia v poiskakh idei: Analiz pressy*, ed. Georgii Satarov (Moscow, 1997). Western analysts have engaged in similar pursuits; see, for instance, Vera Tolz, "Forging the Nation: National Identity and Nation Building in Post-Communist Russia," *Europe-Asia Studies* 50, no. 6 (1998): 993–1022.

18. Rubtsov, "V ozhidanii idei."

19. Veronika Kutsyllo, "Kakoi ne dolzhna byt' ideia dlia Rossii, uzhe izvestno," *Kommersant-Daily*, Dec. 27, 1996, p. 3.

20. Mikhail Kushtapin, "Premiia vruchaetsia, konkurs prodolzhaetsia," *Rossiiskaia gazeta*, Dec. 31, 1996, p. 1; Gurii Sudakov, "Shest' printsipov russkosti," ibid., Sept. 17, 1996, p. 4.

21. Satarov quoted in Bronwyn McLaren, "Big Brains Bog Down in Hunt

for Russian Idea," *Moscow Times*, Aug. 9, 1997, pp. 1–2; Rubtsov, "V ozhi-danii idei."

22. Iurii Grechishkin, "Akh muzhik, davai poobshchaemsia!" *Rossiiskaia gazeta*, Sept. 10, 1996, p. 3; Valentin Miloserdov, "Vsiu zhizn' ia byl ku-lach'em nedobitym," ibid., Dec. 19, 1996, p. 3; Aleksei Firsanov, "Ne putaite imperiiu chuvstv, bankov ili sala s velikoi derzhava," ibid., Dec. 5, 1996, p. 5.

23. Vladimir Mordashev, "My, konechno, ne Amerikantsy: No ne glupee zhe ikh," *Rossiiskaia gazeta*, Sept. 17, 1996, p. 5.

24. Petr Tiflov, "Daite slovo i 'levym'!" and Nikolai Senchev, "Arresto-van. Rasstrelian. Reabilitirovan," *Rossiiskaia gazeta*, Nov. 14, 1996, p. 3.

25. "Primirit', no kak?" *Rossiiskaia gazeta*, Nov. 21, 1996, p. 4; Anatolii Karpychev, "Proshloe dyshit zatylok," ibid.; Senchev, "Arrestovan."

26. Aleksei Kiva, "Blesk i nishcheta dvizheniia pravozashchitnikov," *Rossiiskaia gazeta*, Feb. 20, 1997, p. 5.

27. For a particularly harsh critique of Solzhenitsyn's return, see Grig-orii Amelin, "Zhit' ne po Solzhenitsynu," *Nezavisimaia gazeta*, Apr. 27, 1994, p. 8.

28. Aleksei Kiva, "Blesk i nishcheta," *Rossiiskaia gazeta*, Feb. 20, 1997, p. 5, and Feb. 21,1997, pp. 4–5. For another typical attack on the role of dis-sidents in contemporary Russia, see Viktoria Sharinova, "Pravozashchit-niki i sovremennaia Rossiia," *Segodnia*, Aug. 17, 1996, p. 10.

29. Andrei Papushin, "Poltorasta let odinochestva," *Rossiiskaia gazeta*, Aug. 23, 1996, p. 28; see also V. N. Ponomarev, "Vspomnim, chto my sla-viane," ibid., Aug. 14, 1996, p. 2, and Aleksei Kiva, "Sleva—liberaly, sprava—generaly. A posredine vintiki?" ibid., May 23, 1997, pp. 8–9.

30. Tsipko quoted in Natal'ia Kuzmina, "Eta zagadochnaia russkaia dusha," *Rossiiskaia gazeta*, Aug. 3, 1996, pp. 2, 7.

31. For a riveting account of the fate of the tsar and his family and of their remains, see Robert K. Massie, *The Romanovs: The Final Chapter* (New York: Random House, 1995).

32. Sophia Coudenhove, "Nicholas II Clears Sainthood Hurdle," *Moscow Times*, Oct. 17, 1996, p. 1; Mikhail Lantsman, "Nikolai II blizok k zachis-teniiu v sviate," *Segodnia*, Oct. 11, 1996, p. 1; Maksim Shevchenko and Sergei Chupin, "Mnenie episkopata," *Nezavisimaia gazeta*, suppl., Oct. 27, 1997, p. 3; Andrei Zolotov Jr., "Bishops Boost Tsar's Sainthood Bid," *Moscow Times*, Feb. 22, 1997, p. 4. In August 2000, the Council of Bishops finally voted to canonize the last tsar. See Andrei Zolotov Jr., "Church Agrees to Canonize Nicholas II," *Moscow Times*, Aug. 15, 2000.

33. See, for instance, Aleksandr Shirokograd, "Nikolai II, informatsiia k razmyshleniia," *Izvestiia*, July 11, 1998, p. 4.

34. Quoted in "Lenin Burial Call Renewed as Faithful Mark 74th Year," *Moscow Times*, Jan. 22, 1998, p. 3. For a fascinating discussion of the role of the dead in postsocialist states in general, see Katherine Verdery, *The Polit-ical Lives of Dead Bodies: Reburial and Postsocialist Change* (New York: Columbia University Press, 1999).

35. Orlando Figes, "Burying the Bones," *Granta*, no. 64 (Winter 1998), p. 98. See also Leonid Radzikhovskii, "Tragediia bez geroia," *Segodnia*, July 16, 1998, p. 2. On the importance of graves, see Kathleen E. Smith, *Remembering Stalin's Victims: Popular Memory and the End of the USSR* (Ithaca: Cornell University Press, 1996), pp. 156, 163–165.

36. "Krestnyi khod," *Segodnia*, June 18, 1997, p. 2; Grigorii Sanin, "Dinastiiu Romanov preslediuit krasnye ekstremisty," ibid., July 21, 1997, p. 7.

37. Viktor Trushkov, "A teper' vozhdia na plakhu?" *Pravda*, Jan. 21, 1992, pp. 1–2.

38. After August 1991, democrats repeatedly exploited Communists' fears by escalating rhetoric about burying Lenin whenever they became alarmed by KPRF behavior, as after the October events in 1993, on the eve of the 1995 parliamentary elections, and when the Duma threatened to impeach Yeltsin in July 1999. Poll cited in Dmitrii Pinsker, "Zakhoronit v liuboi tsenoi," *Itogi*, Aug. 19, 1997, p. 57.

39. Andrei Zolotov Jr., "Church Defends Skipping Tsar Burial," *Moscow Times*, June 12, 1998; Alice Lagnado, "Tsar Funeral Priest Chosen," ibid., July 9, 1998; "Patriarch Lashes Out against Interment of Tsar's Remains," ibid., July 15, 1998; Alice Lagnado, "Romanovs Stay Away from Tsar Burial," ibid., July 10, 1998.

40. Bronwyn McClaren, "President Will Attend Tsar Burial," *Moscow Times*, July 17, 1998.

41. "Rossiia prostilas' s poslednim imperatorom," *Rossiiskaia gazeta*, July 18, 1998, p. 1.

42. Ibid.

43. Indeed, a year later, the grave of the royal family was largely ignored by tourists and neglected by the city administrators responsible for its upkeep. See Marina Golovanivskaia and Andrei Sinitsyn, "Mogilu poslednego russkogo tsaria zabyli," *Kommersant-Daily*, July 17, 1999, p. 1.

44. Michael Kammen, *Life in the Past Lane: Historical Perspectives on American Culture* (New York: Oxford University Press, 1997), p. 204.

Chapter 9. Patriotic Divisions

1. The Duma voted 327 to 69 and 256 to 102: Iurii Nevskii, "Duma snova progolosoval za Zheleznogo Feliksa," *Kommersant-Daily*, Dec. 5, 1998, p. 2; Iurii Nikoforenko quoted in "Vozvrashchenie Feliksa," *Moskovskie novosti*, Dec. 8, 1998.

2. Quoted in Chloe Arnold, "Duma Wants Founder of KGB Resurrected," *Moscow Times*, Dec. 3, 1998.

3. Svetlana Ofitova, "Na Lubianku Dzerzhinskii vriad li vernetsia," *Nezavisimaia gazeta*, Dec. 8, 1998, p. 3.

4. "Dzerzhinskii zashchitit FSB ot prestupnosti," *Kommersant-Daily*, Dec. 3, 1998.

5. When the proposal came up for a second reading in July 2000 in the new Duma, it fell short of passing by some 30 votes: Siuzanna Farizova,

"Derzhi Derzhinskogo! Gosduma ne podderzhala pamiatnik," *Kommersant-Daily*, July 8, 2000, p. 1.

6. Aleksandr Iakovlev, "Simvol terrora," *Literaturnaia gazeta*, Dec. 9, 1998, p. 1.

7. Catherine Wanner, *Burden of Dreams: History and Identity in Post-Soviet Ukraine* (University Park: Pennsylvania State University Press, 1998), p. xxvi.

8. Michael Schudson, *Watergate in American Memory: How We Remember, Forget, and Reconstruct the Past* (New York: Basic Books, 1992), pp. 205, 211–212.

9. The number of people who celebrate the defeat of the coup attempt has continued to drop: "Few Mark Failed Soviet Coup at Rally on 7th anniversary," *Moscow Times*, Aug. 20, 1998; Grigorii Nekhoroshev, "Vosem' let so dnia GKChP: Zashchitnikov Belogo doma vse men'she," *Nezavisimaia gazeta*, Aug. 21, 1999, p. 2.

10. "Obrashchenie prezidenta B. N. El'tsina k grazhdanam Rossii 31 dekabria 1999 goda," *Kommersant-Daily*, Jan. 5, 2000, p. 1.

11. Peter Rutland, "Putin's Path to Power," *Post-Soviet Affairs* 16, no. 4 (2000): 343.

12. Vladimir Putin with Nataliya Gevorkyan, Natalya Timakova, and Andrei Kolesnikov, *First Person* (New York: Public Affairs, 2000), p. 42; "Vladimir Putin: Lozung 'kolbasa i svoboda!' ne mozhet byt' natsional'noi idei," *Izvestiia*, Sept. 2, 1999, p. 1. See also Putin's plan for revitalizing mandatory patriotic education, "Gosudarstvennaia programma 'Patriotich-eskoe vospitanie grazhdan Rossiiskoi federatsii na 2001–2005,'" *Rossiiskaia gazeta*, Mar. 12, 2001, p. 4.

13. Oksana Yablokova, "Anthem Dispute Shows House Divided," *Moscow Times*, Nov. 21, 1999, p. 4; "Putin Presses for Stalin's Anthem," ibid., Nov. 29, 1999, p. 4

14. Quoted in Patrick Lannin, "Yeltsin Derides Anthem Proposal as Vote Looms," *Moscow Times*, Dec. 8, 2000, p. 4.

15. Patrick E. Tyler, "Soviet Hymn is back, Creating Much Discord," *New York Times*, Dec. 6, 2000. p. A1.

16. J. Samuel Valenzuela, "Democratic Consolidation in Post-Transitional Settings: Notion, Process, and Facilitating Conditions," in *Issues in Democratic Consolidation*, ed. Scott Mainwaring, Guillermo O'Donnell, and J. Samuel Valenzuela (Notre Dame: University of Notre Dame Press, 1992), pp. 78–80.

17. Vladimir Voinovich, "I moi gimn," *Izvestiia*, Dec. 7, 2000, p. 1. See also Masha Lipman, "My Russia, 'Tis of Thee," *Washington Post*, Nov. 6, 2000, p. A35. For a contrary opinion on the need for an anthem with words, see Boris Vladimirov, "Nemoi gimn," *Izvestiia*, Aug. 5, 1999, p. 5.

18. On the new lyrics, see David Hoffman, "Russians to Sing of God, Not of Lenin," *Washington Post*, Dec. 31, 2000, p. A23.

Index